SPRINGSTEEN
ALBUM BY ALBUM

RYAN WHITE

INTRODUCTION BY
PETER AMES CARLIN

STERLING
New York

STERLING
New York

An Imprint of Sterling Publishing Co., Inc.
1166 Avenue of the Americas
New York, NY 10036

ISBN 978-1-4549-1280-4

Distributed in Canada by Sterling Publishing
c/o Canadian Manda Group, 664 Annette, Street
Toronto, Ontario, Canada M6S 2C8

Created and produced by
Palazzo Editions Ltd, 2 Wood Street
Bath, BA1 2JQ, United Kingdom
www.palazzoeditions.com

Publisher: Colin Webb
Art Director: Emma Wicks
Editor: James Hodgson
Photo Editor: Dave Brolan

Please see picture credits on page 287 for image copyright information

For information about custom editions, special sales, and premium and corporate purchases, please contact
Sterling Special Sales at 800-805-5489 or specialsales@sterlingpublishing.com.

Manufactured in China

4 6 8 10 9 7 5

www.sterlingpublishing.com

Page 1: Portrait by Tom Hill, August 1975, shortly before the release of *Born to Run*.
Page 2: Portrait by Danny Clinch, 2010.
Endpapers: Spectrum, Philadelphia, September 1984.

CONTENTS

"THE REASON I'M RUNNING FOR PRESIDENT IS BECAUSE I CAN'T BE BRUCE SPRINGSTEEN."

BARACK OBAMA, 2008

INTRODUCTION

BY PETER AMES CARLIN

These days the world sees Bruce Springsteen in gilded light. The voice of the common man. The personification of basic American virtues. Touched by inspiration, Springsteen sings the working-class electric: the sound of dreams born, pursued, and crushed, only to be born again.

Tales of Springsteen's religious revival–esque concerts have evolved from cultist babble to widespread cliché to a truism acknowledged by the president of the United States. "I'm the president," Barack Obama declared in 2009, "but he's the Boss."

Not bad for a shy kid from a crumbling industrial town in central New Jersey. Raised poor in a hardworking but troubled family, the schoolboy Springsteen glimpsed the face of Elvis on TV and saw his own transcendence. Given an electric guitar at fifteen he practiced ceaselessly, then spent the next seven years playing with bar bands and building a reputation as the hottest lead guitarist between the Jersey Shore and the state of Virginia. In the winter of 1971–1972 the twenty-two-year-old packed up his guitar and a sheaf of newly written songs and took them to the cultural gatekeepers in New York City.

At first glance his ambitions seemed ridiculous. Longhaired, stick thin, and shivering in his torn jeans and a dirty sweatshirt, he could barely meet your gaze, let alone conduct a conversation beyond *Hey, how ya doin?* But once Springsteen picked up his guitar … *boom.* He was the king of the alley, the lucky young matador, the loser who found the keys to the universe in a rusted-up, piece-of-shit car. Also a visionary lyricist with a piercing eye into society's darkest crevices and a wild energy that seemed to crackle the air around him.

At least, that's how it seemed to the cadre of industry pros who quit their jobs, mortgaged their homes and/or moved across the country to take a role in the artist's quest. When Springsteen landed a contract with Columbia Records in mid-1972 the same fever gripped renowned talent scout John Hammond (discoverer of Benny Goodman, Billie Holiday, Bob Dylan, et al.), label chief Clive Davis, and a feverish cult of staffers whose passion for the new artist compelled them to jump on sofas and curse out colleagues who refused to hear the true spirit of rock 'n' roll in Springsteen's craggy voice.

The doubters got the first laugh. Promoted widely as a son-of-Bob Dylan, Springsteen created no commercial ripples when his debut album, *Greetings from Asbury Park, N.J.*, was released at the start of 1973. The funkier, more conceptual *The Wild, the Innocent & the E Street Shuffle* failed similarly ten months later. Meanwhile Springsteen toured ceaselessly, dragging his band of Jersey Shore regulars—most of whom had played with him since they were all teenagers—up, down, and across the Eastern Seaboard and the Midwest, hitting every bar, roadhouse, and small theater that would have them. Weeks, months, and then years of soul-battering, low-wage work, but increasingly important when it all got retold as part of a hero's journey.

Springsteen was nothing if not wired for rock 'n' roll heroism. Still entranced by that childhood vision of the spotlight-sanctified Elvis, he chased that promise, and commitment, into all of his shows, performing with a passion forceful enough to leave a trail of converts in his wake.

More than a few turned out to be music writers whose published ecstasies helped draw more about-to-be-converts to the shows, but none could compete with leading rock critic Jon Landau's Vesuvian response to a show in Cambridge, Massachusetts in May 1974. "I have seen rock and roll future," he proclaimed, "and its name is Bruce Springsteen."

The future arrived a year later, riding a tsunami of pent-up media adoration fed both by the hard-eyed romanticism in the long-awaited *Born to Run* and the Arthurian saga of the artist's quest for greatness. Springsteen, dressed for the occasion in a classic rebel's leather jacket, torn shirt, and Elvis Presley Fan Club button, leans on the shoulder of saxophonist Clarence Clemons, and beams conspiratorially as his African-American brother-in-music unleashes what looks like a gut-busting riff. And from there the He-is-risen reviews, the dueling *Time* and *Newsweek* covers, a rocket ride to the number-three slot on the *Billboard* album charts, and almost immediately the creepy undertow of mainstream success: busted relationships, bitter litigation, and existential crises.

Locked out of the recording studio for two years owing to a contract conflict, Springsteen went back on the road, furthering his reputation as a wildly inspired performer. Celebrated afresh for the battered-but-not-beaten *Darkness on the Edge of Town* in 1978 and then breaking through to hit singles and multi-platinum sales with 1980's party-like-you're-dying-cos-you-are *The River*, the revivalist rocker ventured to Europe, where the unexpected fervor came with a political edge. In the age defined by US president Ronald Reagan's militaristic Cold War strategy, Springsteen presented the better-natured face of America—the saviors of World War II rather than the imperial provocateurs of World War III.

Now living the Elvis vision he'd imagined as a boy, Springsteen ventured into his heart's most haunted corners to exercise his darkest impulses in the home-recorded *Nebraska*. The deliberately anti-commercial move added ballast to the star's reputation for depth, which seemed particularly useful with his 1984 ascension to the filigreed ether of global stardom.

The new album was called *Born in the U.S.A.*, and it ushered in a Springsteen re-created as a kind of everyman superhero—from his radically Herculean physique to his thigh-grabbing jeans and white T-shirt to the fire-engine-red kerchief headband ornamenting his forehead. The album's dance-friendly songs shimmered with synthesizer lines, while its lead single, "Dancing In The Dark," came with a glossy video featuring a beautiful young model. Plays for commercial success don't come much more obvious, and hardly ever more explosive. By the end of 1984 everyone in the world seemed to know what those Springsteen maniacs had been yammering about for so long. The *Born in the U.S.A.* album sold fifteen million copies at home and millions abroad while global demand for concert tickets sent the tour into the world's most cavernous stadiums, often for multiple shows. Too enormous to be a simple rock star, Springsteen gained folk-hero proportions. More than a top-drawer rock star or the chief minister in the First Church of Rock 'n' Roll, he was now the spokesman for the working class, the living exemplar of old-fashioned American muscle, grit, and might. And he was also a political symbol claimed by candidates and editorialists from every position on the

partisan spectrum. Conservatives from Reagan on down noted the thundering chant that powered the album's title track—*Born in the U.S.A.! I was born in the U.S.A.! I'm a cool rockin' Daddy in the U.S.A.!*—and took it to be gung-ho, unquestioning patriotism.

Only that was the absolute reverse of what Springsteen intended. "Born In The U.S.A." was actually about the American government's failure to care for its military veterans, rendering each chorus more bitterly ironic than the last. And the rest of the album told the whole story in the terms of shuttered factories, derelict storefronts, unemployed workers, deserted lovers, and broken-down lives. Meanwhile Springsteen studded the stadium shows with the bleakest of the *Nebraska* songs, tracing a line from corporate and political malfeasance to the shattered communities his characters inhabited. And when it came to presidents, prime ministers, and governments, Springsteen made his feelings clear when introducing his live cover of Edwin Starr's Vietnam-era hit "War": "In 1985 blind faith in your leaders, or anything, could get you killed."

Springsteen mostly steered clear of specific issues and candidates, choosing instead to support and steer donations to local food banks at each concert. And while he contributed vocals to the USA for Africa fundraiser "We Are The World" in 1985 and to old friend and guitarist Steve Van Zandt's far more gutsy South African apartheid protest "Sun City," Springsteen's political impulses still took a backseat to his lifelong commitment to his art, and the spiritual uplift he'd always sought in it. The late-1986 release of a three-CD/five-record live collection made headlines around the world for the Beatlemania-like response by merchants and frantic customers alike.

And that was the end of Springsteen's run as the globe's reigning rock musician.

Springsteen returned in 1987 with *Tunnel of Love*, an intimate collection of songs celebrating, dissecting, and mourning the marriage he'd recently entered with actress and model Julianne Phillips. Again setting the tone with the album cover, Springsteen posed in citified cowboy finery, the silver tips of his bolo tie gleaming along with the cool yellow body of the convertible behind him. He seemed a continent away from the Jersey Shore (though that was actually where they shot the photograph), anticipating the road that would take him to the opposite coast working without his longtime comrades and with no fixed sense of where he was headed, or why.

So came Springsteen in the nineties: the Hollywood Hills crusader in search of a battle to wage. He'd started the crusade by dismissing the E Street Band, then spent two-plus years producing a sleekly detailed studio album (*Human Touch*) that was easily eclipsed by the raw collection that had erupted from him in the next three weeks (*Lucky Town*). A year-long tour with new musicians left fans both thrilled (Bruce is back!) and dismayed (who are *those* guys?), then a year's worth of experimenting with electronic sounds ended with a shelved album and a song ("Streets Of Philadelphia") that won an Academy Award and took Springsteen back to the upper reaches of sales charts around the world. After that came the stripped-down *Ghost of Tom Joad*, a tonal successor to *Nebraska* that presented the artist in academic garb, girding stark tales of southwestern outcasts with a bibliography citing the authors and publications that had moved him.

As ever, Springsteen's empathy and moral and artistic instincts seemed pure, but as one longtime fan wrote: "I bet he didn't need to read a newspaper to write 'Born To Run.'"

Eventually Springsteen's road led back to New Jersey, and then to the E Street Band, whose 1999 Reunion tour played like the reformation of an American institution; its rehearsals fodder for daily news reports and its launch covered by national magazines and global TV news. Paradoxically, the step backward restored Springsteen's cultural currency. Along with his lifelong pursuit of rock 'n' roll communion (freshly described in the new show-closer called "Land Of Hope And Dreams"), Springsteen made headlines in mid-2000 by introducing "American Skin (41 Shots)," a song mourning the accidental killing of an African immigrant by New York Police Department officers. The song spurred political controversy in New York, but when terrorists struck the city and the rest of the nation on September 11, 2001, it was Springsteen's *The Rising* that came with the force of a national monument. And in 2008 his early endorsement of Barack Obama's presidential campaign is still seen as a key turning point in the race.

Springsteen has worked constantly over the last fifteen years, switching from E Street Band–driven rock to downbeat solo ruminations (*Devils & Dust*) to front-porch folk songs with the Seeger Sessions Band (named for the Pete Seeger tribute album for which their first song was recorded) back to mainstream rock and beyond. Springsteen's 2012 speech and performance at SXSW (South by Southwest), America's preeminent alt-rock convocation, dominated that year's festival and sent a new generation of fans

into the thrall of *Nebraska* and all of the beyond-the-fringe visions and nightmares lurking on his other albums.

For years a regular presence at the Rock and Roll Hall of Fame annual celebrations, with his 1999 induction to the gilded ranks Springsteen sealed his status not just as a legend but a kind of alpha-legend: the free world's rocker laureate. And all of it sounds so overblown and smug. The whole *point* of rock 'n' roll is to destabilize the institutions and blow their legends to smithereens. Even at sixty-five years old, Springsteen keeps this call to arms simmering in his gut.

"Rumble, young musicians, rumble! Open your ears and open your hearts. Don't take yourself too seriously, and take yourself as seriously as death itself."

That was Springsteen, a fever-eyed, battle-hardened veteran, talking to every musician in the room at South by Southwest, and everywhere else, too.

"Don't worry. Worry your ass off. Have ironclad confidence, but doubt—it keeps you awake and alert. Believe you are the baddest ass in town, and, you suck! Be able to keep two completely contradictory ideas alive and well inside of your heart and head at all times. If it doesn't drive you crazy, it will make you strong."

And of course he was talking to himself, too. Another album had just come into being, another mammoth world tour was about to start. And, more pressing than anything else, he had a show to play in a few hours.

"And stay hard, stay hungry, and stay alive. And when you walk on stage tonight to bring the noise, treat it like it's all we have. And then remember, it's only rock 'n' roll."

NEW JERSEY HOME

"PEOPLE THOUGHT I WAS WEIRD
BECAUSE I ALWAYS WENT AROUND
WITH THIS LOOK ON MY FACE.
I WAS THINKING OF THINGS, BUT I WAS
ALWAYS ON THE OUTSIDE LOOKING IN."

BRUCE SPRINGSTEEN, 1979

1949

September 23: Bruce Frederick Springsteen born, Long Branch Hospital, Long Branch, New Jersey—a first child for Adele and Doug Springsteen.

1951

Winter: Birth of Springsteen's first sister, Virginia (Ginny). Doug and Adele give up their small apartment and move in with Doug's parents, Fred and Alice, on Randolph Street, Freehold, New Jersey.

1954

October: Doug and Adele purchase their own house on Institute Street, Freehold.

1955

Fall: Springsteen joins the St. Rose of Lima school, Freehold.

c. 1956

Inspired by seeing Elvis Presley on *The Ed Sullivan Show*, Springsteen takes a few formal lessons on the acoustic guitar.

1961

July: Adele takes her children to see Chubby Checker play at the Steel Pier, Atlantic City.

1962

February 8: Birth of Springsteen's second sister, Pamela. Fred and Alice Springsteen die within a few months of each other.
November: The Springsteens move to a larger, rented house on South Street, Freehold.

1963

Fall: Springsteen enrolls at Freehold Regional High School.

1964

January: Hearing the Beatles play "I Want To Hold Your Hand" rekindles his musical ambitions.
Summer: Buys his own acoustic guitar and starts learning it in earnest.
December 25: Receives his first electric guitar, a $60 Kent, as a Christmas present.

1965

Spring: Joins his first band, the Rogues, and performs in public for the first time, at the Freehold Elks Club, but loses his place in the band soon after.
June: Joins the Castiles as lead guitarist.
Summer and fall: The Castiles hone their skills at a number of local dance concerts booked by their manager, Tex Vinyard.

1966

May 18: The Castiles record their first (and only) single, "Baby I"/"That's What You Get."
Fall: Springsteen meets Steve Van Zandt, guitarist for rival band the Shadows.

1967

June 19: Springsteen's overlong hair causes him to be banned from his high-school graduation ceremony.
September: Joins Ocean County Community College in nearby Toms River.
October 22: Bart Haynes, the Castiles' original drummer, is killed on active service in Vietnam.

1968

c. Winter: Pregnant, Ginny gets married to her boyfriend, Michael "Mickey" Shave.
Winter: Springsteen suffers a concussion in a motorcycle accident.
early August: A major drugs bust in Freehold leads to the arrest of most of the Castiles (though not Springsteen himself) and is the catalyst for the breakup of the band immediately after.
August 10: Springsteen's new group, Earth, plays its first gig at Le Teendezvous, New Shrewsbury.

1969

February 14: Earth's last performance, at the Italian American Men's Association Clubhouse, Long Branch.
February 23: An early-hours jam at the Upstage Club, Asbury Park, leads to the formation of Springsteen's new band, Child, with Vini Lopez (drums), Danny Federici (keyboards), and Vinnie Roslin (bass)
February/March: Carl "Tinker" West, a surfboard entrepreneur, becomes Child's manager and gives the band a rehearsal space in his factory.
April 2: Child plays its debut show, at the Pandemonium club, Wanamassa.
June: Doug and Adele (and Pamela) relocate to San Mateo, California, leaving Springsteen on his own in the family home in Freehold until he invites bandmates Lopez and Federici to move in with him.
August 15–17: Child plays a three-night residency at the Student Prince, Asbury Park, which prevents the band from taking up an invitation to perform at the Woodstock festival.
September: The rent having run out on his family home, Springsteen, Vini Lopez, and Danny Federici move in to West's surfboard factory.
early November: Upon learning of the existence of another group called Child, the band members come up with a new name, Steel Mill.
December 31: The band heads west to play the End-of-the-Sixties New Year's Eve party at countercultural hotspot the Esalen Institute in Big Sur, California.

1970

January 13: A performance at the Matrix, San Francisco, is enthusiastically reviewed by the *San Francisco Examiner,* which gains the attention of Bill Graham, the city's major music promoter.
February: Graham offers Steel Mill a recording contract. Unwilling to sign away publishing rights, the band decides to decline.
February 18: Springsteen meets Nils Lofgren for the first time, at the legendary Fillmore West, San Francisco.
February 24: Steel Mill plays the last gig of its California trip, at the College of Marin in Kentfield, before driving back east.
February 28: Vinnie Roslin plays his final concert as a member of Steel Mill, at the Free University, Richmond, Virginia.
March 27: The band plays the Hullabaloo in Richmond with Steve Van Zandt filling in on bass for the recently fired Roslin.
August: Springsteen invites Robbin Thompson, lead singer of fellow Jersey Shore band Mercy Flight, to join Steel Mill and share front-man duties.
August 29: The band supports Roy Orbison at the Nashville Music Festival.
early September: Having found himself in the wrong house at the wrong time, Vini Lopez is arrested in a major drugs bust.
September 11: Steel Mill plays an outdoor benefit gig at the Clearwater Swim Club, Atlantic Highlands, New Jersey, to raise money for Lopez's legal fees. The concert ends in a near-riot.
early October: Lopez is released from jail and rejoins the band.

1971

January 23: Steel Mill plays its farewell gig at the Upstage.
February–March: Springsteen tries out members for a new band; a seventeen-year-old Patti Scialfa is rejected as a backing singer on account of her age.
March 27: An extended "party band" lineup called Bruce Springsteen and the Friendly Enemies plays its only show, opening for the Allman Brothers at the Sunshine In, Asbury Park.
May 14 and 15: Now called Dr. Zoom and the Sonic Boom, Springsteen's big band plays another two shows, back at the Sunshine In and then at Newark State College in Union, New Jersey.
July 10: Debut of the nine-piece Bruce Springsteen Band at Brookdale Community College's Nothings Festival.
July 11: The band's set at the Sunshine In supporting Humble Pie is so rapturously received that the headliners have to be talked out of fleeing the venue without performing.
September 4: Springsteen meets Clarence Clemons when the Bruce Springsteen Band and Clemons's band, Norman Seldin and the Joyful Noyze, play at neighboring clubs in Asbury Park.

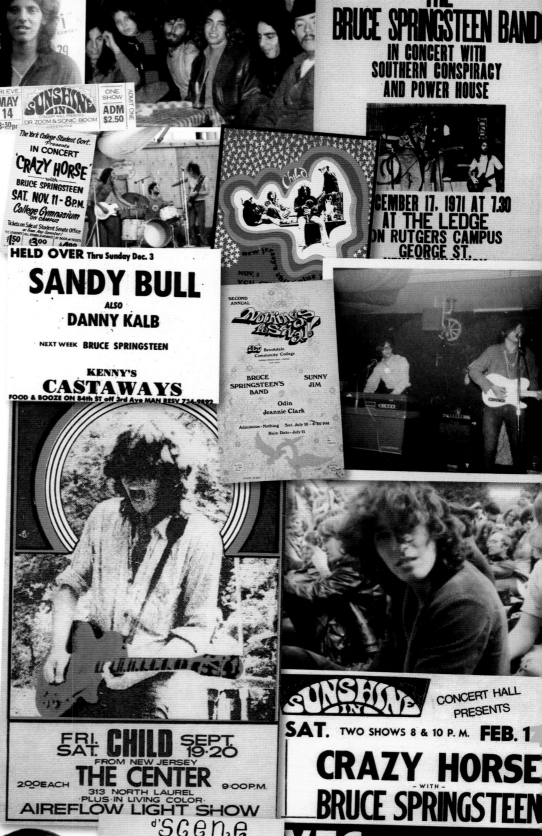

In the beginning, every musician has their genesis moment."

Bruce Springsteen was standing behind a lectern on a stage in the fourth-floor ballroom of a convention center in Austin, Texas. He was sixty-two years old, an icon doing a job the title sometimes requires. He was giving a speech. Specifically, the keynote address at the 2012 SXSW music conference. The sleeves of his blue dress shirt rolled up for work, he tackled a trio of inextricable stories: his, rock 'n' roll's, and America's.

"Mine was 1956, Elvis on The Ed Sullivan Show.*"*

Elvis. The poor white kid from Mississippi who took gospel, R&B, blues—black music—and mixed it with country, shook his hips and put a match to the culture. Elvis made the world take sides. You were with him or against him. Though that choice proved nothing but kindling, too. Sullivan said Elvis would never play his show; Sullivan paid Elvis $50,000 to play his show.

"It was the evening I realized a white man could make magic, that you did not have to be constrained by your upbringing, by the way you looked, or by the social context that oppressed you. You could call upon your own powers of imagination, and you could create a transformative self."

Not that "transformative self" was part of Springsteen's vocabulary in 1956 (or 1957, the other date he's given as the first flash of greatness before his eyes). To the six- or seven-year-old in front of the black-and-white television, Elvis, more than anything, must have looked like a lot of fun. Elvis was expansive and unlike anything in Springsteen's world, which at that point fit snugly in a few blocks of the blue-collar town of Freehold, New Jersey.

"The poor man's South that Elvis knew took strength from community," Greil Marcus wrote in *Mystery Train.* That community, Marcus wrote, was "organized by religion, morals, and music."

The way the South worked on Elvis, Freehold worked on Springsteen from the moment he was born on September 23, 1949. The joyous spirit, the restlessness, the darkness, and the drive that define Springsteen were constant childhood companions.

Twenty-two years before Springsteen was born, his father's elder sister, Virginia, was killed in a road accident. She was five; Douglas Springsteen was not quite two. As Doug's parents, Fred and Alice, mourned, the young boy was first neglected, and then shipped off to be cared for by relatives.

He returned home, but his family had fallen into despair and disrepair. Doug eventually quit school, got a factory job, and then joined the military, spending his part of World War II driving a truck until

"EVERYONE CHANGED THEIR IDEAS ABOUT EVERYTHING AFTER ELVIS. ABOUT RACE, ABOUT SEX, ABOUT GENDER DESCRIPTIONS, WHAT YOU COULD LOOK LIKE, WHAT YOU COULD WEAR."

Bruce Springsteen, 2011

returning to Freehold in 1945 to do not much of anything. Then he met Adele Zerilli. She got his attention. "I couldn't get rid of him," she said in 2011. In that way, at least, Doug exhibited some of the determination that would come to characterize his son.

Adele had her own complicated story. She grew up in relative comfort thanks to her father, Anthony, a charismatic and rakish lawyer. Two things happened to disrupt that: the Depression, and an embezzlement conviction that sent Anthony to Sing Sing prison.

But he bought a small house before he served that sentence. His three daughters lived there, made do the best they could, and kept their exuberant personalities intact. Dancing helped. They were always dancing.

Adele's joy and Douglas's demons wed in February 1947. He went to work in a Ford factory and she went to work as a secretary. Bruce arrived and then his sister, Ginny, less than two years later. Jammed for

Above, left: Bruce and Ginny Springsteen, live from the carousel, 1954.

Above, right: Yearbook photo from his senior year at Freehold Regional High School, 1967.

Page 14: With his eyes set on better days, 1971.

Page 15: Asbury Park, 1973.

space, they turned to Fred and Alice and their beaten old house on Randolph Street, a house Bruce would describe in an unreleased song titled "Randolph Street" as standing "like World War II." The only heat was an old stove that would hiss when Bruce shot it with his squirt gun. There, the "love was crazy," he'd sing.

Bruce became the replacement for the daughter Fred and Alice had lost so many years earlier. On Randolph Street, it was Bruce who mattered most. Almost everything was done for him, and he could do almost anything he wanted.

Adele's job, and her sense of purpose, was steady, but the rest of the adults in Bruce's life tended to drift through the world. Doug's work came and went. Fred, an electrician referred to in "Randolph Street" as a "master of the art of electricity," would scavenge for busted-up radios and then fix and resell them.

To this mix, add religion, in the shape of the nearby Catholic church. Weddings and funerals. Shadows and brightness. "It was filled with terror and mystery and poetry and power that was way beyond my understanding," Springsteen said on stage in 2005, "but you absorbed it anyway." He absorbed everything.

Before Elvis, there was a kitchen radio catching signals from New York and Philadelphia. Doo-wop, the sound "of silk stockings rustling on backseat upholstery," he told the SXSW audience. This was the music drifting from gas stations and cars, pool joints and factories.

There were novelty songs like "Purple People Eater" and "They're Coming To Take Me Away, Ha-Haaa!," delicious musical junk foods. In 1961, the Springsteens took a trip to Atlantic City to see Chubby Checker do "The Twist." That same year, a rug factory that once employed Doug—and so many others in Freehold—moved to North Carolina.

Roy Orbison and Johnny Cash arrived. Then Bob Dylan. Phil Spector made his name synonymous with his Wall of Sound. Soul music ignited the imagination. "It was music of sweaty perspiration, and drenched demands for pleasure and respect," Springsteen said. "It was adult music, it was sung by soul men and women, not teen idols."

If you yearned for something else, something more—even if you had no idea what exactly it was—how could you ignore anything?

The year 1964 began with the Beatles on Sullivan and ended with the *T.A.M.I. Show* in theaters. Teenage Awards Music International featured

Chuck Berry, the Beach Boys, Jan and Dean, Marvin Gaye, the Supremes, Smokey Robinson, the Rolling Stones, and, most famously, James Brown. Brown at his scorched-earth best.

"If you simply watch that, that's all you need to know," Springsteen said of Brown's performance. "It's almost true that it's all you need to know."

Meanwhile, out of deep concern for the children of America who were possibly being led astray by this new art form, the FBI opened an obscenity investigation into the Kingsmen and their hit version of "Louie Louie."

In his bedroom, guitar in hand, checking his moves in the mirror, Springsteen couldn't get enough. He practiced, and practiced, and then practiced more. He joined his first band, the Rogues. He played one show, at the Freehold Elks Club. They opened with the Beatles' version of "Twist and Shout." Springsteen was fired shortly after the gig. He practiced more. He joined his second band, the Castiles (named after a favored brand of shampoo). They wanted him to learn more lead guitar.

Top: "You ain't nothin' but a hound dog …"?

Above: The incomparable James Brown lighting up the *T.A.M.I. Show*, December 1964.

Left: When the Beatles invaded American homes on the *Ed Sullivan Show* in February 1964, Springsteen was among the millions of awestruck viewers.

He went home and went to work. He learned *a lot* of lead guitar. That was 1965.

The United States' involvement in Vietnam began to escalate. Dylan went electric at the Newport Folk Festival. The Animals had a hit with "We Gotta Get Out Of This Place."

"It was the first time I felt I heard something come across the radio that mirrored my home life, my childhood," Springsteen said.

The Castiles picked up a mentor and a manager in Gordon "Tex" Vinyard, who lived next door to the band's drummer, Bart Haynes. They played covers mostly, Sam and Dave's "Hold On, I'm Comin'" and Jimi Hendrix's "Fire," but also stuff like Glenn Miller's "In The Mood."

In 1966, the Castiles recorded two originals—"Baby I" and "That's What You Get"—co-written by Springsteen and the band's other guitarist, George Theiss. They played wherever there was a gig: schools, supermarkets, a swim club, the Elks Club, the roller rink, a *mental hospital*, and the Café Wha? in Greenwich Village.

Springsteen became a part of the scene, collecting friends and future collaborators. Guys like Steve Van Zandt who could argue all night about a chord change, or a fashion change. There's no mythical story about how the two met. They were simply too similar not to meet. Van Zandt, like most everyone else, sensed in Springsteen the combination of talent and focus that could lift him far beyond New Jersey's little joints.

Doug moved through jobs and moods. At night, he'd sit alone in the darkened kitchen, drinking beer and smoking, the glow of the cigarette the only light in the room. He cut a stark image of tortured isolation. When he wasn't distant he was doing what so many parents did—wondering what the hell his son was thinking.

As for Adele, Springsteen would cover her a few years later in the unreleased "Family Song": "My momma she's a rainbow, come to give them thunderclouds a rest."

The clash between the stoic World War II generation and their free-spirited kids didn't skip the Springsteens or their town.

In early 1968, Springsteen was in a motorcycle accident that left him concussed. His mother hired a lawyer to prepare a civil suit against the driver involved. In an effort to clean Springsteen up for court—and give him a good story to tell on stage one day—his father brought a barber to the hospital to cut his hair. That summer, Freehold's police department raided homes across the city, going after kids they suspected of using drugs.

The violence of the era was equally inescapable. In 1967, Haynes was killed in Vietnam. In April 1968, Martin Luther King Jr. was assassinated in Memphis, the same city from which Elvis had emerged. Rioting erupted in August the same year at the Democratic National Convention in Chicago. The culture broke into a hard sprint, with the kids trying to put as much distance as possible between them and their parents, who weren't eager to let them run. There was a charge in the air.

"Thing is, it was the biggest paradigm shift in the world," Van Zandt said in 2011. "Ever. I think five hundred years from now history will be divided between pre-sixties and post-sixties. I really do. Everything changed."

The Castiles did what teenagers do. They drifted apart and they broke up. Earth, Springsteen's

"THE CASTILES STARTED OUT AS LITTLE FREEHOLD GREASERS, AND WE ENDED UP WITH, YOU KNOW, YOU'RE TALKING 1967 WHERE WE WERE ALL LONG-HAIRED HIPPIES."

Bruce Springsteen, 2011

Left and above: In May 1966, as a member of the Castiles, Springsteen recorded his first single, "Baby I"/"That's What You Get."

Opposite: Rocking a heavier sound with Steel Mill, c. 1970.

short-lived power trio in the make and wake of Cream, was next. Earth played long, jammed heavy, and Springsteen, backed by thousands of hours of practice, began to build a reputation as New Jersey's own guitar god.

That mattered in February 1969, when Springsteen walked into the Upstage Club in Asbury Park and asked if he could plug in. More than forty years later, he described Austin, overflowing with musicians for SXSW, as being "like some teenage music junkie's wet dream." In 1969, that was the Upstage. It was the kind of place that opened late, and stayed open later. It was where you went to jam after the gig. It pulsed with energy.

Springsteen took the stage and vaporized the place. Musicians filled in around him and the jam began. From that night came a new band that included drummer Vini "Mad Dog" Lopez (who, seeing Springsteen's promise, pushed for the group), and keyboardist Danny Federici.

The band was Child, which eventually became Steel Mill. With the exception of a few months in the summer of 1969 after Springsteen's parents and their third child, Pamela, packed up and moved to California leaving a few months of prepaid rent in Freehold, the band lived and rehearsed in a surfboard shop owned by their new manager, Carl "Tinker" West. Lopez was the link between band and manager. West was a literal rocket scientist—an aeronautical engineer, to be exact—and demanding. The rule was this: If they were making surfboards in one room, the band better be playing in the other. No problem.

They worked, and they wrote. Long songs, heavy songs. Prog rock, Southern rock, rock that picked you up by the neck and shook you around. Epic, sprawling numbers like "The Wind And The Rain," a breakup song that could stretch to twenty minutes, crashing at the crowd in waves. That was a tight little pop hit compared to "Garden State Parkway Blues," which could clock in at nearly thirty minutes.

Main photo: Child plays a Labor Day festival on Long Branch beach, September 1, 1969.

Inset: After breaking up Steel Mill in early 1971, Springsteen formed a series of larger bands including Dr. Zoom and the Sonic Boom.

The song displays Springsteen's early interest in working-class themes, and references the Rolling Stones' chaotic and deadly 1969 Altamont show by way of mentions of Hells Angel Sonny Barger and one sawed-off pool cue.

"The War Is Over" was the kind of moody antiwar song that seemed to write itself in those days. It didn't matter that Springsteen was an apolitical shore rat. The times shaped the art.

What he said was secondary anyway. The music Steel Mill was playing, its energy and ambition—Springsteen's energy and ambition—was the draw. And they drew thousands. West got them in front of larger and larger audiences, and Springsteen was a rock star. They packed East Coast venues. They headed west to San Francisco and auditioned for Bill Graham. They opened for Grand Funk Railroad, Chicago, and Black Sabbath. They backed Roy Orbison at a festival in Nashville. Already booked for a local show, they turned down an invitation to play Woodstock.

They even had their own *incident*. In September 1970, local police crashed a Steel Mill gig at the Clearwater Swim Club. "Whether or not it was a riot or a melee or a ruckus or a case of overreaction by police to a real or imagined threat from the young concertgoers is still being argued," the *Courier*, a weekly paper, wrote. Federici, who pushed a stack of speakers over on some police and then escaped, earning his nickname the Phantom, ended up wanted for assault. Copy under a photo of Van Zandt notes, "His mother was there."

As funny as it looks in print now—a reproduction was included in Robert Santelli's 2006 book *Greetings from E Street*—the clash was unnerving at the time. In the aftermath, Springsteen began playing more solo gigs while simultaneously thinking ever bigger creative thoughts. After a holiday trip to California to see his family, Springsteen returned to New Jersey, broke up Steel Mill and put together the Bruce Springsteen Band.

Vini Lopez stuck around on drums. Van Zandt, who'd stepped in to take up bass for Steel Mill, switched back to guitar. David Sancious took over keys (Federici was out), and Garry Tallent was on bass. But Springsteen didn't stop there. He added horns, and backup singers.

As he prepped that band, he also threw together Dr. Zoom and the Sonic Boom, consisting of almost

"I COULDN'T BELIEVE HOW GOOD HE WAS. VINI LOPEZ AND I LOOKED AT EACH OTHER. WE WERE BOTH THINKING THE SAME THING: WE HAD TO FORM A NEW BAND, AND SPRINGSTEEN HAD TO BE IN IT."

Danny Federici, 2006

the full roster of music characters he'd picked up over the past few years. Included in that group was a singer named John Lyon, who'd come to be known by his nickname, Southside Johnny.

As good as the Bruce Springsteen Band was—and it took the power of Steel Mill and added jazz, funk, and soul flourishes to songs that were beginning to show off some narrative chops—it was a financial beast. Even when he was forced to pare the lineup down from ten to five members, the audience wasn't there. The force and popularity of Steel Mill was a tough act to follow, and Springsteen was still shuffling through roles—songwriter, guitarist, bandleader, band member—trying to figure out what he wanted to be.

"This was a moment where I had to make a choice," Springsteen said in 2011. "And I chose the voice you hear on *Greetings from Asbury Park*."

Overleaf, main photo: Clarence Clemons, the "Big Man," stands tall at the Los Angeles Coliseum before the last show of the Born in the U.S.A. tour, October 7, 1985. A prominent figure in the early seventies New Jersey club scene, Clemons eventually joined Springsteen's band in 1972.

Overleaf, inset: This door stays on its hinges, 1978.

THE BIG MAN
JOINS THE BAND

One day, there was no Clarence Clemons.
The next, there was the E Street Band. Is that an
oversimplification? Yes. Does the timeline work?
Not quite. But do we really want to know exactly
how it went down the night Clemons joined the
band? Don't we deserve a little magic?

Maybe Bruce Springsteen and Steve Van Zandt were
alone on the boardwalk, bundled against the cold
when a mysterious figure cut through the chill. "And
what was worse, it was four in the morning, and
I wasn't sure, but Steve said he was definitely carrying
a saxophone," Springsteen said in a 1975 retelling.

Metaphorically speaking, it would explain the heat
Clarence Clemons brought to the music, wouldn't it?

"The real one is the best," Clemons said in 2009 while
promoting his part-fact, part-fiction autobiography *Big
Man: Real Life & Tall Tales*. (His bio in that book reads,
"Clarence Clemons is Clarence Clemons.")

In that version, it was also a dark and stormy night,
the wind howling outside the Student Prince in Asbury
Park. Clemons, there to check out this Springsteen
character he kept hearing about, opened the door and
a nor'easter took the thing right off its hinges, sending
it halfway up Kingsley.

That left Clemons, the former football player,
standing with his saxophone, silhouetted by lightning
in the doorway, thunder announcing his entrance.

"That was very true," he said.

Why would anyone want to know anything else?
Springsteen insists that's how it happened, but, writing
in the foreword to Clemons's book, acknowledges
that "mere facts will never plumb the mysteries of
the Big Man."

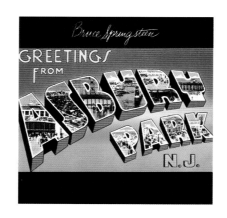

GREETINGS FROM ASBURY PARK, N.J.
1973

"AT THE END OF THE DAY, I JUST THOUGHT WHAT I WAS DOING ON MY OWN WAS MORE INTERESTING. THERE WAS MORE OF AN ORIGINAL VOICE IN IT."

BRUCE SPRINGSTEEN, 2011

1971

Fall: Tinker West ceases to be Springsteen's manager, but introduces him to Mike Appel.

December: Springsteen writes new material including "It's Hard To Be A Saint In The City" while visiting his family in California.

1972

February: Plays his new songs to Mike Appel and his production partner, Jimmy Cretecos, who immediately offer to become his new managers.

March: Signs up with Appel and Cretecos's newly formed management company, Laurel Canyon.

May 2: Auditions successfully for legendary Columbia A&R man John Hammond.

June 9: Appel and Cretecos sign a recording contract between Laurel Canyon and Columbia, under which Springsteen is a subcontractor.

July–September: Recording of *Greetings from Asbury Park, N.J.*, at 914 Sound Studios, Blauvelt, New York.

July 5: The Bruce Springsteen Band plays a benefit concert for 1972 Democratic presidential candidate George McGovern at the Cinema III theater in Red Bank, New Jersey.

October 21: Clarence Clemons plays his last gig with Norman Seldin and immediately joins Springsteen's as-yet-unnamed band.

October: Danny Federici teams up with Springsteen again, not having played regularly with him since Steel Mill.

October 28: The new lineup plays its first concert, at West Chester College, Pennsylvania.

December 7: The band performs a special gig in the chapel at Sing Sing prison.

1973

January 5: Release of *Greetings from Asbury Park, N.J.* (Highest chart position on release: US 60; UK 41).

Right: Springsteen picked up this postcard of Asbury Park in its heyday and convinced John Berg, Columbia's chief designer, to adapt it for his debut album.

Page 27: With a sheaf of new material, Springsteen made the jump from stage to studio without missing a beat. Here shown in 1973.

The first time Bruce Springsteen's name appeared in *Rolling Stone* was on March 15, 1973. Springsteen's debut, *Greetings from Asbury Park, N.J.*, had been out for more than two months—and the record wasn't mentioned. Springsteen pops up in "Random Notes" as an aside to news about John Hammond, "director of talent acquisition at Columbia Records," who suffered a heart attack after Springsteen played Max's Kansas City in New York.

Hammond told *Rolling Stone* it was the result of too much work and a bug he picked up in Paris. "His doctor, however, disagreed. He says it was due to Hammond's enthusiasm at the Springsteen show."

That's pretty much how it went that year. Bruce Springsteen generated all manner of big talk, but his album was an afterthought.

Released on January 5, 1973, *Greetings* proudly announced itself as a New Jersey record. The cover was a reproduction of a colorful postcard Springsteen found on the Shore. On the back, framed like a postage stamp, a photo of a scruffy-looking Springsteen grinning, or gritting his teeth. It's not clear which. Inside, the sounds of adventure, romance, and heartbreak set at the circus by the shore—with a side trip or three into the big city.

By way of introduction, Springsteen tried to jam everyone he'd met, everything he'd done, and everything he wanted to be into "Blinded By The Light," the album's playful opening track and first single. Crazy musicians, tempting and tempestuous women (one with a trigger-happy dad), grumpy authoritarian figures, assorted goofball antics, and all Springsteen's ambition piled into the song and came tumbling out as soon as the needle hit the groove.

"I wanted to get blinded by the light," he said in a 2005 taping of VH1's *Storytellers*. "I wanted to do things I hadn't done, see things I hadn't seen. ... It was really a young musician's tale."

In late 1971, with the Bruce Springsteen Band struggling to find an audience, Tinker West took Springsteen to New York to meet Mike Appel and Jimmy Cretecos. West had stepped away from his role as manager, but like everyone in Springsteen's world, he believed in the musician and wanted to help.

West called a friend who told him about Appel and Cretecos, contract songwriters with Pocketful of Tunes, a publishing company that, among other projects, provided songs for the hit television show *The Partridge Family*. They were looking to diversify. They were looking for talent.

"YOUR EARLY SONGS COME OUT OF A MOMENT WHEN YOU'RE WRITING WITH NO SURE PROSPECT OF EVER BEING HEARD. UP UNTIL THEN, IT'S JUST YOU AND YOUR MUSIC. THAT ONLY HAPPENS ONCE."

Bruce Springsteen, 1998

West set up a meeting, picked up Bruce, and headed into the city. Springsteen sat down with an acoustic guitar and played Appel two songs—"Baby Doll" and "Song To The Orphans"—both pulled from his notebook of singer-songwriter material. These weren't built for rowdy nights in sweaty bars. These were coffee-house songs, born from the writing style he'd turned to in search of something unique to him, and to the detriment of the kind of income, however modest, that kept him relatively comfortable in the Steel Mill days.

"That was the first time, no eating money, no money," Springsteen said in 2011. "I just felt that was where I needed to be at the time. That was the best I had to offer."

Appel wanted more than what he heard, but he'd caught enough to be intrigued. He told Springsteen to keep writing.

Left: John Hammond, the legendary Columbia A&R man who recommended Springsteen to the label, where he has remained ever since.

Opposite: On stage, March 1973. When Springsteen auditioned the previous year, it was the power of his acoustic-guitar playing and the poetry of his lyrics that excited Hammond.

West and Springsteen loaded up for a drive to California for the holidays. The rest of the underworked members of the Bruce Springsteen Band planned a move to Virginia, a dependable market going back to the Steel Mill days, where their names carried some weight.

Springsteen and West parted on the West Coast and Springsteen went to work, even going so far as searching out musicians in that scene and contemplating his own move. When he finally returned to New Jersey in mid-January, he'd written a couple dozen songs, only a few of them with the band in mind. His head and his pen were interested in solo work.

He wrote "Randolph Street," the story of life in Fred and Alice's house. A sequel of sorts, "Family Song," wrestled with the bad times and embraced the better times that had followed his family's move west. "You could say it took California to bring us close," Springsteen sings.

"Two Hearts In True Waltz Time," "Saga Of The Architect Angel," "Visitation At Fort Horn," "Street Queen," the titles alone hinted at the short films flickering in Springsteen's imagination.

In February, Springsteen rang up Appel, made the trip back into Manhattan, and sat down again with his guitar. This time, the effect was similar to that first night at the Upstage when Springsteen plugged in and stopped time.

Appel cleared his world of anything that wasn't related to the business of Bruce Springsteen. Appel's commitment was pure, absolute, and bombastic.

Late in 1972, talking to *Crawdaddy!* writers Peter Knobler and Greg Mitchell about a Springsteen show at Sing Sing prison, where Bruce's grandfather had once done time, Appel described Springsteen as "a combination of Bob Dylan, Chuck Berry, and Shakespeare." Jesus must have felt left out. Then again: "I always thought of myself as John the Baptist, heralding Bruce's coming to the world," Appel said in Dave Marsh's 1979 biography *Born to Run: The Bruce Springsteen Story*.

Springsteen got back with the band for a few last gigs, and then, without fanfare or a farewell show, became a solo artist.

Appel went to work, starting at the top of the food chain. Basically, he badgered his way into John Hammond's office. This was no small accomplishment. After all, Hammond had discovered Billie Holiday,

Benny Goodman, and Bob Dylan. This, to Appel, was a pitch point: *You discovered Dylan? You think you know music? My guy's better.* An obnoxious pitch point, but one nonetheless. Appel walked in and made it.

Hammond didn't much like Appel. In a fit of foreshadowing, Springsteen didn't much like the hype. Everyone liked what happened next.

Springsteen grabbed an acoustic with a cracked neck and lit into "It's Hard To Be A Saint In The City," a street-corner strut packed with juxtaposition that slowly trades its confidence for a panicked frenzy. He's "the king of the alley" and the "prince of the paupers." The sisters "fell back and said 'Don't that man look pretty?'" in one line, while the next introduces a cripple crying out for nickels and pity. The devil appears like Jesus as the street chases the singer down into the subway where things only get worse. The song picks up a

> "LAST WINTER I WROTE LIKE A MADMAN. PUT IT OUT. HAD NO MONEY, NOWHERE TO GO, NOTHING TO DO. DIDN'T KNOW TOO MANY PEOPLE. IT WAS COLD AND I WROTE A LOT. AND I GOT TO FEELING VERY GUILTY IF I DIDN'T."

Bruce Springsteen, 1973

Opposite: Backstage at Max's Kansas City in New York, 1973.

Left: Mike Appel (center) with his young charge and Columbia boss, Clive Davis. Springsteen said of Appel: "I needed somebody else who was a little crazy in the eyes because that was my approach to it all."

claustrophobic rhythm to where it seems he might never escape. Until he does, bringing the song home like a breath of fresh air.

Having won Hammond's attention, Springsteen came back the next day, recorded a batch of demos and soon Columbia head Clive Davis was celebrating him, too. In a great shuffling of lawyered-up paperwork that would become significant down the line, Laurel Canyon Ltd., the company set up by Appel and Cretecos, signed a deal with Columbia. Springsteen would record for Columbia through Laurel Canyon.

And Springsteen would do this as a solo singer-songwriter, or so they thought. That's what the suits had seen and heard, or had they? There's video of Springsteen on stage at Max's Kansas City in September 1972. He's awkward in his banter, but there's a gleam and a grin as he starts "Henry Boy," from which he'd borrow some meter and melody for "Blinded By The Light." His playing, even on an acoustic, is electric. You can hear it as well on the Columbia demos released in 1998 on the *Tracks* box set. There's too much energy; he couldn't possibly be only a folk singer.

Now signed and with a record to make, Springsteen made his reveal. He needed a band. And not just any band, either. Not studio session players. He needed *his* band, in all its ragged majesty. "We were like a band of hobos from New Jersey," Garry Tallent recalled in 2011.

Tallent got the call to bring his bass. David Sancious was brought in on piano and organ, and Lopez on drums. Notably absent was Van Zandt, who was told he wouldn't be needed after the first day of recording at 914 Sound Studios. That was July. In August they turned the album over to CBS and Davis, who handed it back. There wasn't a single.

Springsteen went back to Asbury Park, to his apartment above an abandoned beauty salon. He knocked out "Blinded By The Light," and "Spirit In The Night," the tale of a late-night adventure to Greasy Lake co-starring his girlfriend at the time, Diane Lozito (as Crazy Janey), and a cast of typically nicknamed characters like Hazy Davy, Wild Billy, Killer Joe, and G-Man.

Springsteen returned to the studio (playing bass and piano now, too), with Lopez, and Clarence Clemons on sax. Satisfied this time, Columbia released the record and introduced Bruce Springsteen to the world.

Greetings was a compromise—between label and artist, artist and himself. Springsteen might have had to go it alone to find his voice, and that voice might have been what Columbia bought into, but there was no reason to stop there.

"I THINK I WAS VERY CAUGHT UP IN THE TIME ALSO— WITH THE ONE MAN, YOUR GUITAR, YOUR SONG. I WAS IN THE MIDDLE OF THAT REINVENTION OF MYSELF."

Bruce Springsteen, 2011

The suggestion in "Growin' Up," when Springsteen finds the "key to the universe in the engine of an old parked car," is that everything he needed was nearby. Continuing his metaphor, he had to strip that engine to its parts and rebuild it.

"Spirit In The Night" and "Blinded" highlight Clemons's role as the spark plug, and among the tales Springsteen would eventually weave into extended versions of "Growin' Up" was one of he and Clemons on a mystical journey in what might well have been that car.

"Mary Queen of Arkansas" is like a circus love song, one character "a lonely acrobat," the other "not man enough for me to hate or woman enough for kissing." It's about a guy in love with a transvestite. "The Angel" wears the scars of the times, the song's eponymous protagonist "followin' dead-end signs into the sores."

"For You" and "Lost In The Flood" are the album's epics. "Lost In The Flood," with its nuns running pregnant through Vatican halls "pleadin' immaculate conception," tangles Catholic and wartime imagery. "That pure American brother, dull-eyed and empty-faced," Springsteen sings.

"For You" is a suicide ballad, Springsteen's increasingly impassioned vocal building to the lyric, "So you left to find a better reason than the one we were living for." It's a desperate moment, a what-could-be echo from "Mary Queen Of Arkansas" and the first-person exclamation, "but I was not born to live to die."

Backstage at Max's Kansas City, 1973. Springsteen played the legendary New York club venue more than forty times in 1972 and 1973.

"I DON'T LIKE IT AND IT'S HARD TO LIVE WITH. I MEAN, I RESENT IT WHEN I HEAR IT ABOUT ANYONE."

Bruce Springsteen, on being called the New Dylan, 1973

"Does This Bus Stop At 82nd Street?" paints a wide-eyed view of New York in motion, sex and mystery just the other side of the window.

Rolling Stone returned to the topic of Springsteen in a little more depth on April 26, 1973, this time in a piece titled "It's Sign Up a Genius Month" (which still didn't name the album).

"He's much further along, much more developed than Bobby was when he came to me," Hammond said, feeding the marketing campaign the label had already launched comparing Springsteen to Bob Dylan.

Dylan was just the most inescapable influence. When *Rolling Stone* finally did review *Greetings*, Lester Bangs detected traces of the Band and Van Morrison. The review was mixed, with Bangs describing Springsteen's singing as "sorta like Robbie Robertson on Quaaludes with Dylan barfing down the back of his neck." But also, "Hot damn, what a passel o' verbiage," and closing with a request to keep an eye on Springsteen: "He's not the new John Prine."

Prine had been a recent New Dylan. Loudon Wainwright III was a New Dylan. Elliott Murphy was a New Dylan. Lots of New Dylans. "And the old Dylan was only thirty," Springsteen said in 2012.

Blame Dylan for some of that. He was so good, and such a cultural force, that of course the industry was going to go looking for more versions of him to sell. And the artists couldn't avoid his influence any more than the bean counters. "The way Elvis freed your body, Bob freed your mind," Springsteen said in his 1988 speech inducting Dylan into the Rock and Roll Hall of Fame.

The writing on *Greetings* owes an undeniable debt to Dylan's ability to turn the seemingly banal into something romantic. In Dylan's 2004 book *Chronicles*, he sketches the view from a window during a blizzard: a guy scraping frost off the window of a car, a priest "in a purple cloak ... slipping through the courtyard of the church," a woman dragging laundry up the street.

"There were a million stories, just everyday New York things if you wanted to focus in on them," he wrote. "It was always right out in front of you, blended together, but you'd have to pull it apart to make any sense of it."

Greetings is packed with such deconstructions. Out the window of that bus, Springsteen could have seen just another sketchy porn theater. Instead, he saw "tainted women in Vistavision," and that's before Mary Lou "rides to heaven on a gyroscope."

There were similarities, but they weren't the same. Go back to 1965, when Dylan famously sat in front of reporters in a television studio in San Francisco and toyed with a press conference. Reporters worked to heap meaning on him; he insisted he was nothing but a song-and-dance man. Maybe yes, maybe no. One of Dylan's greatest talents has always been his elusiveness. It's allowed him cover to do whatever he wants, good, bad, or indifferent.

Springsteen hadn't had a moment of indifference, and hasn't since. *Greetings* might have been a compromise, but it was done in the service of the big picture. He knew who he was, and where he was going. Only the exact path was unclear. Mike Appel, John Hammond, Clive Davis, and Columbia Records signed a solo singer-songwriter, and Springsteen could play the part.

"But I was a wolf in sheep's clothing," he said.

When *Greetings* was released in January 1973, its creator was one of the few people to pick up a copy.

THE WILD, THE INNOCENT & THE E STREET SHUFFLE

1973

"BY THE TIME THE SECOND RECORD CAME, I SAID, 'LET'S BRING THE NOISE.' EVERYBODY WAS LIKE, ABSOLUTELY."

BRUCE SPRINGSTEEN, 2011

1973

February: Springsteen's first single, "Blinded By The Light"/ "Spirit In The Night," fails to make the charts.

February 5: David Bowie sees Springsteen playing Max's Kansas City in New York City and later that year becomes the first person to record cover versions of his compositions ("Growin' Up" and "It's Hard To Be A Saint In The City").

February–March: The band plays a short tour of the West Coast.

May: Clive Davis (president of Columbia) is fired, which weakens Springsteen's position at the record company.

May–June: Springsteen gets his first taste of playing big arenas, as the support act on Chicago's early summer mini-tour.

May–September: Recording of *The Wild, the Innocent & the E Street Shuffle* at 914 Sound Studios.

July 27: Springsteen plays an underwhelming set at a Columbia sales convention in San Francisco.

September 28: First night of what might loosely be described as The Wild, the Innocent & the E Street Shuffle tour, at Hampden-Sydney College, Virginia; touring would continue until March 1975.

November 5: Release of *The Wild, the Innocent & the E Street Shuffle* (US 59, UK 33).

Above: Liberty Hall, Houston, March 1974.

Right: "Whoah-oh, everybody form a line!"—Clarence Clemons, Danny Federici, Springsteen, Vini Lopez, Garry Tallent, and David Sancious, August 1973.

Page 39: Portrait by David Gahr from the cover shoot, 1973.

Early in 1973, not long after *Greetings* was released, Springsteen did a radio interview in Maryland. What, he was asked, do people do in Asbury Park?

"Not too much," he told WHFS. "Nobody goes there anymore. The average age is old people."

With *Greetings*, Springsteen had deliberately associated himself with New Jersey and Asbury Park. He might have had Manhattan-sized ambition, but he was a Jersey Shore artist. With his next record, he was going to expand the map. *Greetings* took its title from a postcard. *The Wild, the Innocent & the E Street Shuffle*, released just eleven months later, was one part Jersey Shore, two parts Hollywood.

The Wild and the Innocent was a 1959 Western starring Audie Murphy as a mountain trapper named Yancy, and Sandra Dee as Rosalie. She runs away from her family and joins him as they hit the big city. Adventure and mayhem ensue.

The rest was all Springsteen. "I wanted to invent a dance with no exact steps," he wrote in his 1998 lyric collection, *Songs*. "It was just the dance you do every day and night to get by."

He saw it going down all around him: in the streets, in the bars, and on the road as he traveled with his band. Springsteen was doing it himself. They were all doing "The E Street Shuffle."

Springsteen based "The E Street Shuffle" on "The Monkey Time," a 1963 R&B hit written by Curtis Mayfield, recorded by Major Lance, and bearing no relation at all to Bob Dylan. It opens in a state of discord, horns arguing with each other about who knows what? Maybe the old singer-songwriter versus bandleader debate. Whatever it was, they reach an agreement, fall into harmony, and give way to a funky electric-guitar shuffle.

Then Springsteen: "Sparks fly on E Street when the boy-prophets walk it handsome and hot."

The "teenage diplomat" of "Blinded By The Light" was back, but he brought friends this time, and they weren't short on confidence. Nor should they have been. "The group fairly steams with fresh energy," Peter Knobler and Greg Mitchell wrote in *Crawdaddy!* in March 1973. "The *next* album should be unbelievable!" they added.

The next album should have changed everything. The next album didn't change much of anything. Not outwardly, at least.

By the beginning of 1973, after a year spent touring heavily in a few, mostly East Coast, areas—Boston, Philadelphia, New York—the crowds were growing. Springsteen was playing with a power and passion that made critics combust. If not completely outrunning it, Springsteen was putting a little distance between himself and the New Dylan hype. On stage, he was undeniable and not a lot like anyone who had picked up the newly released *Greetings* would expect.

"You folks are probably saying, 'What's this folk singer doing dressed up so fancy?'" Springsteen said as members of the band filled the stage. Bassist Garry Tallent went for his tuba, Danny Federici readied his accordion. They were at the Main Point in Bryn Mawr, just outside Philadelphia.

He joked about finding Federici at a Lawrence Welk show, "playing so good I asked him if he wanted to join the band."

Springsteen paused.

"This is a circus song, as are most of our numbers."

Everyone laughed, and Springsteen strummed into an early version of "Wild Billy's Circus Story," Federici doing his best to turn the accordion into a calliope and bring the whole crazy scene—Missy Bimbo, the flying Zambinis and the rest—to life.

> # "YOU DON'T WANT TO GET TOO SELF-CENTERED. IT'S EASY TO DO, YOU KNOW, BECAUSE PEOPLE ARE ALWAYS SHOVIN' YOU IN YOUR FACE."
>
> Bruce Springsteen, 1973

Student Prince
911 Kingsley St., Asbury Park

Presents

BRUCE SPRINGSTEEN

Mon. thru Wed,
776-9837

Opposite: A less pensive Springsteen than the shot finally chosen for the front cover.

Left: Audie Murphy and Sandra Dee in *The Wild and the Innocent*, 1959.

Federici's reappearance had more to do with necessity than anything else. After work on *Greetings* was done, David Sancious headed back to Virginia where he had a job and a record of his own to finish. Springsteen called Federici, who had been left behind in the Steel Mill-to-Bruce Springsteen Band transition, to fill out the band.

Federici needed a little more than a phone call to come running, however. As recounted by Robert Santelli in *Greetings from E Street*, Federici wanted to know he wasn't going to get burned again, that this wouldn't be another Steel Mill.

Springsteen's answer: "Well, we've got a record to promote this time."

They hit the road in two vehicles, doing multi-night runs in dependable markets. Brucebase, a website dedicated to details of Springsteen's career, lists four nights at the Main Point, seven nights at Paul's Mall in Boston, four nights at My Father's Place in Roslyn, New York, five nights at the Quiet Knight in Chicago, and six nights back in Manhattan at Max's Kansas City.

The first night at Max's, on January 31, 1973, was recorded for the *King Biscuit Flower Hour* radio program. From that night, "Bishop Danced" would eventually end up on *Tracks*, the 1998 outtakes box set. Sadly missing was Springsteen's introduction: "Kind of a nonsense song. It's about a bishop and his wife and this violin player in West Virginia. It's about how their daughter lost her mother to mathematics while on a business trip in Detroit."

On May 1, Springsteen was back in California. Los Angeles this time (and by plane), for a show presented by Columbia Records, playing a forty-minute set between the opener, Dr. Hook & the Medicine Show, and the headliner, New Riders of the Purple Sage. Three of the songs from that set were released with the 2005 making-of-*Born to Run* documentary *Wings for Wheels*.

"Thundercrack" had become the acetylene torch set to most every show they played. Written for Springsteen's girlfriend, Diane Lozito, the song mirrored their fiery relationship. Even the introduction could sting. During one of the Main Point shows, Springsteen noted from the stage that his girlfriend was in attendance. "She's here with her sister," he said. "I'm going to do this for her sister."

In Los Angeles, they stretched "Thundercrack" past the ten-minute mark, Springsteen, eyes flashing, showing off on guitar with Lopez thundering behind him

"IN PERFORMANCE THINGS CRYSTALLIZE THAT DO NOT ON AN ALBUM. I THINK, TO KNOW WHAT I'M TRYING TO DO, WHAT THE BAND IS, YOU HAVE TO SEE IT."

Bruce Springsteen, 1974

almost note for note. The camera catches Clemons shouting. Springsteen and Lopez pile on and pick up steam. Manic energy coils, ready to strike. Springsteen comes out of that solo and swings toward Clemons, gives him a nod, and the two play a soaring melody. In moments like that, the word hype seems to have been criminally applied to Springsteen. It can't be hype if it's true.

At the end of May, they played the first of twelve opening dates for Chicago. Big shows in cavernous barns built for hockey and basketball. Faced with short sets and the distracted crowds that greet openers, Springsteen was miserable, telling Appel after the tour he was done with arenas. He'd play clubs or theaters and perform his full show for people who wanted to see him.

They did just that—until July 27, when it was back to California. This time they landed in San Francisco. The occasion was a CBS sales convention, a chance to impress the office staff who'd be charged with working *The Wild, the Innocent & the E Street Shuffle*.

Stuck following Edgar Winter and what could have been (but wasn't) called His Explosions and Lasers Spectacular, Springsteen opened quiet with "4th Of July, Asbury Park (Sandy)."

Joe's Place, Cambridge, Massachusetts, January 5, 1974. Springsteen toured throughout 1974, tirelessly building his fan base and playing to bigger and bigger audiences.

"GENERALLY GOOD BANDS COME OUT OF NEIGHBORHOODS AND OUT OF VERY SPECIFIC GEOGRAPHICAL BOUNDARIES AND LOCATIONS. THINK OF ANY BAND YOU LOVE, THEIR BACKSTORY IS SOMEWHAT SIMILAR."

Bruce Springsteen, 2011

Another song heavy on acoustic guitar and accordion, it finds Springsteen weary of the old scene, casting the people there as "stranded." Longing for an escape to anywhere and trying to talk his girl into coming along, Springsteen declares, "This boardwalk life is through."

It left the room cold and annoyed John Hammond, but it's hard to deny the subversive humor of the choice. Then, rather than the tight three-song set everyone else played, Springsteen went on for forty minutes, further alienating the audience.

Talking to writer Paul Williams in 1974 about the Chicago tour, Springsteen said, "It had nothing to do with anything that had anything to do with me, those big arenas." You couldn't expect him to find himself in a sales meeting, either. He had his ideas, his vision for his music, and the whole thing would rise or fall with those. If that meant "Thundercrack" didn't make the new album, fine. If it meant "The Fever," a lustful, humid R&B ballad had to go from the final track list, so be it. Springsteen had a specific story in mind and, unlike *Greetings*, no one was going tell him how it should be soundtracked.

The Wild, the Innocent & the E Street Shuffle came together in sessions stretching from May through September 1973. Back from Virginia, Sancious rejoined the band, expanding its sound and eventually inspiring its name. His mother lived on E Street.

Released in November, the album was described by *Rolling Stone* as "[taking] itself more seriously. The songs are longer, more ambitious and more romantic." Sancious and Clemons were singled out in a band that's "essentially an R&B outfit—

funky-butt is Springsteen's musical *pied-à-terre*." The album had far more in common with the Bruce Springsteen Band than it did the coffee-house croon that defined *Greetings*.

The shortest song, the album-launching shuffle, was, at four minutes, twenty-six seconds, too long for AM radio. Four songs clock in longer than seven minutes, and the record closes with the nearly ten-minute "New York City Serenade."

"Kitty's Back" sounds like a riot in a jazz club started by a stripper (Springsteen pulled the title from a passing marquee). But if Kitty was coming home, the rest of the record suggests packing up. Both "4th Of July, Asbury Park (Sandy)" and "Wild Billy's Circus Story" play like glances back over the shoulder on the walk out of town, the latter ending with an "All aboard, Nebraska's our next stop."

If "Thundercrack" had to be tossed to the outtake bin, at least it was in the service of "Rosalita (Come Out Tonight)." Flush as ever with Springsteen's sense of nickname—Jack the Rabbit, Weak Knees Willie, Big Bones Billie—the song has a hero determined to bust his girl free of parental bonds. His promise is the future, and that one day it'll all be funny. "Because the record company, Rosie, just gave me a big advance!" Springsteen shouts.

"Incident On 57th Street" and "New York City Serenade" are sketches from the city, screenplays in waiting. "Incident" is a love story, a *West Side Story*, starring Spanish Johnny and Puerto Rican Jane. As with "Sandy," all the old charms are fading. Sitting on a fire escape, Johnny yells down to the kids in the street, "Hey little heroes, summer's long but I guess it ain't very sweet around here anymore."

The as-yet-unnamed E Street Band in their natural habitat on the Jersey Shore, August 1973.

"New York City Serenade" combined two songs, "New York City Song" and "Vibes Man," to add one more goodbye to the album's arc. "Sometimes you just gotta walk on," Springsteen sings.

His artistic world was expanding and Springsteen was outgrowing the Jersey Shore, as a setting for his stories if not as a home. The economy and unrest of the early seventies had taken its toll on Asbury Park. The town was closing up. The Upstage had shut down. The music didn't match this backdrop, no matter how pensive Springsteen looked on the album cover. And he looks awfully pensive on the album cover, but it's the photo on the flip side that tells the story.

It's a group shot, and one that's full of sideshow charm. Clemons stands at the far left, shirt open, white handkerchief around his neck. Springsteen is next, in a tank top, jeans, and blue Converse sneakers. Sancious, barefoot and sitting,

looks like a jazz album. Federici, in a button-down shirt, might have just gotten in from the night before. Tallent has shed his shoes, too. Standing behind them all, in an open Hawaiian shirt and sporting a drophandle mustache, is Lopez looking more like Jimmy Buffett than a madman.

These were the pirates Springsteen was going to stake his career on, not the suits at Columbia who were wavering in their support (especially since Clive Davis had been sent packing). As with *Greetings*, Springsteen needed his guys, the guys who knew his music, and his language. "The localism of it was important to me," he said in 2011.

Radio would catch on at some point, or it wouldn't. Springsteen was going to take his music out and go door to door if that's what it took to make people care about rock 'n' roll the way he cared about rock 'n' roll. He had the parts.

Above: With Jon Landau, whose article in the *Real Paper* gave Springsteen a boost just when he needed it.

Left: When Columbia president Clive Davis departed from the label in May 1973, Springsteen's career had been left in the balance.

He knew he had the parts, and the tools to put them together right.

"I told them I'd been playing in bands for eight years and by myself for two, three months," Springsteen told Knobler and Mitchell. "They forgot about the eight years and went with the two months."

That story came packaged under the headline "Who Is Bruce Springsteen and Why Are We Saying All These Wonderful Things About Him?" Even Springsteen was scratching for the answers, but he was getting closer all the time. In the 1974 interview with Paul Williams, he talked about all the artists he grew up listening to, and how they seemed to stall, creatively speaking. "They'd make the same statement every record, basically, without elaborating on it much."

He'd moved his work forward with *The Wild, the Innocent & the E Street Shuffle*, but the weight he felt, that "boulder on his shoulder" from "Blinded By The Light," still pressed down. Finances were tight, and Springsteen had created a number of extra obstacles in the name of creative freedom.

Six weeks on from the release of the new record, Springsteen and the guys were back in Asbury Park playing three nights at the Student Prince to earn a little Christmas money. They'd done the same thing in 1971.

"If I didn't know it was good, I never would have stuck with it," Tallent said in 2011.

But the guys *knew*. Like Appel knew. Like Tinker West had known. Like just enough supporters at Columbia knew, too. They knew they were right, and everyone else was wrong. They fought to keep Springsteen on the road. They fought to make sure the label didn't drop him before a third album. They saw how that weight manifested as determination and responded in kind.

What they needed was a little help.

It didn't take much. A mention in an alternative newspaper—the *Real Paper*—was all, by a writer called Jon Landau who was having a hard go of it himself. A guy who was looking for something to believe in, and ran into the one guy who made people believe.

Immortalized on the back cover of the album, David Gahr's group portrait perfectly captures the solidarity and ragtag charm of Captain Bruce and his crew.

BORN TO RUN

1975

"THE BOTTOM LINE IS, IN ADDITION TO MAKING A GREAT RECORD, HE ALSO MADE THE RECORD HE NEEDED TO MAKE AT THAT POINT. THAT DIDN'T HAPPEN BY ACCIDENT."

JON LANDAU, 2011

1974

Winter
Columbia advances only enough money to record a single, based on which the company would decide whether to commit to a third album.

January
Recording of early versions of "Born To Run" and "Jungleland."

February
Springsteen fires Vini Lopez from the band after the drummer loses his temper one time too many. Ernest "Boom" Carter takes over.

Spring
Around this time, the band becomes known as the E Street Band for the first time.

April 10
Springsteen meets Jon Landau backstage at a gig at Charlie's Place, Cambridge, Massachusetts.

May–October
First phase of recording of *Born to Run*, at 914 Sound Studios.

May 22
Publication of Landau's famous "rock and roll future" column.

July 12–14
During a three-night, six-show run at the Bottom Line in New York City, "Born To Run" is well received by music-industry insiders.

August
David Sancious and Boom Carter leave the E Street Band and are replaced by Roy Bittan and Max Weinberg.

Winter
Jon Landau visits Springsteen in Long Branch and they bond over their shared music obsession.

1975

March
Recording of *Born to Run* resumes at the Record Plant in Manhattan and Jon Landau becomes a co-producer.

July
Born to Run recording eventually comes to an end.

July 20
First night of the Born to Run tour, at the Palace Concert Theater in Providence, Rhode Island; featuring Steve Van Zandt's live debut as a member of the E Street Band.

August 13–17
Another residency at the Bottom Line stokes pre-release excitement.

September 1
Release of *Born to Run* (US 3, UK 17) to universally positive reviews.

October 16
Robert De Niro catches one of the band's shows at the Roxy in West Hollywood and is believed by some to have got the idea for his "Are you talkin' to me?" improvisation in *Taxi Driver* from Springsteen's between-song patter.

October 20
Springsteen appears on the covers of *Time* and *Newsweek* in the same week.

November 18
Plays his first concert outside the United States—at the Hammersmith Odeon in London, the start of a week-long European mini-tour.

Top: A detour to Pauls Valley, Oklahoma, September 17, 1975.

Above: Monmouth Arts Center, Red Bank, New Jersey, October 11, 1975.

Left: Alex Cooley's Electric Ballroom, Atlanta, Georgia, August 21, 1975.

Far left: The Bottom Line, New York City, August 1975.

Page 51: Beginning to make it big. Sunset Boulevard, Los Angeles, 1975.

You could get away with calling the *Real Paper* just a weekly publication. But Jon Landau wasn't just another critic. He was in charge of *Rolling Stone*'s review section. He was of a group—with Greil Marcus, Dave Marsh, Lester Bangs, Paul Williams, and a few others—that made rock criticism mean something. And Landau had produced records—by the MC5 and Livingston Taylor. Labels courted his opinion. Landau's words had weight, and he knew it.

What he was far less certain of in the spring of 1974 was what, if anything, any of that meant.

Springsteen had his own questions. "What do you do when your dreams come true?" he asked in the 2005 documentary *Wings for Wheels: The Making of Born to Run.* "What do you do when they don't?"

"Is love real?"

Less poetic but far more immediate was one more: How are we going to pay all these bills? "Oh, we owe like a mint," Springsteen said to Williams in an October 1974 interview.

The pattern that had established itself in 1973 hadn't changed as the midway point of the next year approached. The crowds grew in numbers and enthusiasm. Reported cases of the vapors reached near epidemic proportions in the critical community. Records barely sold and radio lagged except in a few key markets with activist DJs. To the roiling internal conflicts, Springsteen could add the pressures of being in charge. The boss, if you will.

All or none of these things could have been on his mind in early April when he wandered outside Charlie's Place during a four-night Boston stand. In the front window was the largely ecstatic *Real Paper* review of *The Wild, the Innocent & the E Street Shuffle.* Springsteen braced himself against the cold and started to read. "Impassioned and inspired street fantasy." That was good. Weak drumming and poor production? Not as much.

One problem had already been fixed. After a fight in February between Vini "Mad Dog" Lopez and Mike Appel's brother, Springsteen had fired Lopez. Ernest "Boom" Carter, a friend of pianist David Sancious, was now behind the kit.

Springsteen was still standing in front of the review when a voice asked him what he thought. It was Landau, who had written the review. They spoke for a few minutes, and more after the show. And the next day on the phone. Springsteen wanted to know more about production.

"That was the beginning," Landau said in 2011.

The beginning of more than either could possibly know. So they weren't strangers, and Landau had an idea what was in store when Springsteen returned to Boston on May 9 to open for Bonnie Raitt at the

"EVERYONE SAW A LITTLE OF THEIR HOPES AND DREAMS IN THAT RECORD."

Roy Bittan, 2005

Harvard Square Theater. Two shows that night, and Springsteen would have his full set. Landau decided to hit the late one, went home, sat down, and let it all out.

"It's four in the morning and raining," is how Landau led a piece that would yield arguably the most famous line in the history of rock criticism. "I'm twenty-seven today, feeling old, listening to my records, and remember that things were different a decade ago."

You can almost hear Springsteen's voice singing words not yet written: "So you're scared and you're thinking that maybe we ain't that young anymore."

"Through college, I consumed sound as if it were the staff of life," Landau wrote. "... Whether it was a neurotic and manic approach to music, or just a religious one, or both, I really don't care."

It really didn't make any difference. Seventeen is carefree. Twenty-seven is worried. Landau made music his business, and so it became a business. He was sick (Crohn's disease), and enduring a crumbling marriage. He had an adult life with adult problems, and rock 'n' roll was never supposed to be about adulthood. It was supposed to kick and thrash and scream obscenities at adulthood.

And don't forget what had happened during the ten years in question, from the Beatles in 1964 to 1974's continued mess in Vietnam and the growing Watergate scandal in Richard Nixon's White House.

"Nobody was that young anymore," Springsteen said in a 2005 taping of VH1's *Storytellers.*

Landau walked into the Harvard Square Theater disillusioned. He left rededicated. On May 22, *Real Paper* readers picked up Landau's column, and there it was: "I saw rock and roll future, and its name is Bruce Springsteen. And on a night when I needed to feel young, he made me feel like I was hearing music for the very first time."

Danny Federici, Clarence Clemons, and Springsteen take their bows at the Hammersmith Odeon, London, November 18, 1975. This was the E Street Band's first overseas performance.

Double portrait by Eric Meola
from the *Born to Run* shoot, 1975.

He did hear one piece of music for the very first time. Springsteen unwrapped a work-in-progress that set out in search of answers to *his* questions, a muscled-up mission statement titled "Born To Run." In Springsteen, Landau saw someone who could take every glorious feeling he'd had about rock, and make it feel new again. There was a purity in this man's belief, and "Born To Run" was the most pure expression yet.

What Landau wrote was "almost Dickensian, with its spoofing allusion to the spiritual resurrection of Scrooge," Dave Marsh wrote in *Born to Run: The Bruce Springsteen Story*, "but other versions made it seem as though Landau were attempting to write advertising copy." What the other versions got wrong, almost always, was the phrasing. Even Springsteen's website is mistaken: "I have seen the future of rock and roll," it reads. It's a small but important distinction.

Not that direct quotations couldn't be turned into advertising copy. The pros at Columbia Records read Landau's "Loose Ends" column and saw promotional future. They ran up television spots re-emphasizing the first two records while a man with a Serious TV Voice read "rock and roll future." One poster, highlighting Landau's copy, featured Springsteen's image juxtaposed godlike against a brilliant blue sky and puffy white clouds.

No longer the Next Dylan, Springsteen was the Next Savior. This is the kind of thing that can drive a publicity-averse guy a little nuts. And it did. It also gave him a shot of confidence at an important moment, when he needed to know his music meant something to someone other than himself.

That connection was real and meaningful, but the rest was marketing at its most infuriating. The design team could put his head in the clouds, but those vacations in the stratosphere were going to have to wait. "Gotta have your feet on the ground if you're going to make it," he told the *Storytellers* crowd. "Can't be fantasy land."

The making of *Born to Run* was anything but.

With the spotlight back on his career, and the label behind him, he needed a new record. In *Songs*, Springsteen described the words of "Born To Run" coming to him as he sat playing guitar in his tiny rental house in West Long Branch, New Jersey. Maybe he'd seen it painted on a car cruising the circuit in Asbury Park some Saturday night. Maybe it came from some old movie he'd caught on television.

The recording of "Born To Run" started in May 1974 at 914 Sound and stretched, off and on, into October. That's the song, not the album. "Anytime you spend six months on one song, there's something not quite right," Van Zandt said in *Wings for Wheels*. He added a wry grin, because he's Van Zandt and torturous is not his suit. Springsteen wore it well … well, he wore it.

"'Born To Run' was kind of set up by the golden age of those richly arranged rock records," Springsteen said.

He was working on a singing voice that was as close as he could get to Roy Orbison's. Orbison was "the true master of the romantic apocalypse you dreaded," Springsteen said at SXSW.

For Springsteen, the music of "Born To Run" evoked Phil Spector's recordings, his Wall of Sound, all-time-everything gems like the Ronettes' "Be My Baby," and the Crystals' "Then He Kissed Me," which Springsteen and the band had been playing live with a quick flip of the pronoun to "She."

Top left: A rare moment of peace on the tour bus.

Center left: Springsteen and Steve Van Zandt—a great team on and off stage, but not the most gracious victors. Lee Dorsey's Ya Ya Lounge, New Orleans, September 1975.

Bottom left: A Big Mac in the Big Easy, September 1975.

"Phil's records felt like near chaos," Springsteen said at SXSW, "violence covered in sugar and candy, sung by the girls who sent Roy-O running straight for the antidepressants. If Roy was opera, Phil was symphonies, little three-minute orgasms, followed by oblivion."

That oblivion is what Springsteen was afraid of, what the couple at the heart of "Born To Run" is in a dead sprint from. All they see is a future where possibilities diminish rather than multiply, where before you know it you're the one sitting alone in a dark kitchen with smokes and beers wondering where it all turned wrong. There's one solution: "We gotta get out while we're young," Springsteen sings.

Gone are the boardwalk characters with colorful nicknames. Just plain old Wendy and the song's unnamed narrator making their move past the amusement park rising "bold and stark" onto the highway "jammed with broken heroes." They aren't

alone. Everybody's running, and "there's no place left to hide."

Not for them, and not for Springsteen. With no promise of another, the new record had to be *the* record. It had to say all the things Springsteen needed to say. It had to capture all the music he had in his head. "His desire [was] for this to be his last will and testament," Landau said in 2011.

No one said it. Everyone felt it. "Born To Run" bore the brunt of it. Springsteen was writing and rewriting lyrics. He was composing note after note after note, and then building on those compositions and piling up instruments. Glockenspiel? Glockenspiel.

In July 1974, the band played six concerts in three nights at the Bottom Line in New York City. The record company packed the shows with tastemakers; the tastemakers were impressed. Springsteen didn't let up. Executives heard "Born To Run" and loved it. Springsteen didn't let up.

Above: *Born to Run* took significantly longer to record than Springsteen's first two albums combined.

"I JUST LOVED THE SOUND OF THAT VOICE AND I SAID, 'WELL, HERE I GO.' I DIDN'T GET THERE, BUT I GOT SOMEPLACE."

Bruce Springsteen,
on his shot at Roy Orbison's voice, 2011

Right: With Elvis's badge on his jacket and Roy Orbison's voice on his mind, Springsteen drew on the past to produce the sound of "rock and roll future."

Overleaf: The defining album-cover photo by Eric Meola—youthful rebellion with a grin.

"I HAVE NO IDEA WHAT IT MEANS TO THIS DAY, BUT IT'S IMPORTANT."

Bruce Springsteen, on "Tenth Avenue Freeze-Out," 2005

The following month, Sancious announced he was leaving the band to make his own record and taking Carter with him. Springsteen didn't let up, but he did have to audition new members.

Responding to an ad in the *Village Voice*, drummer Max Weinberg and pianist Roy Bittan became the newest members of the E Street Band. Both had been playing gigs since they were kids. Weinberg had had it drilled into him from a young age that he was to be well dressed and on time. He knew nothing of the "rock and roll future" quote and brought a minimalist kit to the audition. He stood out for that reason and for his ability to follow Springsteen. What he noticed immediately is that *everyone* followed Springsteen, and Springsteen was all business. "The sense of seriousness, I'd never experienced that," Weinberg said in 2011.

Bittan had seen the E Street Band before, and, like most everyone, left the show awestruck. "I could tell where they were going," he said. "I could sense they needed to be more of a rock 'n' roll band."

With the new additions, the E Street Band was exactly that. Sancious and Carter were jazz cats, with a feel for eclecticism, flair, and improvisation. Weinberg and Bittan put even more of the focus on Springsteen.

The band kept touring. They had to pay the bills. And Springsteen was struggling to write.

"It gets harder because it's more personal," he told critic Robert Hilburn during a tour stop in Los Angeles that summer.

Early versions of "Jungleland" began to work their way into the set. Early in 1975, the band played a song called "Wings For Wheels," which later evolved into "Thunder Road." Finally, in March, Springsteen returned to the studio, but not to 914 Sound.

Since their first meeting, Springsteen and Landau had talked a lot. Landau's role in Springsteen's career grew, and one of his first contributions was getting the band to a better studio, the Record Plant in New York City. There they went to work, obsessively. Landau eventually took the title of co-producer with Springsteen and Appel.

Van Zandt rejoined the organization when one day, lying on the floor listening to a playback of the horn section on "Tenth Avenue Freeze-Out," he bluntly told Springsteen he thought the arrangement sucked. Challenged to do better, Van Zandt popped up and did just that. On the spot.

The clock ticked toward the planned start of the Born to Run tour in July, though it's a small miracle no one killed all the clocks out of frustration. By the time July arrived, the band was working in multiple studios. Exhausted and crazy, they worked seventy-two hours straight until they stepped into the van to drive to Providence, Rhode Island for the first night

of the tour. Clemons barely finished his work on "Jungleland" before walking out the door.

Never had a packed van seemed so invigorating. They were done. Or were they? Famously, engineer Jimmy Iovine brought the test pressing to Springsteen on tour. He was so upset with the sound he threw the record in the pool and threatened to scrap the album. "Why do people suffer?" Springsteen said in *Wings for Wheels*. "Because we have to." Appel and Landau went to work, talked him down, and only then were they finished with one of the all-time great rock records, and the most important album of Springsteen's career.

Born to Run is about "that one endless summer night," Springsteen said in *Wings for Wheels*. Countless times over the years he's described it as an invitation. On stage in Detroit in 2009, introducing a performance of the entire album, he said, "It started a lifelong conversation that I've had with you, and you've had with me."

Its impact began with the cover, shot by Eric Meola. Wrapped in a black leather jacket, his soon-to-be iconic 1950s Fender Esquire-Telecaster mutt hanging low (Elvis button on the strap), Springsteen's a flashback— to Marlon Brando, to James Dean. He's youthful rebellion with a grin as he leans on Clemons's shoulder. It's more than a grin, though. There's admiration.

There's friendship. And don't overlook the racial composition. "A friendship and a narrative steeped in the complicated history of America begin to form and there is music already in the air," Springsteen wrote in the foreword to Clemons's 2009 book *Big Man*.

The story fades in on "Thunder Road," the title pulled from a 1958 Robert Mitchum movie. The setting could be the Jersey Shore, but it could be anywhere else, too. "The screen door slams, Mary's dress waves," and who doesn't know that sound? It's the same in Kansas as it is in California. The deal is simple, Mary can waste her summer "praying in vain," or jump in the car and take a ride. "It's a town full of losers and I'm pulling out of here to win," Springsteen sings. The music soars and Clemons's saxophone seems capable of blowing away any roadblock that might stand in the way.

"Tenth Avenue Freeze-Out" is the band's story, Springsteen as Scooter and all alone until "the change was made up town and the Big Man joined the band." What then? The two are going to "bust this city in half." What is a Tenth Avenue Freeze-Out? Springsteen never did figure it out, and it doesn't matter.

"Night" explodes with energy as it sheds day's frustrations. During business hours, "you're just a prisoner of your dreams." Under cover of darkness, there is possibility and mystery.

The E Street Band in full cry on the Born to Run tour.

"Backstreets" remains one of Springsteen's most powerful songs, a story of friendship, betrayal, and youthful innocence unfairly and inevitably encroached upon by the real world ("Well, after all this time to find we're just like all the rest"). It's hot and humid, and there isn't even a hint of a breeze to help cool the emotions.

"Born To Run" opens side two with Carter blasting the band's way into the song. "She's The One" takes Bo Diddley's beat and applies it to a tangle of lust and more complicated emotions. Yes, she's telling lies. Yes, he'd like to leave her. No, he won't. There was a time when "her love could save" him "from the bitterness." He's not letting that go easily.

"Meeting Across The River" is a story Springsteen might have taken much longer to tell earlier in his career, but it comes in on *Born to Run* at under three-and-a-half sparsely arranged minutes. The song's two main characters, one hell bent on one last score, the other in need of some convincing, are both trying to be something they're not. "Change your shirt, 'cause tonight we got style," Springsteen sings.

Of course, he needed the space for "Jungleland," one last nine-and-a-half-minute epic about the warfare of the streets. The vividly nicknamed Magic Rat might connect the song to Springsteen's earlier work, but the "barefoot girl sitting on the hood of a Dodge drinking warm beer in the soft summer rain," is as simple and as beautiful as his writing gets.

Lester Bangs, who'd written *Rolling Stone*'s mixed assessment of *Greetings*, reviewed *Born to Run* for *Creem*. "In a time of squalor and belittled desire, Springsteen's music is majestic and passionate with no apologies," Bangs wrote.

In *Rolling Stone*, Greil Marcus published maybe the second most famous sentence about Springsteen. Of *Born to Run*, he wrote, "It is a magnificent album that pays off on every bet ever placed on him—a '57 Chevy running on melted-down Crystals records that shuts down every claim that has been made."

In October, Springsteen made the covers of both *Time* and *Newsweek*. Van Zandt bought a stack and thought it was great. Springsteen saw that stack and split for his hotel room.

Time took the straight-ahead approach, focusing on Springsteen's story, his music, and his place as "Rock's New Sensation." *Newsweek* chose to feature on the process of Springsteen's rise. "Making of a Rock Star" was the headline. Sure, *Born to Run* had sold 600,000 copies by then and reached number three on *Billboard*'s album chart, but, it was noted, the record company had spent $200,000 promoting it, with another $50,000 planned by the end of the year.

The promotional machine did exist. It wasn't some existential manifestation. After packing more Bottom

"SEEING YOUR FRIEND ON TIME AND NEWSWEEK IS COMPLETELY SURREAL. JUST IMAGINE."

Steve Van Zandt, 2011

Line shows in August, that machine moved Springsteen out to Los Angeles in mid-October for a run of gigs at the Roxy that were press packed and star studded. *Newsweek* referred to the shows as "the official investiture," atypical verbiage for a story about rock 'n' roll.

Springsteen was plenty aware of what was going on, and who was (and wasn't) in the audience. "There ain't nobody here from *Billboard* tonight," he said during one of his shows as the band rolled into "Spirit In The Night." He sounded relieved. He even managed to joke about having his billboard put on a truck to take back to New Jersey to sit in front of his house as a "that'll show her" to an old girlfriend.

But the physics of celebrity isn't any different from physics. For every action, there is an equal and opposite reaction. "Out here in the Midwest," Bangs wrote in his *Creem* review, "where at this writing Springsteen has not even toured yet, you can smell the backlash crisp as burnt rubber in the air."

From across the Atlantic, Andrew Tyler took care of that on behalf of *New Musical Express*. He was also at those Los Angeles shows. He wasn't impressed with Springsteen. "His harp playing's every bit as dumb as Dylan's," and "Springsteen's knotty, out-of-tune voice," and so on. Tyler gave Springsteen six months until he would be either wiped out or an also-ran and left the reader on an ominous note from Springsteen himself: "I used to feel I always was in control, but now I'm not so sure."

FINALLY. LONDON IS READY
BRUCE SPRINGSTEEN
AND THE E STREET BAND

ODEON

FINALLY. LONDON IS READY FOR …

"From the 'very' anxious heavens of our first transatlantic flight we descended into … well … hell, as I would soon come to know it," Springsteen wrote in 2005, when the November 18, 1975 show at London's Hammersmith Odeon was released on DVD.

If the publicity machine whirring in the United States was wearing Springsteen down, it broke him when he arrived for the first time in Europe. He took one look at the marquee—"Finally. London is ready for Bruce Springsteen and the E Street Band"—and had had enough.

Telling the host "you're welcome" is no way to show up at a party. Springsteen tore down and then tore up the "rock and roll future" posters that lined the walls. He yanked promotional flyers off of seats. Later, he walked on stage to a room packed with "show us what you got."

In 1999, writer Eric Alterman described the performance as "near comatose." That's how the story was passed down, and for a long time, even Springsteen's memory was that they didn't play well. The video says differently. "Thunder Road" opened the show, Springsteen still as a statue, bundled in a black leather jacket and stocking cap.

But then Clemons shuffles to the intro of "Tenth Avenue Freeze-Out," finely attired in a white hat and white suit with red flower in his lapel. Springsteen flashes a grin at Van Zandt, who's dressed in a red suit with a white flower in lapel (white hat, red band). Between them, Springsteen looks like a dock worker who wandered into a wedding band. From there, the set erupts. "Born To Run" and "It's Hard To Be A Saint In The City" are played breakneck. "Backstreets" is a gut punch. "Detroit Medley" is pure celebration.

"With the keys to the kingdom dangling in front of us and the knife at our neck, we'd gone for broke," Springsteen wrote. Still, they wouldn't return to Europe for another six years.

DARKNESS ON THE EDGE OF TOWN

1978

"YOU DON'T KNOW IF THIS MIGHT BE THE LAST RECORD YOU EVER MAKE. THERE'S NO TOMORROW. THERE'S JUST THIS MOMENT."

BRUCE SPRINGSTEEN, 2010

→11

→10A

KODAK SAFETY FILM 5063

→10

→9A

KODAK SAFETY FILM 5063

→9

→14

→13A

KODAK SAFETY FILM 5063

→13

→12A

KODAK SAFETY FILM 5063

→12

→11A

1975

December: Springsteen checks his 1972 contract with Laurel Canyon for the first time and does not like what he discovers.
December 31: Last night of the Born to Run tour, at the Tower Theater, Philadelphia.

1976

March 25: First night of the Chicken Scratch tour, at the Township Auditorium in Columbia, South Carolina.
May 28: Last night of the Chicken Scratch tour, at the US Naval Academy, Annapolis, Maryland.
July 27: Springsteen files a lawsuit against Mike Appel.
July 29: Appel countersues, which prevents any new recording work.
September 26: First night of the Lawsuit tour, at the Arizona Veterans Memorial Coliseum, Phoenix.
November 4: End of the first leg of the tour, at the Palladium, New York City.

1977

January: Unable to record their own music, Springsteen and the E Street Band play on Ronnie Spector's single "Say Goodbye To Hollywood."
February 7: The Lawsuit tour resumes at the Palace Theater, Albany, New York.
February 19: The Manfred Mann's Earth Band cover of "Blinded By The Light" hits number one in the US.
March 25: Last night of the Lawsuit tour, at the Music Hall, Boston.
May 28: Springsteen reaches an out-of-court agreement with Appel and signs a new contract with Columbia soon after.
June: Recording of *Darkness on the Edge of Town* begins at the Atlantic Studios, New York City, relocating to the Record Plant in September.
August: Two days after the death of Elvis Presley, Springsteen makes an epic desert road trip through Utah and Nevada with Van Zandt and photographer Eric Meola.

1978

January: End of the *Darkness* recording sessions.
April: Patti Smith's version of "Because The Night" reaches number thirteen in the US (and number five in the UK).
May 23: First night of the Darkness on the Edge of Town tour, at Shea's Buffalo Theater, Buffalo, New York.
June 2: Release of *Darkness on the Edge of Town* (US 5, UK 16).
July 7: A memorable concert at the Roxy, West Hollywood includes for the first time "Twist And Shout" and "Raise Your Hand."
Summer: Springsteen appoints Jon Landau as his full-time manager.
August 21–23: Plays three straight sellouts at Madison Square Garden, New York City.
August 24: Publication of major *Rolling Stone* cover story "Bruce Springsteen Raises Cain" by Dave Marsh.

1979

January 1: Last night of the Darkness tour, at the Richfield Coliseum, Richfield, Ohio.

Some distance down Thunder Road, a car sat in the rain. Disillusionment steamed the windows. Tires rushed past on wet pavement. And a packed house at the Monmouth Arts Center in Red Bank, New Jersey fell silent as melancholy filled the summer night.

Springsteen, accompanied by a lonely piano, was quietly setting himself in that scene: "When the promise was broken, I was drunk and far away from home, sleeping with a stranger in the backseat of a borrowed car."

He'd put the characters from "Thunder Road" in a car and sent them out into the world. Then life got complicated.

Springsteen debuted "The Promise" in Red Bank on August 3, 1976, dropping it between "Born To Run" and "Backstreets" in a section of the set that began with a burst of defiance (a cover of the Animals' "It's My Life") buoyed by the limitless possibility "Thunder Road" implied.

"Thunder Road" had been the promise—a promise, anyway. It was hope just past the horizon. Get in the car, go, and don't look back. Just follow the sax solo to a better life. The success of *Born to Run* should have been the happily ever after.

"The weirdest anomaly of success is that it requires compromises never demanded of failure," Dave Marsh wrote in *Born to Run: The Bruce Springsteen Story*. By that point, Springsteen was being driven to compromise more than he'd ever dreamed, and he was fighting back.

"I started playing to get as much control of my life as I could, and that's what I felt slipping away, and that's what was scaring me," Springsteen told Dave Herman in a 1978 *King Biscuit Flower Hour* interview.

A week before Springsteen performed "The Promise," he had filed suit against Mike Appel, charging, among other things, fraud and breach of trust. Two days later, Appel countersued and stopped Springsteen from entering the studio with Landau to begin work on the follow-up to *Born to Run*. He could do this because Springsteen recorded for Appel's Laurel Canyon, and Laurel Canyon was the signatory on the Columbia contract, not Springsteen.

Appel and Springsteen had three contracts: production, publishing, and management. All three favored Appel. In the 2010 documentary *The Promise: The Making of Darkness on the Edge of Town*, Springsteen described the deals as naïve. "Bound to be destructive," he said.

For all the financial stakes in play—Appel had gone to Columbia for a $500,000 advance against *Born to Run*'s royalties, not to mention all the future money that seemed certain, and all the debt that had

"IT'S A SONG ABOUT FIGHTING AND NOT WINNING. IT'S ABOUT THE DISAPPOINTMENTS OF THE TIME. I FELT TOO CLOSE TO IT."

Bruce Springsteen, on "The Promise," 2010

piled up—it was control that drove Springsteen. No one was going to tell him who he could work with, or dictate any other terms of his artistic life.

"These are the things I would have fought to the death for," Springsteen said. "Whatever it was, I was going to take it the whole way."

And he was going to have to do it not only against a friend, but a friend with heels built to dig just as deep as his. In a 2011 interview, looking back on their earliest days together, Springsteen said of Appel, "I needed somebody else who was a little crazy in the eyes, because that was my approach to it all."

Neither had softened in the interim. The conflict was going to take a while to resolve, and who knew how much time Springsteen had? He'd had a hit, but how long would the world wait to see if he had another one in him?

He'd just survived one make-or-break album, and now here was the executioner, back again, whistling and waiting at the guillotine. It's no wonder Springsteen had come to identify with the noir heroes up on the screen, and in the books he was increasingly digging into. "The sand was always shifting underneath them," he said.

The Born to Run tour had ended on New Year's Eve 1975. A two-month run starting at the end of the following March that became known as the Chicken Scratch tour rolled through some of Springsteen's softer markets in the southern states, including Memphis, where he and Steve Van Zandt took a cab to Graceland and then hopped the fence to see if Elvis was home. He wasn't.

In late September 1976, the so-called Lawsuit tour began. Opening night was in Phoenix at the Arizona

Opposite: At home in Holmdel, New Jersey, where he wrote the songs for *Darkness*. Portrait by Eric Meola, 1977.

Page 69: Contact sheet from Frank Stefanko's photo shoot for the album cover.

Pages 70–71: Springsteen shows off his pinball wizardry to Clarence Clemons, Roy Bittan, and Steve Van Zandt.

Veterans Memorial Coliseum, the band's first full arena show. They wrapped with six nights at the Palladium in New York City that followed two nights at another arena, the Spectrum in Philadelphia. Springsteen's reluctance to play such large venues, grounded in artistic ideals, had to eventually yield to financial realities.

Another nearly two-month run of shows took place in early 1977. It was the only way Springsteen could keep the organization's lights on. And even then things were tight. He'd moved to a farmhouse in Holmdel, New Jersey, one big enough for the band to set up and rehearse in and remote enough they could play all night. They'd eat together around one long table, Springsteen and Van Zandt holding things down at one end. Songs piled up.

Finally, in the middle of the night on May 28, 1977, the lawyers sealed the deal. Appel got cash, and his cut from the songs published through Laurel Canyon. Springsteen got complete control.

A week after the settlement, Springsteen, the E Street Band, and Landau headed into the studio to begin the follow-up to *Born to Run*.

Born to Run had found its voice in the history of rock 'n' roll. Marsh, reviewing the August 1975 Bottom Line shows for *Rolling Stone* had called Springsteen "the living culmination of twenty years of rock 'n' roll tradition." The next album would dig deeper into American culture. Springsteen had become interested in the Great Depression–era Dustbowl struggle of the Joad family in *The Grapes of Wrath*—as told by director John Ford. (Springsteen had not yet read John Steinbeck's novel.) Country music, and especially Hank Williams, had become a new obsession. "The grim recognition of the chips that were laid down against you," he said at SXSW. "Country's fatalism attracted me."

Springsteen's personal darkness was scribbled in his notebooks, a "we're sure we're gonna die tonight" here, a "God's angels can tear this town down and blow it into the sea" there. "As soon as you've got something, they send someone to try and take it away" made it into "Something In The Night." His words flashed with anger and disappointment.

Above: Taking their bows at the Springfield Civic Center, Springfield, Massachusetts, August 22, 1976. From left to right: Clarence Clemons, Springsteen, Max Weinberg, Garry Tallent, Steve Van Zandt, Roy Bittan, and Danny Federici.

Opposite: Strutting in the stalls during the Darkness on the Edge of Town tour, 1978.

"ADULT LIFE IS A LIFE OF COMPROMISE, AND THAT'S NECESSARY. THERE ARE A LOT OF THINGS YOU SHOULD BE COMPROMISING ON; THERE ARE SOME ESSENTIAL THINGS WHERE YOU DON'T WANT TO COMPROMISE."

Bruce Springsteen, 2010

Then, on August 16, 1977, Elvis died, a cautionary tale of celebrity and excess. "And it was hard to understand how somebody who took away so many people's loneliness, could end up feeling so lonely," Springsteen said on stage in 1984. "There's all kinds of isolation that can kill you." A few days later, Springsteen, Van Zandt and photographer Eric Meola flew to Utah, rented a convertible and drove the "rattlesnake speedway" through what would become "The Promised Land," Meola capturing the "dark cloud rising from the desert floor" in a stunning collection of photographs.

The making of *Born to Run* dragged on because of too many options on just a few songs. Pace of production on the new album suffered from too many songs. Dozens. Some of the best were given away. Patti Smith took "Because The Night." Robert Gordon got "Fire," a slow burner Springsteen had originally written with Elvis in mind.

DAILY NEWS

ELVIS PRESLEY DIES AT 42

Singer Suffers Heart Attack

Berkowitz Pleads Innocent; Plans Insanity Defense

Report Carter Picks Ala. Judge As FBI Chief

Elvis: Idol of Millions—Series Starts on page 2

Southside Johnny and the Asbury Jukes, Van Zandt's other project, got a couple. "The Promise" didn't make the cut. A stack of damn-near perfect, soulful pop tunes didn't go anywhere, left to wait for ... never, as far as Springsteen knew at the time.

"He has the extraordinary discipline and willpower to be extreme like that and get away with it," Van Zandt said in 2011. "And he does get away with it; he can throw away his best songs and still make a great album."

Springsteen could also drive everyone to the point of collapse, mentally and physically. And he kept writing. In footage shown in *The Promise*, Van Zandt comically asks Springsteen what he's going to sacrifice to make room for yet another pull from the notebook. "Remember," Springsteen says, "there's always room to throw out." What he was left with by spring 1978 was a collection of songs about challenges, identity, and choice.

The lives on *Darkness* are isolated. Nothing comes easy. "I wanted my new characters to feel weathered, older, but not beaten," Springsteen wrote in *Songs*.

"ALL THE HYPE IN THE WORLD [IS] NOTHING COMPARED TO A KI[D] TELLING ANOTHER KID, 'MAN, [YOU] SHOULD'VE SEEN THAT!'"

Bruce Springs[teen]

Opening the album, "Badlands" refuses to lose, taking a sense of helplessness and spitting it back in the face of anyone who would dare get in the way. "I want control right now," Springsteen sings. "You better listen to me, baby." How do you get there? Hard work. Love. Faith. A little hope and the understanding "that it ain't no sin to be glad you're alive." No matter how anyone tries to make you feel.

In "Adam Raised A Cain" and "Factory," Springsteen began to reach out to his father. A howling rocker, "Adam Raised A Cain" throws haymakers at a simple fact of life: Father and son aren't that different. Not with "the same hot blood burning in our veins." The path is laid out, you do what your daddy did, and that wasn't much. "Daddy worked his whole life for nothing but the pain," and he's left with a house to wander "looking for something to blame." That something is the son. "Factory" moves like the slow march of work weeks fading into months and years. Day after day, the view is the same: "I see my daddy walking through them factory gates in the rain." There's a toll ("factory takes his hearing"), but also a reward to be gained from the sense of purpose ("factory gives him life").

The anticipation that pulsated underneath *Born to Run*'s "Night" has been drained from "Something In The Night," replaced with a weary loneliness. Rock 'n' roll, old and reliable, offers respite when turned up so loud it overwhelms one's thoughts, but the relief is temporary and Springsteen is left "running burned and blind," shouting into the abyss.

"Candy's Room" is home to a prostitute and decorated with "pictures of her heroes on the wall." Darkness lights the path to her, and "there's a sadness hidden in that pretty face." What's clear is the song's narrator loves her, and wants to be loved. "In the darkness there'll be hidden worlds that shine," he sings. "When I hold Candy she makes these hidden worlds mine." For her part, she tells him he's got a lot to learn.

"Racing In The Street" charts the path from carefree youth to weighty adulthood in as many years—three—as it took Springsteen to get from *Born to Run* to *Darkness*. The guy gets the girl, but "she stares off alone into the night, with the eyes of one who hates for just being born." Those two find some peace in the end as they head to the ocean to "wash these sins off our hands."

"The Promised Land" is a statement of faith: "I believe in the promised land." And belief is nice, but it doesn't get you far. The guy in the song gets up every day, goes to work. "I've done my best to live the right way," and still the clouds pile up on the horizon and threaten "to blow everything down." You either stand firm, or you end up like the character in

"I INTENTIONALLY STEERED AWAY FROM ANY HINT OF ESCAPISM AND SET MY CHARACTERS DOWN IN THE MIDDLE OF A COMMUNITY UNDER SIEGE."

Bruce Springsteen, 1998

"Streets Of Fire," lied to and ambivalent—"a loser down the tracks."

"Prove It All Night" is an after-hours reminder that hard work doesn't stop when you punch the clock at the end of the shift.

"Darkness On The Edge of Town" makes the album's most important point: The darkness is necessary. Life is hard. Everything worthwhile is hard. "Tonight I'll be on that hill 'cause I can't stop," Springsteen promises. "I'll be on that hill with everything I got."

He'll risk everything for what he wants. Springsteen already had. "My characters stand unsure of their fate, but dug in and committed," Springsteen wrote in *Songs*. "By the end of *Darkness* I'd found my adult voice."

Darkness on the Edge of Town was released on June 2, 1978 and shot into *Billboard*'s top ten. It didn't stay there. "Prove It All Night," the album's first single, didn't do much, either. Springsteen's initial idea to let the album roll out without much promotion—an overreaction to the over-promotion of *Born to Run*—wasn't a particularly good one.

"I mean, the records ain't going to sprout legs and walk out of stores and jump onto people's record players and say 'Listen to me'" Springsteen told Dave Herman. So they did press. They shot live footage for a television commercial. Radio stations broadcast shows that were quickly bootlegged and have become part of his live legend.

"Driving all night, chasing some mirage." A refueling stop in Valmy, Nevada, during Springsteen's epic road trip with Steve Van Zandt and photographer Eric Meola in August 1977.

Dave Marsh was invited along for shows in Los Angeles at the Forum and then the Roxy. The result was a *Rolling Stone* cover story—Springsteen's first. Springsteen walks the beach, leads a raid to vandalize his own billboard six stories above the Sunset Strip, and gives *Los Angeles Times* critic Robert Hilburn cold sweats as he tries to figure out how to write about the Roxy show after already claiming the Forum gig to be "one of the best events ever in Los Angeles."

This time, rather than flip out about so much praise, Springsteen had a little fun with it. "See all that fancy stuff in the papers about me?" Marsh quoted him from the Forum show. "Big deal, huh? I gotta tell you, I only levitate to the upper deck on Wednesdays and Fridays."

The Darkness tour would come to be a cornerstone in Springsteen's mythology. They played fast and hard. Every night. The shows stretched past three hours. The sound checks would sometimes last longer as Springsteen would go from section to section checking the sound himself.

"Prove It All Night" picked up an extended piano intro, Springsteen ripping through it with a guitar solo. "Backstreets" remained an emotional centerpiece, Springsteen building a heartbroken story of betrayal into the song's middle section. "And like everything in those days, you promised, and you lied," Springsteen sang softly in San Francisco. "Didn't you?" The music builds, Springsteen seethes. The song slams to a halt, and falls back into "Backstreets." That night, they followed up with "Rosalita (Come Out Tonight)" then "Born To Run" then "Detroit Medley" then "Tenth Avenue Freeze-Out" then "Raise Your Hand" then "Quarter To Three." Exhale.

"His MO was always that we were going to slug it out until we dropped," Roy Bittan said in 2011. Not just Springsteen. Not just the band. *Everyone*. "Someone carries me out," he joked with a crowd in Saginaw, Michigan. "You guys got to walk out on your own."

In 2009, Springsteen and the band set up in the Paramount Theater in Asbury Park to run through *Darkness* from start to finish. The theater was empty, the performance beautiful. By then, the songs had established themselves as the emotional core of Springsteen's work. No matter the decade, whatever the news, those songs endured.

He put himself through the process because he had to. Some compromises you can make. Others you can't. "More than rich," he said, "more than famous, more than happy, I wanted to be great."

Above: "We ain't done yet …" The spellbinding show at the Forum, Los Angeles, July 5, 1978.

Opposite: Portrait by Lynn Goldsmith, 1978.

THE PROMISE

Had the whole sordid affair never gone down, had Springsteen not sued Mike Appel, and Appel not filed a countersuit, had the operation rolled along harmoniously, the follow-up to *Born to Run* would have been fun.

"I was still held in thrall by the towering pop records that had shaped my youth and early musical education," Springsteen wrote in the notes to *The Promise*, a double album of twenty-two castaways from the *Darkness* era released in 2010.

Tracks like "Save My Love," "The Little Things (My Baby Does)," "Gotta Get That Feeling," "Talk To Me," and "Spanish Eyes" are full of longing, and humor, and the heat of another summer night—maybe the night after *Born to Run*.

In contrast to the loneliness and weight of adult life which consumed *Darkness*, this collection is full of characters looking for a connection. "If you hold me tight, we'll be riders on the night," Springsteen sings in "Rendezvous," its very title more communal than anything on *Darkness*. He's still got that hint of Roy Orbison in his voice, and Clarence Clemons works his simple, soulful magic. Springsteen could have been celebrated for his pop writing long before he finally was.

"It's a part of himself he completely takes for granted," Steve Van Zandt, the man most frustrated by the decisions of the late 1970s, said in 2011, "but it's the most accomplished part."

"Rattlesnake Speedway" by Eric Meola. Just off Highway 80, Nevada, August 1977.

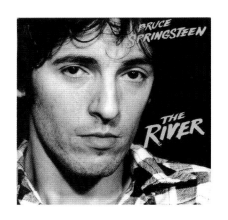

THE RIVER

1980

"I WANTED A RECORD THAT COMBINED
THE FUN ASPECT OF WHAT THE BAND
DID ALONG WITH THE STORY
I WAS TELLING."

BRUCE SPRINGSTEEN, 2011

1979

February: The Pointer Sisters' version of "Fire" reaches number two in the US.

March: Recording of *The River* starts at the Power Station.

September 21 and 22: Springsteen headlines two benefit concerts for MUSE (Musicians United for Safe Energy) at Madison Square Garden on the eve of his thirtieth birthday.

November: Release of the *No Nukes* live album from the MUSE shows, containing the first official live recordings of the E Street Band.

1980

May: End of recording sessions for *The River*.

July 18: Release of the *No Nukes* concert movie.

October 3: First night of the River tour, at the Crisler Arena, Ann Arbor, Michigan.

October 17: Release of *The River* (US 1, UK 2).

December 27: Springsteen's first top-ten single in the US, "Hungry Heart"/"Held Up Without A Gun," peaks at number five.

1981

March 5: End of the first North American leg of the River tour, at the Market Square Arena, Indianapolis, Indiana.

April 7: Start of Springsteen's first major European tour, at the Congress Centrum, Hamburg, West Germany.

June 8: End of the European leg of the River tour, at the Birmingham International Arena, Birmingham, England.

June 20: The entire E Street Band plays at Max Weinberg's wedding reception in New Jersey.

July 2: The River tour resumes Stateside, at the Brendan Byrne Arena, East Rutherford, New Jersey.

August 20: The tour's first date of six at the Los Angeles Memorial Sports Arena is designated a benefit concert for the Vietnam Veterans of America Foundation.

September 14: After almost a year, the River tour finally ends, at the Riverfront Coliseum, Cincinnati, Ohio.

September 24: Clarence Clemons gets married in Hawaii with Springsteen as best man, and the E Street Band headlines another wedding reception.

Right: Letting off steam on the roof of the Power Station during the meandering *River* sessions.

Page 87: Two years on from *Darkness*, and back in front of the cabbage rose wallpaper.

The son of former slaves, Rufus "Tee-Tot" Payne grew up in New Orleans in the late nineteenth century. He picked up his nickname, from the cocktail of tea and homemade whiskey he carried in a flask, in Georgiana, Alabama, where he could be found playing music on street corners, enthralling the kids that would follow him around. That's where Payne met a young Hank Williams. Payne taught Hank a few chords, and almost certainly how to play them with style. He probably also passed down the tune "My Bucket's Got A Hole In It."

In *Songs*, Springsteen wrote he was singing just that song in a New York hotel room when inspiration struck. "I drove back to New Jersey that night and sat up in my room writing 'The River.'" Most likely, as Dave Marsh pointed out in a 1981 story for *Musician*, Springsteen was also listening to "Long Gone Lonesome Blues," which tells of a man who goes down to the river and decides to die—only to jump in and find "the doggone river was dry." Hank's voice howls into a lonely night, looking for something, anything, to believe in.

"As Jerry Lee Lewis, the living, breathing personification of both rock and country said, 'I've fallen to the bottom and I'm working my way down,'" Springsteen said at SXSW in 2012. "So that was hardcore working man's blues."

In 1979, on the far side of two major successes (three if you count getting past the lawsuit) and undeniably now a Rock Star, Springsteen could have been expected to come up for air, a little sun, maybe a drink or two in the back of a limo. *Born to Run* had been his shot at the title, and it at least put him in the fight. *Darkness* had been a reaction to the aftermath, a battle for his artistic soul. Having won that, having proven he could do it his way, he could relax.

Or he could spend time in low-down country songs, diving deeper into the questions they raised. "Why is there a hole in the bucket?" he said at SXSW. More pressing: How do you deal with the problems the hole presents? The one thing you can't do is shrug off the hole and party.

"Because," Paul Nelson wrote in *Rolling Stone*'s review of *The River*, "[Springsteen] realizes that most of our todays are the tragicomic sum of a scattered series of yesterdays that had once hoped to become better tomorrows." And tomorrows are not infinite.

After a few months off, Springsteen and the E Street Band moved back into the studio in March 1979 planning to record quickly. Eighteen months later *The River* was finished.

In between, they played only two shows, benefits at Madison Square Garden in September 1979 known as the "No Nukes" concerts. With the near-catastrophic partial meltdown in March at Pennsylvania's Three Mile Island nuclear power plant as a backdrop, Musicians United for Safe Energy (MUSE), led by Jackson Browne, Bonnie Raitt, Graham Nash, and others, organized the shows. The concerts would be filmed for a movie and recorded for an album. Only two artists passed on writing statements for the program—Springsteen and Tom Petty.

For Springsteen, his presence was enough. "What I wouldn't have done is offer the power of my band casually," he said in 2011. He'd given thought to the issue. The first song they recorded for the new album, the urgent "Roulette," was inspired by Three Mile Island and marked by one of Springsteen's most furious vocal performances. In it,

Above: After "No Nukes," Springsteen continued to support anti-nuclear events. Here with Gary U.S. Bonds during Survival Sunday at the Hollywood Bowl, June 14, 1981.

Left: Springsteen refuses medical assistance in his James Brown–inspired stretcher routine during the second "No Nukes" concert. Madison Square Garden, September 22, 1979.

the stakes grow with the addition of a wife and kids, a house, and there's the inescapable fear that it could all go wrong at any moment, that we're all just chips in another player's far bigger—and riskier—gamble.

But, with the two shows bumping up against his thirtieth birthday, giving him one more reason to think about adulthood, Springsteen left "Roulette" on the shelf and instead debuted a much more personal song, "The River," a narrative driven by the story of his sister Ginny and her husband.

There's the life that's planned out for you. "They bring you up to do like your daddy done," Springsteen sings. There's the life you plan for yourself. Then there's life. That's "The River," a narrative sketch about the upheaval that happens. The song's couple faces an unplanned pregnancy, gets married, and tries to grind it out. The economy tanks. Jobs are lost and the future looks nothing like

anyone said it would. "Is a dream a lie if it don't come true, or is it something worse?" Springsteen asks. Like the couple in "Racing In The Street" who pack up and head to the ocean to be reborn, the guy in "The River" heads toward water. "Though I know the river is dry"—just as Hank found it.

If the themes were a continuation of *Darkness*'s search for control and identity, the studio approach wasn't much different, either. Springsteen had a lot of songs, and more every day. Early in the process, Steve Van Zandt sensed another marathon and decided he'd rather pass. Instead Springsteen made him co-producer, and if that helped the sound, it did nothing for the pace.

"He'd come in every day with four new songs," Van Zandt said in 2011. "Not finished, but a great riff, great chord change, sometimes half done. But sometimes more than that; four, five, six songs a day."

Performing Maurice Williams and the Zodiacs' 1960 doo-wop hit "Stay" with Jackson Browne and Tom Petty at "No Nukes," September 22, 1979.

"THE ESSENCE OF WHAT BRUCE DOES IS THE HARDEST KIND OF WORK—DIGGING, DIGGING, DIGGING INTO HIMSELF, LOOKING FOR SONGS. YOU GOTTA LET YOURSELF SINK INTO THAT, AND IT'S NO FUN."

Chuck Plotkin, 2011

They were all in the room, and they'd work through the ideas. Again and again. Through this change and that change, new solos, new lyrics, new arrangements. "So basically, instead of going in and recording a record, we were going in and recording rehearsals," Max Weinberg said in 2011. They cut live, and they made a lot of noise working as close as they could to the way they did on stage.

From deep in Springsteen's magical stack of sounds emerged some chords and a riff based on "Dawn (Go Away)," a top-five hit for the Four Seasons in 1964 (which, coincidentally, was recorded while they were caught up in a royalty dispute of their own). Springsteen thought the song a little too pop, a little too light. Van Zandt and Jon Landau thought it was a hit and, more importantly, that it was time for a hit. Springsteen had given "Fire" to Robert Gordon, and the Pointer Sisters had turned it into a number-two song in early 1979. The previous year, Patti Smith got "Because The Night" and that had gone to number thirteen. In 1977, Manfred Mann's Earth Band released "Blinded By The Light" and it went to number one.

"This is our fifth album, we've paid our dues, you can get away with a hit single if it's the right one," Van Zandt said. "And this felt right." And so was born "Hungry Heart," the happiest sounding song you'll ever hear about a guy leaving his family.

Tapes piled up. So many tapes that staff had to be dispatched to buy a massive road case to hold them all. There were songs that were written just after *Darkness*, that wear that album's themes like shadows: "The River," "Hungry Heart," "Point Blank," "The Ties That Bind," and "Stolen Car."

Time and again, Springsteen's characters are handed a setback to see how they deal with it. "The River" leans toward sad acceptance. "Hungry Heart" sends its protagonist hard after whatever the heart desires. In "Point Blank" it's all about the "little white lies" we tell ourselves to make the pain go away for a while, but it always comes back. And in "Stolen Car," the heartbreak of what could have been, but wasn't, manifests itself in recklessness, that guy stealing a car and driving around hoping to get caught.

With "Independence Day," Springsteen again goes head-on at his relationship with his father, managing to both forswear the same dark fate, and take some responsibility for the tumult, as if perhaps it was his arrival that sapped the energy from his father's hopes. "I swear I never meant to take those things away," he concludes.

Into 1980 they worked, adding lighter fare—"Out In The Street," "Crush On You," "Cadillac Ranch," "I'm A Rocker," "Ramrod," "You Can Look (But You Better Not Touch)"—the kind of songs that would drive an arena crazy if the band ever got out of the studio and back on the road. Eventually, Springsteen was left with only one option: a double album.

Released in October 1980, *The River* was complicated, and a hit. It sold more than one and a half million copies before Christmas, and "Hungry Heart" worked its way up to number five on the *Billboard* singles chart. Van Zandt and Landau were right.

After the tightly wound narratives of *Born to Run* and *Darkness*, *The River* was, as one might expect with twenty songs, more expansive.

Opposite: A moment of introspection. Portrait by Frank Stefanko, 1978. Stefanko shot the covers for both *The River* and *Darkness on the Edge of Town*.

Overleaf: On the roof of the Power Station, March 1980.

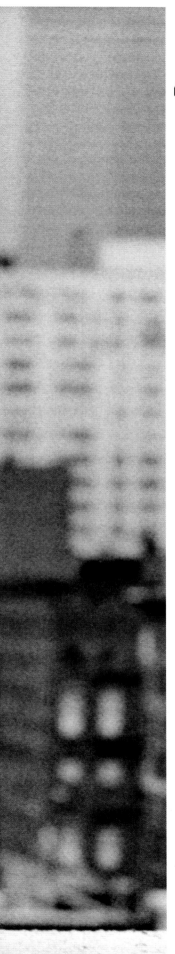

"I WAS INTERESTED IN WHAT ADULTHOOD MEANT. THAT WAS A LIFE THAT I WAS NOT LIVING, BUT I WAS ON THE OUTSIDE OF IT LOOKING IN. I ADMIRED IT IN A LOT OF WAYS."

Bruce Springsteen, 2011

"I tried to accept the fact that, you know, the world is a paradox, and that's the way it is," Springsteen told Dave DiMartino for a story that appeared in *Creem* in January 1981. "Let there be sunlight, let there be rain," Springsteen shouts over a raucous crowd on "Sherry Darling."

Springsteen returned to the idea of community and moved away from the isolation that permeated *Darkness*. "The Ties That Bind" doesn't believe for a second that tough-guy talk about going it alone. Walking tough? "You're walking blind." "Two Hearts" takes up a similar space. "Once I spent my time playing tough-guy scenes," Springsteen sings, suggesting no more. And yet "Jackson Cage" paints daily life as a crucible and asks how you're going to handle it: "Are you tough enough to play the game they play?" Or are you just going to let them run you down? It's the difference between determination and false bravado. "The Price You Pay" puts it another way: Can you make the choices you have to make and "learn to sleep at night"?

The sets are familiar enough. Cars and highways, small towns populated by confused boys and lots of little girls. But then the sets rarely change in real life. The characters just grow up. Casting "Mary" as the co-star in "The River" connects it to "Thunder Road." The woman pushing the baby carriage down the street in "I Wanna Marry You" could easily be the same woman Springsteen used to describe during the live introduction to the band's cover of Manfred Mann's "Pretty Flamingo." Then she was attracting the attention of horny guys hanging out on the street. Now? He can't make all her dreams come true, "But maybe, darlin', I could help them along."

"Fade Away" and "Drive All Night" stumble confused and alone, untethered from what had been a meaningful connection. "When I lost you, honey, sometimes I think I lost my guts too," Springsteen sings on "Drive All Night."

The romanticism of his earlier work had grown up. "To me, 'romantic' is when you see the realities ... but you also see the possibilities," Springsteen said in his interview with DiMartino.

Springsteen closed the album with "Wreck On The Highway," a title he got from a country song Dorsey Dixon wrote in 1937 and Roy Acuff recorded in 1942. Springsteen puts his character at the scene of a bloody accident on an archetypal two-lane highway. The album fades out with the image of that guy in bed, watching his wife or girlfriend sleep while imagining the knock on another door where another wife or girlfriend is getting the worst news of her life.

"We have a finite amount of time to come together, to do the things we need to do and want to do, to love the people we want to love and to have the opportunity to raise and guide, to do our work," Springsteen said in 2011. "Really that was, to me, a little quiet meditation on how I felt about my life at the time, the beginning of that clock ticking."

As the reviews rolled in, Springsteen began to be compared not just to rock stars, but to cultural heavyweights like John Steinbeck (in *Rolling Stone*) and Francis Ford Coppola (in *Time*). "The heathens raged in Ann Arbor as they haven't for years," the *Michigan Daily* wrote after the opening night of the tour in early October, "perhaps not since Dylan played here in '74."

"I DON'T THINK, 'IF I DON'T PLAY GOOD TONIGHT, AT LEAST I PLAYED GOOD LAST NIGHT.' IT'S LIKE THERE'S NO TOMORROWS OR YESTERDAYS. THERE'S ONLY RIGHT NOW."

Bruce Springsteen, 1981

On November 5, the day after Republican Ronald Reagan won the presidency, Springsteen looked out across a crowd in Tempe, Arizona and made as explicit a political statement as he had to that point in his career, "I don't know what you guys think about what happened last night, but I think it's pretty frightening. You guys are young, there's going to be a lot of people depending on you coming up." Then he counted into "Badlands."

A month later, Springsteen and the E Street Band played Philadelphia the night after John Lennon was murdered in New York. "It's an unreasonable world and you have to live with a lot of things that are just unlivable," Springsteen said from the stage. They ended the show with "Twist And Shout," the first song Springsteen ever learned. "I have never seen a human being exert himself the way Springsteen did

that night in Philly," *Rolling Stone*'s Fred Schruers wrote in his cover story from February 1981.

Having been forced to pare down their normal set to ninety minutes for the "No Nukes" shows, to exhilarating effect, Van Zandt told Marsh he figured they'd do the same on the tour. "What we ended up doing is adding ninety minutes to the show we already did."

Any kid in that crowd could be seeing the band for the first time, Springsteen figured, and so the show had to be great. Every night. All the time. "It's like there's no tomorrows or yesterdays," he told DiMartino.

For the first time since their brief visit after *Born to Run*, the band returned to Europe (albeit delayed even then owing to exhaustion brought on by the US run). A *Sunday Times* piece in May 1981 noted that in the UK alone there were 300,000 applications for 105,000 tickets. Springsteen broke big in Europe and got a different view of America and being an American, two slightly different things that were increasingly present in the perception of Springsteen by both others and himself. There was the creeping suspicion that he could be more than a rock star, that he could "help inspire the country as a whole in the ways already suggested in his music," which is how the *New York Times*'s John Rockwell put it.

Inspired by Joe Klein's 1980 biography of Woody Guthrie, Springsteen had added the revered folksinger's "This Land Is Your Land" to the set, finding in it so many of the themes that defined *The River*. On New Year's Eve 1980 at the Nassau Coliseum in Long Island, New York, he put the song between the Creedence Clearwater Revival Vietnam-era "Who'll Stop The Rain" and "The Promised Land." Introducing Guthrie's classic, Springsteen spoke of his father, how he'd let the world rob him of joy, and hope. "And every day people are going to be trying to take it away from you, and every day you gotta fight for it," Springsteen said. "So this is a fighting song."

A few days earlier, a piece by Greil Marcus appeared in *New West*. It drew a line from Lester Bangs's assertion that Elvis would be the last thing we agreed on as a country to a piece Jon Landau had written about Bob Dylan and the way the Vietnam War had permeated his *John Wesley Harding* album. Marcus turned to Springsteen and the election of Ronald Reagan, hypothesizing that Springsteen's next album would find fuel in that one event. "Those songs likely will not comment on those events," Marcus wrote, "they will, I think, reflect those events back to us, fixing moods and telling stories that are, at present, out of reach."

Above: Portrait by Frank Stefanko, 1978.

Opposite, top: "Out in the street, I just feel all right" . . .

Opposite, center: . . . but back home it's a different story.

Opposite, bottom: Making a connection during the River tour, 1980.

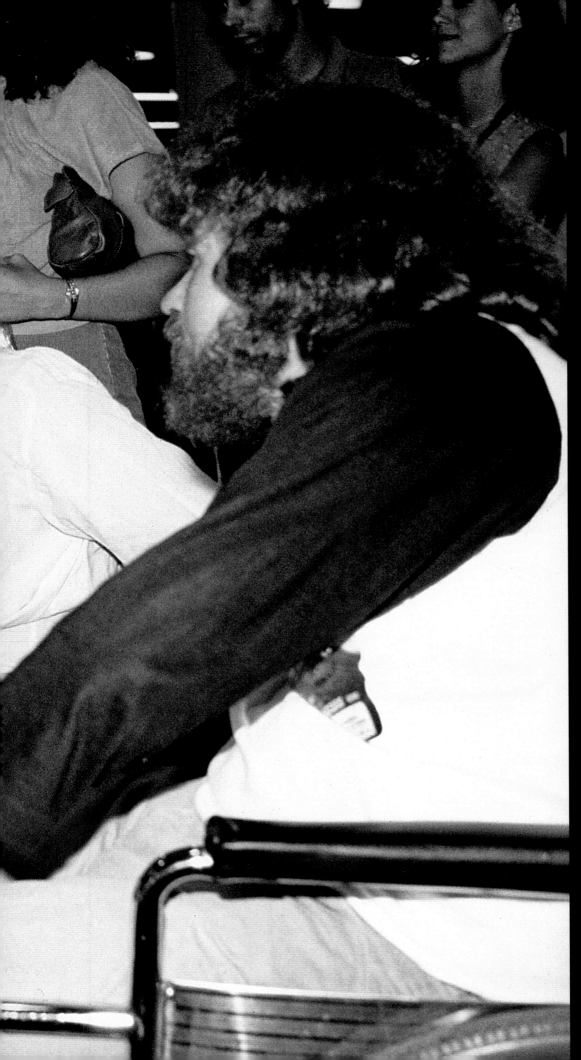

BRUCE SPRINGSTEEN, ACTIVIST

"Hello. Listen. Listen for a second," Springsteen said, trying to calm a crowd that was, by then, like all the crowds, crazy. "Tonight we're here for the men and women who fought the Vietnam War."

The show at the Los Angeles Memorial Sports Arena on August 20, 1981 was not just another show. A few years earlier, on a road trip through the southwestern desert, Springsteen had picked up a copy of Ron Kovic's Vietnam memoir *Born on the Fourth of July*. A few days later, in Los Angeles, he met Kovic by chance, and through Kovic he met Bobby Muller, president of the Vietnam Veterans of America Foundation.

When Springsteen heard the organization needed money, he arranged for the first of a six-night Los Angeles stand to double as a benefit. This wouldn't be a case of simply applying the power of the E Street Band (as he'd done with the "No Nukes" shows), or making a brief political statement (as in Arizona after Reagan's election), it was Springsteen in front on the issue with all the dedication his career implied.

Springsteen introduced Muller with a speech that laid plain the importance of the cause, likening it to when you see someone being beaten in the dark, and you have to decide whether to step in or just walk on by to avoid the trouble.

"Well, Vietnam turned this whole country into a dark street, and unless we're able to walk down those dark alleys and look into the eyes of the men and the women who are down there and the things that happened, we're never going to be able to get home, and then it's only a chance," he said.

He also played a set that, decades down the road, still ignites the heart and imagination when the bootleg rolls, a fierce, purposeful performance that marked the beginning of an involvement in causes big and small that continues to this day.

Backstage at the Vietnam Veterans of America Foundation benefit, Los Angeles Memorial Sports Arena, August 20, 1981.

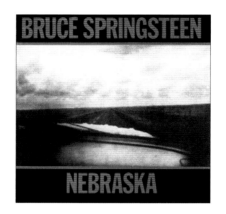

NEBRASKA

1982

"I WANTED THE MUSIC TO FEEL LIKE
A WAKING DREAM AND THE RECORD
TO MOVE LIKE POETRY. I WANTED
THE BLOOD ON IT TO FEEL DESTINED
AND FATEFUL."

BRUCE SPRINGSTEEN, 1998

1982

January 3: Springsteen records most of the songs for *Nebraska* in one day at his home "porta-studio" in Colts Neck, New Jersey.

January–May: First phase of recording of *Born in the U.S.A.* in New York at the Power Station and the Hit Factory.

June 12: Performs with Jackson Browne at the Rally for Disarmament in Central Park, New York City.

June: Steve Van Zandt starts to spend less time with the E Street Band, changes his stage name to Little Steven, and forms his own band, the Disciples of Soul.

August 10: At the wedding reception of his old friend Southside Johnny (John Lyon), Springsteen puts in a guest appearance with the groom's band, the Asbury Jukes.

September 20: Release of *Nebraska* (US 3, UK 3).

October: Donates the song "Pink Cadillac" to Bette Midler, but does not like the recording and so does not allow it to be released.

December 31: Another wedding reception performance, this time for Van Zandt; the Reverend Richard Penniman (aka Little Richard) conducts the ceremony, and Percy Sledge sings "When A Man Loves A Woman" as bride and groom walk down the aisle.

Above: The sparse, mainly acoustic sound wrong-footed fans.

Page 101 and right: From David Kennedy's cover shoot for *Nebraska*, an album on which Springsteen explored the dark recesses of his memory.

Early in 1982, Springsteen made the trip into New York City from the house he was renting in Colts Neck, New Jersey. He had with him a cassette tape, the kind you'd buy at a drugstore, and handwritten notes to deliver to Jon Landau. On the cassette was a collection of fifteen songs Springsteen had recently recorded at home on a four-track machine he'd sent his guitar tech to purchase. They'd mixed the demos on a boom box with a dubious history.

"A lot of ideas, but I'm not exactly sure where I'm going," Springsteen wrote. He must have been encouraged, because he included a drawing of a stick figure playing a guitar and smiling. But there was plenty of hedging, too. "They might not hit you right away," he warned Landau in the cover letter.

The memo continued song by song, offering insight, inspiration and details about different takes. "Johnny 99," a track about a down-on-his-luck character who gets drunk, shoots a "night clerk," and asks the judge to sentence him to death, was described as "kinda fun!"

Landau had sent Springsteen a script for a movie that writer and director Paul Schrader was making: "Born in the U.S.A." "Which I did not have a chance to read yet," Springsteen wrote, "but I did whip up this little ditty purloining the title."

Springsteen assured Landau that his "Reason To Believe" was not the 1965 Tim Hardin song. "Open All Night" was "very hard to perform," and "State Trooper" was "kinda weird." Of "Losin' Kind," Springsteen wrote, "Can't seem to find a better punch line." Which is funny, because it had a pretty good punch line.

A thematic cousin to "Johnny 99," "Losin' Kind" starts when a guy meets a girl outside a bar. They go dancing, get drunk, get a room, go back out, and rob a roadhouse where our hero hits someone "too hard," and then hits him again. The couple speeds off into the night—until the narrator wraps the car around a telephone pole. He steps from the wreckage into the wrong end of a cop's .45. The cop tells him, "Son, you're lucky to be alive."

"Sir," he replies, "I'll think that one over, if you don't mind."

Springsteen came home from the River tour a worldwide star. Unlike after *Born to Run* and *Darkness*, this time he had the bank account to prove it. He had the freedom to do whatever he wanted, go wherever he liked. He used that freedom to return to Freehold and stalk his childhood. "I'd always drive past the old houses I used to live in," he said on stage in 1990. "Sometimes late at night."

In the darkness, the ghosts Springsteen had been running from since Elvis captured his imagination

caught up, and no amount of money was going to buy them off. On stage he could play until they were exhausted, but the stillness of post-tour life left him at their mercy.

He turned back toward his earliest experiences, the sense of failure and loss that defined life in his grandparents' house on Randolph Street. The demons that had haunted his father all those lonely nights in the kitchen began to work on Springsteen, too. The album that became *Nebraska*, the album that was on that cassette Springsteen carried to New York, was born from the shadows of his past cast long to his present.

When he began recording on January 3, 1982, he started with the title track, listed in the notes he sent Landau as "Starkweather (Nebraska)."

At home one night, Springsteen caught Terrence Malick's 1973 movie *Badlands*. It's based on the story of Charles Starkweather and his girlfriend, Caril Ann Fugate, who took off from Lincoln, Nebraska in January 1958, killing ten people (and two dogs) before they were caught in Wyoming. Starkweather was twenty when he was executed the following year. The story stuck with Springsteen to the point where he called Ninette Beaver, a Nebraska journalist who wrote a book about Fugate.

Above: Caril Ann Fugate and Charles Starkweather, whose murder spree across Nebraska and Wyoming inspired the album's title track.

Opposite: In songs like "Johnny 99" and "Open All Night," Springsteen adopted a 1950s rockabilly style, which Frank Stefanko captured in this 1982 photo shoot.

"You can put together a lot of detail, but unless you pull something up out of yourself it's going to lie flat on the page," Springsteen said during his 2005 *Storytellers* performance for VH1. "You gotta find out what you have in common with that character no matter who they are or what they did."

For help, Springsteen turned to another dark new source of inspiration. Five years before Starkweather went full monster, the Southern writer Flannery O'Connor published one of her most famous short stories, "A Good Man Is Hard to Find." Her Starkweather is an escaped convict named the Misfit, and he comes across a family dragged well off the main road by a false memory. A simple mistake—the grandmother's belief they could find an old house she recalled too late was in Tennessee, not Georgia—dooms them all.

The bulk of the story's dialogue takes place between the Misfit and the grandmother as the rest of the family is marched off into the woods and killed. Asked what first sent him to prison, the Misfit says, "Turn to the right, it was a wall. Turn to the left, it was a wall. Look up it was a ceiling, look down it was a floor. I forget what I done, lady."

Finally, it's just the two of them and O'Connor writes a devastating sentence: "There was not a cloud in the sky nor any sun."

"Everyone knows what it's like to be condemned," Springsteen said. One way or another. And so he sat down in a rocking chair, with two microphones, a twelve-string acoustic guitar, and a harmonica—the root instrumentation of "The River"—and he told another story. "It's after the violence," Springsteen said. "And it feels like it's after his death. There's even a joke." That would be Starkweather asking that Fugate be right there on his lap as the electric chair goes to work. Get it?

Where he found his connection was in the final verse. "They wanted to know why I did what I did. Well, sir, I guess there's just a meanness in this world."

The cold, matter-of-fact style of the title track informs most of the songs Springsteen knocked out in his bedroom. "Johnny 99" and "Atlantic City" both spring from the news.

In 1980, Ford closed its assembly plant in Mahwah, New Jersey, and in "Johnny 99" that's what sends Ralph out into the night and spiraling toward Judge Mean John Brown's courtroom. In March 1981, a Philadelphia mobster named Philip Testa was blown up in his house. His nickname: the Chicken Man.

"Well, they blew up the Chicken Man in Philly last night," is how Springsteen opens "Atlantic City." In both songs, the main character has "debts no honest man can pay." Ralph turns to crime, the guy in "Atlantic City" is about to.

"Mansion On The Hill," borrowing a title from Hank Williams's 1948 country hit "A Mansion On The Hill," casts a child's view up toward what he doesn't (and likely never will) have. In "Used Cars," the kid watches as his mother "fingers" her wedding band and the salesman "stares at my old man's hands." Hands no doubt calloused and worn from the kind of work that never pays for a new car.

"State Trooper" rides shotgun through the night with someone who's packing not only a "clear conscience," but if the low rumble of the music is any indication, bad intentions as well. When he says, "Hey somebody out there, listen to my last prayer," that prayer is for any kind of connection to save him.

"Open All Night" is a much more rambunctious and seemingly less criminal road trip, the song's narrator riding hell bent through the night to get to his girl. He knows who he wants to hear *his* last prayer. It's "mister deejay,"

> # "MY BASIC ATTITUDE IS PEOPLE-ORIENTED, YOU KNOW. KIND OF LIKE HUMAN POLITICS. I FEEL THAT I CAN DO MY BEST BY MAKING SONGS. MAKE SOME DIFFERENCE THAT WAY."
>
> Bruce Springsteen, 1984

Left: Philip "Chicken Man" Testa, the Philadelphia gangster referred to in "Atlantic City."

Opposite: Portrait by David Kennedy, 1982. A similar shot appeared on the album's inner sleeve.

"THE AUDIENCE AND THE PERFORMER HAVE GOT TO LEAVE SOME ROOM FOR EACH OTHER TO BE HUMAN. OR ELSE THEY DON'T DESERVE EACH OTHER, IN A FUNNY KIND OF WAY."

Bruce Springsteen, 1984

and it's rock 'n' roll that will deliver him "from nowhere." It's the rare moment when salvation is even considered.

"Highway Patrolman" casts brothers on opposite sides of the law, but brothers are brothers and a "man turns his back on his family, well he just ain't no good." "My Father's House" opens with a dream and then takes us on one of Springsteen's drives back through Freehold and to the front door of his past, the lights "shining 'cross this dark highway where our sins lie unatoned."

"Reason To Believe" almost mocks those who figure out how to find such a thing. A baby is baptized, an old man dies, and we wonder, "What does it mean?" A groom, deserted on his wedding day, stands watching the river flow on, as it always has, without a care of what's happening on its banks.

When Steve Van Zandt heard the cassette, "I told him, 'I'm sorry, this isn't a demo. You just made your next record,'" he said in 2011.

That doesn't mean they didn't try to turn it into something bigger. Springsteen and the E Street Band convened in the studio and set about recording full-band versions of the songs on the cassette. A few worked. Most didn't. The cassette was better. The ten recordings that made the final track list sounded like they were from another time.

Part of that was the way they were recorded. Neither Springsteen nor his tech, Mike Batlan, knew what they were doing with the Teac Tascam 144 that Batlan had brought to Colts Neck. And the beat box they used to mix the songs had recently been soaked by the waters of the

Navesink River during a boat trip Springsteen had taken with Garry Tallent. Only later—and in the middle of the night—did the beat box spring back to life. It worked, but it had been wounded.

"That's where the darkness comes from," engineer Chuck Plotkin said in 2011. "Everything is slightly below pitch, and slightly slow."

Aside from murderous psychopaths and great Southern writers, Springsteen had become interested in Harry Smith's *Anthology of American Folk Music*, which had been released in 1952. "Johnny 99" makes a nod to Julius Daniels's "99 Year Blues," which is part of that collection, and that collection was important enough to take a co-starring role in the 1960s folk revival that launched Bob Dylan. In *Songs*, Springsteen mentions bluesmen John Lee Hooker and Robert Johnson, guys who made "records that sounded so good with the lights out."

And, of course, there was Springsteen's continued interest in another of Dylan's inspirations—Woody Guthrie. Guthrie's songs were plainspoken, powerful, and political. In Guthrie, Springsteen saw someone else who had tried to answer Hank Williams's question about why the hole was in that bucket. Springsteen also knew he wasn't going to be Guthrie. "I liked Elvis, and I liked the 'Pink Cadillac' too much," he said at SXSW in 2012. "I liked the simplicity and the tossed-off temporary feeling of pop hits … And in my own way, I like the luxuries and the comforts of being a star. I had already gone a long way down a pretty different road."

Opposite: Springsteen grappled with his demons on repeated nighttime drives back to his childhood home in Freehold, where his father had spent long hours brooding in darkness at the kitchen table.

This page: Two of the major musical influences on *Nebraska*—the nocturnal blues of John Lee Hooker (left) and the plainspoken protest songs of Woody Guthrie (right).

Nebraska at least let him walk a few steps in Guthrie's shoes. Released on September 20, 1982, the album was unlike anything in the popular culture and nothing like what had been expected as a follow-up to *The River*, the record that had earned Springsteen millions of new fans. "*Nebraska* comes as a shock," read the *Rolling Stone* review, "a violent, acid-etched portrait of a wounded America that fuels its machinery by consuming its people's dreams."

There would be no tour, just a simple black-and-white video for "Atlantic City" handed over to the fledgling MTV. Springsteen was nowhere to be found in the footage. "An inspired way out of the high-stakes rock 'n' roll game that requires each new record to be bigger and grander than the last," *Rolling Stone* wrote. By skipping part of the process—the part with the expensive studios and high-end production, Springsteen got as close as an artist of his fame could to those first personal recordings when you don't know that there will ever be an audience.

Nebraska was small. The sound was small. The lives were small and confined. Walls to the left and right, ceiling above, floor below. Springsteen sounded like he was whispering his own horror story, an American horror story.

"I really didn't think about what its political implications were," he said in 1990, "until I read it in the newspaper."

Whatever he intended, the album was immediately taken as a reaction to Ronald Reagan's America. At his inaugural pep talk in January 1981, Reagan stood in Washington, DC and sold his vision of the country. In Reagan's America we were all in it together, and this was the greatest place, perfect really, except for the high taxes, and especially the high taxes on the richest. Cut those, and the money will shower on all, cleansing the nation. It was "a mythic, very seductive image … that people want to believe in," Springsteen told *Rolling Stone* in 1984.

The reality in 1982 was high unemployment (above fourteen percent in Michigan, the worst-hit state, where decades earlier the middle-class American Dream had been punched out alongside cars on assembly lines), shuttered factories, and boarded-up downtown windows. The walls were closing in on a lot more people than were knocking them down to add extra rooms to the mansion.

In the *Philadelphia Inquirer*, music critic Ken Tucker wrote: "Springsteen's new songs make

nearly everything else in the top ten sound shabby and weak-willed. *Nebraska* is not music to dance to, or music to escape with; it's music to confront. It forces you to accept or reject its conclusions."

That a record as challenging as *Nebraska* worked its way to number three on *Billboard*'s album chart suggests one brand of acceptance. Time has been even more generous. In 2012, the *New Yorker* called the recording of the album "one of the more mythical events in pop-music history." *Nebraska* is a cornerstone of the modern Americana and alt-country genres. In 1986, with his own star on the rise after releasing his debut album, *Guitar Town*, Steve Earle introduced "State Trooper" at the Bottom Line saying, "This next song was written by a pretty good hillbilly singer from South Jersey."

Twenty-four years later, Earle's son, Justin Townes Earle, playing with Joe Pug, introduced "Atlantic City" saying, "If you don't like Springsteen, then you don't like Woody Guthrie, which means you don't like *songs*."

Johnny Cash covered "Highway Patrolman" and "Johnny 99." Hank Williams's grandson Hank Williams III covered "Atlantic City" on a 2000 tribute album released by Sub Pop that also included work from the likes of Son Volt, Los Lobos, and Ani DiFranco. Emmylou Harris and the National have taken on "Mansion On The Hill." The list is long and cool. Actor Sean Penn took "Highway Patrolman" and turned it into the screenplay for his directorial debut, *The Indian Runner*. In 2006, the New York Guitar Festival opened with a tribute to the album. Among those who helped recreate it live were Michelle Shocked, Meshell Ndegeocello, Martha Wainwright, and Vernon Reid.

All that was to come, however. After *Nebraska* was released, Springsteen took a drive. He ended up, as he had for years, in California, where he now owned a little home, and more recording equipment, and he stayed working on music. He also tracked down a psychiatrist to talk to about the emotional wreckage he'd just released for all the world to hear.

He talked about those late-night drives through his past. Retelling the story in 1990, Springsteen said he asked the psychiatrist why. Why was Springsteen still wandering Freehold?

"Something went wrong and you keep going back to see if you can fix it and somehow make it right," Springsteen recalled the psychiatrist telling him. "I sat there and said, 'That *is* what I'm doing.' And he said, 'Well, you can't.'"

Left: Springsteen rejected the utopian view of America that President Reagan laid out in his 1981 inauguration address.

Opposite: Portrait by Frank Stefanko, 1982.

BORN IN THE U.S.A.

1984

"THE FLAG IS A POWERFUL IMAGE AND
WHEN YOU SET THAT STUFF LOOSE,
YOU DON'T KNOW WHAT'S GOING TO
BE DONE WITH IT."

BRUCE SPRINGSTEEN, 1984

1983

January–February: Solo recording sessions for *Born in the U.S.A.* in a studio installed in Springsteen's house in Los Angeles.

April–June: Full-band sessions for *Born in the U.S.A.* resume at the Hit Factory.

September: Final phase of *Born in the U.S.A.* sessions begins.

1984

February: *Born in the U.S.A.* sessions conclude with the recording of "Dancing In The Dark."

February: Official announcement of Steve Van Zandt's departure from the E Street Band.

May: Nils Lofgren replaces Van Zandt and Patti Scialfa also joins the band on backing vocals.

June 4: Release of *Born in the U.S.A.* (US 1, UK 1).

June 29: First night of the Born in the U.S.A. tour, at the St. Paul Civic Center Arena, Minnesota.

June 30: "Dancing In The Dark"/"Pink Cadillac" hits number two in the *Billboard* singles chart, Springsteen's highest-charting single ever in the US. It would end up as the highest-selling 12-inch single that year.

September 13: Publication of George Will's "A Yankee Doodle Springsteen" article in the *Washington Post.*

September 19: At a New Jersey campaign stop, President Reagan attempts to associate himself with Springsteen.

September 22: Springsteen responds to Reagan when introducing "Johnny 99" at the Civic Arena in Pittsburgh.

October: Meets Julianne Phillips when the tour arrives in Los Angeles.

1985

January 27: End of the first leg of the Born in the U.S.A. tour, at the Carrier Dome, Syracuse, New York.

January 28: Springsteen records vocals for the USA for Africa "We Are The World" charity single.

February 26: Awarded his first Grammy, for "Dancing In The Dark" in the Best Male Rock Vocal Performance category.

March 23: Plays in Australia for the first time as the Born in the U.S.A. tour resumes at the Sydney Entertainment Centre.

April 10: The tour moves on to Japan, another new country for Springsteen, with the first of five nights at the Yoyogi National Gymnasium in Tokyo.

April 23: End of the Japanese leg of the tour, at the Osaka-Jō Hall in Osaka.

May 13: Springsteen marries Julianne Phillips in Julianne's hometown, Lake Oswego, Oregon. Clarence Clemons and Steve Van Zandt are his joint best men.

June 1: Start of the European leg of the Born in the U.S.A. tour, at Slane Castle in Ireland, an outdoor concert with an audience of up to 100,000—Springsteen's biggest show to date.

July 7: Last night of the European leg of the tour, at Roundhay Park, Leeds, England.

July: Springsteen sings on Little Steven's "Sun City" anti-apartheid single and appears in the video.

August 5: Start of the final leg of the Born in the U.S.A. tour, at the RFK Stadium, Washington, DC.

October 2: Fifteen months after it started rolling, the Born in the U.S.A. tour finally comes to a halt at the Los Angeles Memorial Coliseum.

December: *Born in the U.S.A.* becomes the bestselling album of 1985.

1986

February: Springsteen participates in the recording of charity single "We've Got The Love" for Jersey Artists for Mankind.

October 13: Performs at Neil Young's first annual Bridge School Benefit Concert.

November 10: Release of the *Live/1975–85* box set (US 1, UK 4), Springsteen's long-awaited first official live album.

Right: Hitting the heights during the Born in the U.S.A. tour.

Far right: A new country, but the same old attention to detail— checking the sound during the Japanese leg of the tour. Furitsu Taiikukan, Kyoto, April 19, 1985.

Page 113: E Street bandana— portrait by Aaron Rapoport for *Rolling Stone*, 1984.

In spring 1982, Springsteen and the E Street Band were holed up at the Power Station in Manhattan trying to figure out what could be done to punch up the songs that had been put to tape in that Colts Neck bedroom.

Not much, it turned out—at least not until they got to the song Springsteen had whipped up after lifting the title from that script Paul Schrader had sent over. On Springsteen's demo, "Born In The U.S.A." sounds like a nightmare fraying at the edges, his voice echoing out of the dark alley he talked about in Los Angeles the night of the benefit for the Vietnam Veterans of America. It's about broken dreams, broken promises, and the broken spirit of someone who risked everything for his country and got nothing back. "Nowhere to run, ain't got nowhere to go." That he was "born in the U.S.A." made the betrayal that much worse. The deal had been broken.

In the studio, Roy Bittan turned to his new synthesizer and picked up the riff, Max Weinberg summoned thunder, and the band ripped into the song, Springsteen's voice now uncoiled into a full-throated, desperate rage. And just when the band seemed ready to fade out, Springsteen signaled Weinberg to create chaos, counted off the beat, and they slammed back into the song. "Martial, modal, and straight ahead," Springsteen wrote in *Songs*. "Born In The U.S.A." didn't sound like anything they had recorded before.

Over the next three weeks, they knocked out another dozen or so songs. Tacked on to the work they'd done earlier in the year—sessions that included songs for Gary U.S. Bonds and Donna Summer—there was a solid foundation in place for whatever came next. Even when "next" became turning some of the cassette into *Nebraska*, it seemed logical the *next* "next" would be easier than it had been in the past. But of course it wouldn't be easier. Abridging *Rolling Stone*'s "Random Notes" from the period is one way to map a struggle that, miraculously, resulted in a release perfectly timed to catch a cultural wave.

November 25, 1982: "Bruce Springsteen has headed out to Los Angeles to complete his next album with the E Street Band."

May 12, 1983: The album "may make it to stores before summer's end."

September 1, 1983: "Don't bet the rent on it, but Bruce Springsteen may have turned a corner on his next LP."

February 2, 1984: "Not even Bruce Springsteen's own E Street Band knows for sure what's up with his long-delayed new LP."

March 17, 1984: "The LP, says Van Zandt, should be out 'sometime this decade.'"

"A SONGWRITER WANTS TO BE UNDERSTOOD. IS THE WAY YOU CHOOSE TO PRESENT YOUR MUSIC ITS POLITICS? IS THE SOUND AND FORM YOUR SONG TAKES ITS CONTENT?"

Bruce Springsteen, 1998

Springsteen could write a song fast, and, working mostly live, the band could record the song in just a few takes, but the one thing no one could do was stop Springsteen from writing *more* songs. As long as there was another song, he couldn't be sure he was choosing from the best collection of songs. The artistic success of *Nebraska* dared Springsteen to match that album's intensity and, in his mind, he couldn't—or hadn't *yet*.

By the time they pushed into 1984, Springsteen and the band had recorded between sixty and eighty songs. He labored over narrative, but had developed enough self-awareness (or acceptance) to know there were other decisions this time. "I had to say I'm using this one and not that one, because I think this one is going to reach an audience that that one may or may not," he said.

Co-producer Chuck Plotkin suggested an album that began with "Born In The U.S.A." and ended with "My Hometown," a moody time-lapse of a town in decline seen first through the eyes of a child, and then, in the end, that child grown up and with a boy of his own. Given the "whitewashed windows" and "vacant stores," the jobs that are leaving and the knowledge that "they ain't coming back," the adult in the room is giving a good hard thought toward abandoning ship.

Springsteen's natural-wood Fender Esquire-Telecaster hybrid, an essential element of his iconography. In a letter to the *Los Angeles Times* in 2004, he declared that "when that big rock 'n' roll clock strikes twelve I will be buried with my Tele on!"

For Springsteen, the title track was the story. "The rest of the album contains a group of songs about which I've always had some ambivalence," he wrote in *Songs*.

Eight of *Born in the U.S.A.*'s twelve songs would end up pulled from those first, earliest recording sessions of 1982. "Cover Me" had been written for Summer, until it was deemed too good. Springsteen gave her another song, "Protection," played guitar on it (recording in Los Angeles with Quincy Jones), and kept "Cover Me," an out-and-out rocker about finding respite from the world in companionship.

"Downbound Train" and "Working On The Highway" both came from the same cassette as *Nebraska*. "Downbound" is a dark night of the soul in which guy loses job, wife, and self—in that order. "Working On The Highway," originally titled "Child Bride," got a drastic musical rework from its original version. Springsteen stripped the most explicit references to the age of the song's girl and turned into the kind of criminal mischief you can dance to.

"Darlington County," a *Darkness*-era title, put another car on another highway, but replaced the girl with a buddy. The guys hit the road in search of fun, fortune, and women. Boys being boys, one of them,

Wayne, is last seen in the rearview "handcuffed to the bumper of a state trooper's Ford."

An early draft of "Glory Days" shaded the song with the disappointment of a father who'd lost his job and couldn't find his place: "Glory days gone bad, glory days he never had." On the album, old victories— and a few drinks—become a source of strength dosed with a cold reality. "Time slips away and leaves you with nothing, mister, but boring stories of glory days" Springsteen shouts over a barroom groove.

Bittan, again on synth, washes "I'm On Fire" in longing, while Springsteen's lyrics provide the lust. "I'm Goin' Down" covers what happens when the lust, and even the love, fades away. The fickleness of romance is how he'd describe it from on stages around the world.

Had Springsteen found his album sooner—say in early 1982—"Bobby Jean" might never have been written. But the old familiar march began and Steve Van Zandt didn't have it in him. By the time he gave *Rolling Stone* that "sometime this decade" quote, he was preparing his second album with his band the Disciples of Soul.

While the European tour in support of *The River* had been revelatory for everyone in the band, it was especially so for Van Zandt. He realized that when he

Above: A retuned E Street Band welcomed Patti Scialfa (fourth from left), as well as Nils Lofgren (third from right), who came in for Steve Van Zandt.

Opposite: The great outdoors. Despite initial misgivings, Springsteen thrived as a stadium rocker.

"I WAS A BIG FAN OF MEANINGLESS, REPETITIVE BEHAVIOR, AND WHAT'S MORE MEANINGLESS THAN LIFTING A HEAVY OBJECT AND THEN PUTTING IT DOWN IN THE SAME PLACE YOU FOUND IT?"

Bruce Springsteen, 2011

left the United States, he wasn't just a guitar player in a rock band. He was an American, and as such, he was responsible for the actions of the government. His focus broadened beyond rock 'n' roll. As evidence, see those first two politically charged records he made with the Disciples of Soul, *Men Without Women* and *Voice of America*. So Van Zandt left the E Street Band. Springsteen would eventually replace him with guitarist Nils Lofgren (who years earlier had auditioned for Bill Graham the same night as Steel Mill), and then added Patti Scialfa, who had earlier auditioned for Springsteen in 1971, to assist on background vocals.

The presumption, never explicitly stated (even to Van Zandt), was that "Bobby Jean" was about the breakup, about a friendship that had endured since "we were sixteen." It isn't a counter-argument; it's a hug. "Good luck, good-bye," Springsteen concludes. "No Surrender" covers similar ground with a bigger beat.

Nebraska was Springsteen's low-budget art-house masterpiece, his own perfect noir. *Born in the U.S.A.* was the blockbuster, a buddy flick full of car chases and romance and just enough conflict to roughen up the story. The plot was loose, but the plot was secondary. As Springsteen put the finishing touches on the album early in 1984, Jon Landau broke the news that one piece remained missing. They still needed a lead single. Springsteen reacted like a guy who'd already written dozens of songs, and then he calmed down and went to work. If he could tuck a protest song inside an anthem, he could mask his frustration and exhaustion with a dance hit.

"Dancing In The Dark" keeps rock-star hours—waking in the evening, getting to sleep in the morning. At night, the song's protagonist "ain't got nothing to say." When he gets home, he goes to bed "feeling the same way."

"Man, I'm just tired and bored with myself," Springsteen sings, and just how uncomfortable he is in his skin is made clear in the next verse when a gaze at the mirror reveals nothing he wouldn't change. Springsteen had spent a decade in a single-minded pursuit of artistic vision and rock stardom, and he had done so at the expense of every other part of his life. And still he needed one ... more ... song. "There's a joke here somewhere and it's on me," he realized.

When the band assembled in the studio to record the song early in 1984, they again leaned on Bittan and his synthesizer. Weinberg first attacked it the way he had "Born In The U.S.A.," as a big rock song. "I remember Jon Landau coming up behind me in the studio after a couple of takes saying play it like that Michael Jackson song," Weinberg said. "Beat It," which had been a number-one hit a year earlier off Jackson's *Thriller*, was the song in question. That did it. They had their single, and Springsteen had the most commercial album of his career.

"And at the point I got there, I was that guy," he said. "That's where I found myself. You can kid yourself that you're not, but then what have you been doing?"

Released in June 1984, *Born in the U.S.A.* was built for the masses. Bob Clearmountain, who'd worked with David Bowie and the Rolling Stones, had mixed an entire album's worth of material from *The River* that wasn't used. With one exception: "Hungry Heart," Springsteen's biggest hit to date. He mixed all of *Born in the U.S.A.*

For the cover, Springsteen turned to celebrity photographer Annie Leibovitz who stood him in front of an American flag and went to work. The outfit they chose was a classic white T-shirt and blue jeans, a red baseball cap hanging from Springsteen's back pocket; the shot they settled on centered on his butt.

Having heard producer and DJ Arthur Baker's work on the Cyndi Lauper hit "Girls Just Want To Have Fun," Springsteen asked Baker to remix "Dancing In The Dark," "Cover Me," and even "Born In The U.S.A." for the dance clubs. "You've gotta do different things and try stuff," Springsteen told Chet Flippo for *Musician* magazine. "I figured that a lot of people would like it and that the people that didn't like it would get over it. My audience is not that fragile, you know. They can take it."

Then there was the matter of MTV, which had debuted ten months after *The River* was released, and had, in the time it took to make *Born in the U.S.A.*, become an impossible-to-ignore cultural force. After a comical false start for the "Dancing In The Dark" video, which featured Springsteen, alone on an all-black set, swinging his

arms about in a white tank top with black pants, black suspenders, and a black headband while lip-synching to the song, he settled on a "live" treatment pitched by Brian De Palma, director of *Carrie* and *Scarface*.

Springsteen kept the dance moves and the lip-synch, but significantly upgraded the setting when they shot the video in St. Paul, Minnesota on the opening night of the tour. This time dressed in jeans and a white shirt, his sleeves rolled up to show off the work he'd done in the weight room, Springsteen grinned and surveyed the crowd, looking for the spark that'll start the fire the song suggests will help the world make sense. He finds an unknown actress named Courteney Cox, pulling her on stage to dance through the song's fade. (It would be the beginning of a long, successful career for Cox who, a few years later, would play the girlfriend of Michael J. Fox's *Family Ties* character. In 1987, Fox would co-star with rocker Joan Jett in Schrader's *Light of Day*, the movie made from the script once titled "Born in the U.S.A." *Light of Day* carried the name of the song Springsteen eventually sent Schrader.)

The video is cheesy—a stylized version of what had happened at countless Springsteen shows in the past. Only then the women had run on stage without invitation. But the video worked.

Everything Springsteen did in 1984 worked.

Born in the U.S.A. spent the month of July in the number-one spot on *Billboard*'s albums chart, knocking Huey Lewis and the News' *Sports* from the top after only one week. Eventually *Born in the U.S.A.* would be replaced by Prince's *Purple Rain*. The only other

"IT WAS CONTROVERSIAL, BUT IT BROADENED BRUCE'S APPEAL, ESPECIALLY WITH WOMEN AND TEENS."

Jon Landau, on the "Dancing In The Dark" video, 2012

Left: Corny though it may have been, the video for "Dancing In The Dark" made its mark and helped to propel the song to number two—Springsteen's highest placed US single to date.

Opposite: Giants Stadium, New Jersey, August 1985.

Overleaf: Springsteen recruits more than seventy thousand backing singers at Wembley Stadium, London, July 1985.

albums to top the chart that year were *Thriller* and the soundtrack to the movie *Footloose*.

"Dancing In The Dark" would go to number two on the singles chart, the first of seven top-ten hits the album would produce. The tour was bigger still. They played multiple nights at almost every stop—including ten nights at the Brendan Byrne Arena in New Jersey, six nights at the Spectrum in Philadelphia, and seven at the Los Angeles Memorial Sports Arena.

Springsteen stepped out of the rock press, and into celebrity culture, sitting down to chat with *People* magazine, and the television show *Entertainment Tonight*. MTV held a contest where the winner got to be one of his roadies for a day. Springsteen was part of a small group of artists—Prince, Michael Jackson, Van Halen, Madonna—who were working career-defining albums that year. What distinguished him was he was the only rock star in 1984 who could also get caught up in election-year politics.

It started in September when bow-tied conservative columnist George Will used his nationally syndicated newspaper column to prove he could make even rock 'n' roll sound boring. Will cast Springsteen as the kind of self-made man that built the country. "He is no whiner," Will wrote, "and the recitation of closed factories and other problems always seems punctuated by a grand, cheerful affirmation: 'Born in the U.S.A.!'"

Cheerful? Not that Will would be the first to make the mistake. Or even the most prominent. A week later, at a campaign stop in New Jersey, President Ronald Reagan cast America's future in "the message of hope in songs of a man so many young Americans admire." That man, of course, was Bruce Springsteen.

Springsteen understood the power of iconography and knew exactly what he was doing with his. Knew it from the moment he walked into Eric Meola's photo studio with Clarence Clemons and a guitar for the *Born to Run* shoot. Each album cover since had set the mood for what was to come. *Born in the U.S.A.*, with its suggestion of impending fireworks, was no different. But the flag is a hard thing to control. You wrap yourself in it, give people a reason to pump fists in the air, and it's entirely possible they'll be too fired up for the finer points. The version of "Born In The U.S.A." Springsteen chose was, he wrote in *Songs*, the song "in its most powerful presentation." For better or worse.

When it came time to shoot the video, he refused to lip-synch. Shot live (but set to the album track), with Springsteen wearing leather, denim, and some unshaven scruff, the images are less than perfectly aligned with the song. It's a grainy, tough performance interspersed with all-American images

of carnivals and factories, cars, and row upon row of white cemetery headstones. Springsteen no doubt benefited from the patriotism kicked up by Reagan's campaign. The difference was how each defined that particularly loaded word. For Reagan, America was great, always and forever. For Springsteen, it could be, but there was work to do.

Whatever concessions Springsteen had made to mass appeal, he wasn't ready to be anyone's political prop, and especially not Reagan's as he was busy selling an idealized version of a new American dawn. "It's not morning in Pittsburgh," Springsteen told *Rolling Stone* in December 1984. "It's not morning above 125th St. in New York. It's midnight, and, like, there's a bad moon risin'." But when Reagan's opponent, former vice president Walter Mondale, attempted to exploit the misstep to land a political punch or two, he overbalanced. After his campaign managers tried to claim a Springsteen endorsement, they were forced to retract.

Springsteen's politics, while aligning more closely to Mondale than Reagan, had always been more personal than partisan. "Human politics" is how he described them to Chet Flippo. On the Born in the U.S.A. tour, he took time out at shows to direct fans to food banks and other community resources working directly with citizens in need.

Springsteen turned down a fortune (that he already had) from Chrysler, which wanted to put his music in commercials for their cars. He turned down tour sponsorships. He managed to be both in and above the fray. And the hits kept coming. "Born In The U.S.A." peaked at number nine (after "Cover Me" had reached seven). Released early in 1985, "I'm On Fire" went to number six and came with a video that marked Springsteen's first foray into acting. He played a mechanic. "Glory Days" got to number five on the chart, that video capturing Springsteen's not-quite-textbook pitching motion.

As if he didn't already have enough going for him, during a break from touring in May 1985 he married actress Julianne Phillips in a late-night ceremony at a Catholic church in her hometown of Lake Oswego, Oregon.

Predictably, it was all too much for some. "Piety has begun to collect around Springsteen's curly head like mist around a mountain top," James Wolcott wrote in *Vanity Fair*. "The mountain can't be blamed for the mist, but still—the reverence is getting awfully thick."

Springsteen was "too cornball sincere" for Wolcott's "corrupt taste," he wrote, ending on this note: "Virtue, it's a wearisome thing."

For some, but far from all. By the time the tour hit Europe in 1985, it was playing the biggest

"I WAS INTRODUCED BY JAMES BROWN AS MR. BORN IN THE U.S.A. ONE NIGHT. THAT WAS A HIGHLIGHT OF MY LIFE."

Bruce Springsteen, 2011

venues in town, opening in Ireland at Slane Castle before working its way to three nights at Wembley Stadium in London. Every step along the way they were chased by fans and photographers. Back in the United States, the schedule could have belonged to a National Football League team. They moved from stadium to stadium throughout the summer. The hotels were the best. The airplanes were chartered. The days jammed in cars and buses were a distant memory. Inertia took over; all anyone could do was hold on and ride.

Born in the U.S.A. would spend eighty-four consecutive weeks in the top ten and, despite being released in mid-1984, was the highest-selling album of 1985 in the United States. By the time it took that honor, more than ten million copies had been sold (on the way to more than fifteen million). Anything Springsteen had ever set out to do, he'd done. Rock 'n' roll had moved and inspired him. He now was moving and inspiring with rock 'n' roll. On October 2, 1985, the tour wrapped with a fourth night at the Los Angeles Memorial Coliseum, which the year before had been home to the Summer Olympics. Springsteen closed with a cover of Creedence Clearwater Revival's "Rockin' All Over the World" segueing into "Glory Days."

At the show's end, the band walked up the steps toward the Olympic torch. "I remember taking a last look at the crowd, smiling to myself, and feeling like I had never felt before," Bittan told Robert Santelli in 2006. Reflecting on the tour in 2011, Garry Tallent said, "It was going to get real again the next day, certainly a year later. But for that moment, it was unbelievable."

Seeing stars. The dizzying success of *Born in the U.S.A.* was greater than Springsteen could possibly have expected.

LIVE, FINALLY

By the end of the Born in the U.S.A. tour, Springsteen was the biggest rock star in the world, a sex symbol at the age of thirty-six, an unstoppable commercial force. After a decade devoted exclusively to music, he was now married and feeling out a more grownup existence. "I felt like it was the end of the first part of my journey," he told *Rolling Stone* in 1992. It was a moment worth marking.

Bruce Springsteen & the E Street Band Live/1975–85, released in time for Christmas 1986, was the live album fans had anticipated for years. For the most part. A five-record, forty-song collection that stretches from the clubs to the stadiums, it still manages to leave a lot out. Only five songs from the first two albums made the cut, with epics like "Incident On 57th Street" and "For You" being overlooked—though both would show up as B-sides. Extended takes on songs like "Backstreets," some of Springsteen's most powerful live work, were shortened. The collection leaned heavily on *Born in the U.S.A.*, including eight songs from that album as well as a cover of Edwin Starr's "War," a tour staple in 1985. Released as the album's lead single, it went to number eight on *Billboard*'s singles chart, making it eight straight top-ten hits for Springsteen. That run was finally snapped by the follow-up, "Fire," which barely cracked the top fifty.

The release of *Live/1975–85* generated long lines, wads of cash, and a bright media spotlight. It debuted at number one and has since sold more than thirteen million copies (each disc/record counting as a single unit).

Spectrum, Philadelphia,
September 1984.

TUNNEL OF LOVE

1987

"*BORN IN THE U.S.A.* HAD BEEN A LOT OF PEOPLE'S FIRST BRUCE RECORD. SO THEY HEARD *TUNNEL* AS A SHIFT TO THE LEFT. LONGTIME FANS KNEW IT WAS HIM RETURNING."

ROY BITTAN, 2011

1987

January–May: Main phase of recording of *Tunnel of Love* at Thrill Hill East, Springsteen's home studio in New Jersey.

January 21: Gives the induction speech for Roy Orbison at the Rock and Roll Hall of Fame ceremony.

February 6: Release of the Paul Schrader movie *Light of Day*, featuring Springsteen's title song performed by the film's co-stars, Joan Jett and Michael J. Fox.

May–August: *Tunnel of Love* is completed at the A&M Studios, Los Angeles.

July 10: Death of John Hammond, aged seventy-six, the man who had signed Springsteen to Columbia fifteen years earlier.

September 16: The E Street Band plays Danny Federici's wedding reception in Janesville, Wisconsin.

September 30: Filming of *Roy Orbison & Friends: A Black & White Night* at the Cocoanut Grove nightclub in the Ambassador Hotel, Los Angeles. Springsteen appears along with Elvis Costello, Tom Waits, k.d. lang, and others.

October 9: Release of *Tunnel of Love* (US 1, UK 1).

October 22: Springsteen sings Bob Dylan's "Forever Young" at a memorial service for Hammond at St. Peter's Church, New York City.

December 7: Performs at a tribute concert for late singer-songwriter Harry Chapin, held at the Carnegie Hall, New York City.

1988

January 20: Gives another Rock and Roll Hall of Fame induction speech, this time for Bob Dylan.

February 25: First night of the Tunnel of Love Express tour, at the Centrum in Worcester, Massachusetts.

March 2: Springsteen wins a Grammy for Best Male Rock Vocal Performance for "Tunnel Of Love."

May 23: End of the US leg of the tour, at Madison Square Garden, New York City.

June 11: The tour resumes in Europe, at the Stadio Comunale, Turin.

June 15: Paparazzi photographers snap Springsteen and Patti Scialfa on Springsteen's hotel-room balcony in Rome.

June 17: Announcement of Springsteen's separation from Julianne Phillips.

July 19: Plays a memorable pre-reunification concert at the Radrennbahn Weißensee in East Berlin.

August 3: Last night of the Tunnel of Love Express tour, at the Camp Nou, Barcelona.

September 2: First night of the Amnesty International—Human Rights Now! tour, at Wembley Stadium, London.

October 15: The Human Rights Now! tour concludes at the River Plate Stadium, Buenos Aires.

Right: Tunnel of Love Express tour, 1988.

Page 131: Portrait by Neal Preston, 1988.

The December 1988 cover of *Esquire* cast an illustrated Springsteen as "Saint Boss," patron of the square-jawed sad sacks. "Has Fame Crucified Bruce Springsteen?" the headline asked. Tackling the answer, writer John Lombardi piled up more than seven thousand mostly dismissive words under the headline "The Sanctification of Bruce Springsteen and the Rise of Mass Hip." To be sure, it was no longer 1976, the year *Creem* announced "Bruce Springsteen Is Not God (and Doesn't Want to Be)" and *Playboy* followed a few months later with "The Ascension of Bruce Springsteen."

To Lombardi, Springsteen was a construct, a rebel without an edge mass-marketed by egghead rock critics who saw him as "the perfect punk, a street guy with boundless energy who wouldn't beat you up."

"His 'TV' audience has been weaned off depth," Lombardi wrote. "It only wants to mime emotion." And another thing: That audience says "Brooooce"— a lot. And that bugged Lombardi—a lot. Springsteen was safe, carefully calibrated and test-marketed. "In 1988, rock 'n' roll's job is to render frenzy sensible," Lombardi wrote.

A few years removed from His Moment and staring back at himself atop the world in 1985, Springsteen might have accepted some of the critique. "You end up creating this sort of icon, and eventually it oppresses you," Springsteen told *Rolling Stone*'s James Henke in 1992, noting that in New Jersey, he'd become like Santa Claus at the North Pole.

"It's like you're a bit of a figment of a lot of other people's imaginations," Springsteen said. "And that always takes some sorting out."

Someone was bound to take a sledgehammer to the whole damn thing. Lombardi did it in print. But Springsteen did it first, did it better, and did it from the opening notes of *Tunnel of Love*.

"Ain't Got You" is more an admission of what Springsteen had in 1987 than what he didn't. "The fortunes of heaven"? Got those. "Houses 'cross the country honey end to end"? Those too. And in those houses, a whole lot of "priceless art." The watch is diamond, the caviar is weighed by the pound. The car—Mr. Born in the U.S.A.'s car—is foreign. The women are willing, "and everybody wants to be my friend." Sing it, Santa.

Steve Van Zandt *hated* the song, told Springsteen there's no way he could release it. "He said, 'Yeah I can. It's honest, you know?'" Van Zandt said in 2011. "And I'm like, so what? Honesty isn't the final word when it comes to art. In fact, I can make a case that honesty has nothing to do with art, by definition. You're the best representative of

Above: The inevitable backlash. John Lombardi's takedown in *Esquire*, December 1988.

Below: "Better be good for goodness sake"—from Saint Boss to Saint Nicholas.

working-class people since Woody Guthrie. That's your job." Van Zandt recalled a big, loud argument. "Which I lost, again," he said. During his 2005 solo tour, Springsteen would introduce "Ain't Got You" as the answer to the question that's never gone away: What's it like to be the Boss? In that context, the song became a punch line. It got a good laugh. It *is* a funny song, but in October 1987, when *Tunnel of Love* arrived as the long-awaited follow-up to its planet-conquering predecessor, "Ain't Got You" was also a statement. Bruce Springsteen's job had changed. It had to. "I thought it was my responsibility to offer up something different to my fans and to myself," he said in 2011.

He could have gone big again. Michael Jackson did, releasing *Bad* in 1987. But while it sold millions, it didn't sell like *Thriller*, and so he lost what was always going to be an impossible fight. The previous year Madonna had released *True Blue*, with which she found further ways to titillate and instigate, playing a stripper in the "Open Your Heart" video, and taking on the topic of abortion in "Papa Don't Preach." By 1989 she'd be burning crosses in the "Like A Prayer" video, inching closer and closer to the edge, which you can do for only so long. Prince, meanwhile, had set course as Prince—releasing an album a year and dodging any easy musical classification.

Springsteen was older than them all, thirty-eight when *Tunnel of Love* was released, thirty-seven when he wrote and recorded it (mostly) alone at his new home studio in Rumson, New Jersey. He got rid of the flag and the jeans, the T-shirts and leather jackets, and showed up on the cover cleaned up in a black suit, white shirt, and silver-tipped bolo tie. It looked a lot like the suit he wore just before the October release of the record when he joined an absurdly talented group to back Roy Orbison for a television special. Filmed in the Cocoanut Grove nightclub at the Ambassador Hotel in Los Angeles, *Roy Orbison: A Black and White Night* featured, as the core of the musicians, Elvis's TCB Band. And, oh yeah: Springsteen, Tom Waits, Elvis Costello, Jackson Browne, Bonnie Raitt, k.d. lang, and T Bone Burnett. During songs like "Oh, Pretty Woman" and "Ooby Dooby," Springsteen traded guitar licks with James Burton and grinned throughout like the luckiest guy in the world. On that night he might have been.

Hair tight and clothes pressed, Springsteen looked every bit the grown-up. "The cornerstones of [*Tunnel of Love*] were the issues of identity and love," Springsteen said at the taping of VH1's *Storytellers* in 2005. "Who am I? Where am I going to be? Where do I belong? Where am I going to end up?"

Who would he be traveling with? The relationships that mattered most to Springsteen—with his band and with his wife—were being put under stress. He was experiencing "the ambivalence of relationships that had always been an undercurrent in my psychological life," he said.

The characters on the record reflect that conflict. They're not as lonely as their cousins on *Nebraska*, but neither are they partying and shouting "sha la las" like their pals on *Born in the U.S.A.* The dozen songs on *Tunnel* are date-night declarations, and the sighs that cut the silence that can build between two people. They're about strength, and weakness—often within the same moment.

Most explicitly, the internal conflict plays out on "Cautious Man," the story of Bill Horton, "man of the road." Borrowing again from a Robert Mitchum film, this time *The Night of the Hunter* not *Thunder Road*, Bill's knuckles are tattooed.

The luckiest guy in the world. Springsteen shares a mic with his hero Roy Orbison during the filming of the *Black and White Night* television special, September 30, 1987.

Rather than "Love" and "Hate," as in the movie, Bill's read "Love" and "Fear." Horton lets "his cautiousness slip away" when he meets a girl. Guard down, he falls in love, laughing at what he'd become. One night he awakes from a nightmare calling for his wife, and she's right there next to him "a thousand miles away." He gets up and takes a walk down to the highway, to his past, and discovers that's all it is anymore. Bill goes home to his wife, lying in the moonlight, "filling their room in the beauty of God's fallen light."

"If there was some part of myself I was trying to explain, for better or worse, that song describes a good amount of it," Springsteen said.

The inner turmoil of "Cautious Man" is more confrontational in "One Step Up," where it's the "same thing night on night, who's wrong, baby, who's right." Doors slam, they fight dirty, and self-doubt and disappointment dominate. The song's narrator hits the road, but only as far as the closest bar, where he trades looks with a girl across the room. She doesn't appear married "and me, well honey, I'm pretending."

The album's lead single, "Brilliant Disguise," suggests the same betrayal as "One Step Up." Everyone's playing a part, "the loving woman" and "the faithful man." And it works out, as long as no one looks any deeper than the publicity photo. "Two Faces" is a one-sided version of the story, a Jekyll and Hyde of the heart. Sometimes he feels "sunny and wild," but "then dark clouds come rolling by."

"Who is that person sleeping next to me?" Springsteen said of "Brilliant Disguise" during the *Storytellers* taping. "Who am I? Do I know enough about myself to be honest with that person?"

"Tougher Than The Rest" and "All That Heaven Will Allow" offer love's potential reward and another dance. "All you gotta do is say yes," Springsteen sings in the former. "Rain and storm and dark skies, well now they don't mean a thing," he promises in the latter. With just one caveat: *If* there's someone who loves you. Someone "who wants to wear your ring."

Janey, the woman at the heart of "Spare Parts," digs for the strength to raise a child after the father splits to the oil fields of South Texas never to be heard from again. She weighs the options, pawns her engagement ring, and gets to work.

"WHEN I WAS YOUNG, I ALWAYS SAID I DIDN'T WANT TO END UP BEING FORTY-FIVE OR FIFTY AND PRETENDING I WAS FIFTEEN OR SIXTEEN OR TWENTY. THAT JUST DIDN'T INTEREST ME."

Bruce Springsteen, 1992

Eight months before *Tunnel of Love* was released, Springsteen's parents celebrated their fortieth wedding anniversary. The father–son angst that had fueled earlier songs is tempered in "Walk Like A Man," Springsteen's tender acknowledgment that, no matter what else, his father had found a way to make a marriage work. When it doesn't, when not even love is enough, is "When You're Alone."

These matters of the heart, as the title track suggests, make for one hell of a ride. "It ought to be easy, ought to be simple enough," Springsteen sings on "Tunnel of Love," but "the house is haunted." Live with the ghosts, or else. The video for the song, cut up with shots of fire eaters, sword swallowers, snake handlers, and rundown Jersey Shore amusement attractions, promises, via a sign on a chain-link fence, that "This Is Not A Dark Ride." It is a dark ride. Dark enough that Chuck Plotkin heard it for the first time and thought maybe his old pal could use a hand.

Left: For the Tunnel of Love Express tour, a horn section took center stage and Max Weinberg's drums were shifted to the side. The E Street Band as a whole would become increasingly marginalized during this time.

Opposite: Springsteen acts his age in the "One Step Up" video.

Overleaf: "When you're alone you ain't nothing but alone."

Springsteen closes the record with "Valentine's Day," and light in the sky and a guy who just wants to pilot his "big lazy car" home again. Qualified as it is—again the song's narrator awakes scared in the darkness—it's an uplifting end to a quiet, complicated record, "an unsettled and unsettling collection of hard looks at the perils of commitment," Steve Pond wrote in *Rolling Stone*.

Said Springsteen: "The good thing about the record is it said you can *feel* like this and still make a go of it." The better question was whether or not he could make it work.

The tour opened on February 25, 1988 in Worcester, Massachusetts, and it was … different. "After '85 I just didn't know where to take the band next," he said in 2011. "I didn't have an idea. Seemed like we'd reached an apex of what we were trying to do and say." Springsteen had rearranged the band, moving Max Weinberg to one side, bringing Patti Scialfa up front to his right, where Clarence Clemons had been, and moving Clemons to his left. Springsteen added a horn section.

And while it was a small change, the tour's billing, "Bruce Springsteen's Tunnel of Love Express *featuring* the E Street Band," seemed to put some distance between the singer and the musicians who had backed him for so many years. The stage wardrobe matured and darkened. The formerly casual entrance of the band on stage was replaced with a theatrical work-up involving a ticket booth. "It was like a Broadway stage sort of thing," Garry Tallent said.

The introduction to "All That Heaven Will Allow" imagined Springsteen and Clemons chatting on a

park bench. Actually, it didn't imagine the scene. There was a park bench on stage. "What you been up to?" Springsteen would say to Clemons, falling into a "remember when" story like old friends who hadn't seen each other in a while.

Springsteen made a list of some of his biggest songs, "Thunder Road," for example, and dropped them from the set, loading it instead with new songs, and B-sides like "Roulette," which, with its wife and kids and general dread, fit the new album's theme. With Detroit R&B singer Gino Washington's 1964 song "Gino Is A Coward" as inspiration, Springsteen worked up "I'm A Coward (When It Comes To Love)." Noticeably, and predictably given the emphasis on relationships between men and women, Scialfa took on a larger role and attracted more of Springsteen's attention. Way more of Springsteen's attention.

In Rome in June, Springsteen and Scialfa were caught by paparazzi on the balcony of his hotel room looking very much like a couple they weren't supposed to be because Springsteen was married to Julianne Phillips. Except Springsteen had separated from Phillips. With no other option, Jon Landau Management made the announcement on June 17. Shock was feigned (and was in some cases genuine). Yet for all its celebrated virtue, Springsteen's music had always been dominated by inner conflict. Life is messy and relationships are hard, no matter how many people might have made Springsteen their moral compass. Those same people had heard the record, hadn't they?

A month later, the tour rolled into East Berlin to play the other side of the Berlin Wall. Estimates of the size of the crowd have gone as high as 300,000. Springsteen opened with "Badlands" and, for the first time on the tour, broke out "The Promised Land." As others had done before, the Communist government of East Germany attempted to claim Springsteen's support, and Springsteen refused to cooperate. He gave a speech his driver had helped him translate into German. He said he wasn't there to play for any government. He'd planned on saying he was there with "the hope that one day all walls will be torn down." The West German promoter talked Springsteen into changing it to barriers. Either way, there was no mistaking his intent, and then he doubled down, following with a cover

> # "I WAS KIND OF COMING TO GRIPS WITH IT, MY ADOLESCENT IDEA OF ROMANTIC LOVE, AND COMING TO GRIPS WITH THE COMPLEXITY OF WHAT I WAS FINDING OUT."
>
> Bruce Springsteen, 2011

of Bob Dylan's "Chimes Of Freedom." By the end of 1989, the Berlin Wall was largely a memory.

That show featured another first, the first full-band version of "Born To Run" since the Born in the U.S.A. tour. For much of the Tunnel of Love tour, Springsteen had been performing the song accompanied by just an acoustic guitar and a harmonica. He spoke of the evolution of the song, which mirrored the evolution of his career and life.

"I realized, after I put all those people in all those cars, I was going to have to figure out someplace for 'em to go," Springsteen said that April in Los Angeles. What they were looking for, he realized, was a connection. He'd come to learn that "individual freedom, when it's not connected to some kind of community, or friendship, or world outside ends up being pretty meaningless."

"This is a song about two people trying to find their way home."

That he said all this standing alone was not insignificant.

Opposite: On stage with Patti Scialfa during the historic East Berlin show at the Radrennbahn Weißensee, July 19, 1988.

Left: At the Rock and Roll Hall of Fame Awards, January 20, 1988, with wife, Julianne Phillips, and future wife, Patti Scialfa, at his side.

Overleaf: Jawaharlal Nehru Stadium, New Delhi, September 30, 1988.

HUMAN RIGHTS NOW!

Amnesty International's Human Rights Now! tour launched at Wembley Stadium in London on September 2, 1988. If Springsteen had struggled with where to take the band artistically after 1985, the tour allowed him to at least take them places they'd never been geographically.

Also featuring Sting, Peter Gabriel, Tracy Chapman, and Youssou N'Dour, the twenty-date tour raised money for Amnesty and carried a message of human rights to parts of the world Springsteen had never played—South America, Africa, India, and Greece. The sights were new, the atmosphere was collegial, and there was a shared sense of purpose. For the E Street Band, the sets were shorter than they'd ever been, too.

"That was my favorite tour," Clarence Clemons said in early 2011. "When we went to Africa, the whole audience was black. It was the first time I ever saw more than one black person at Bruce's concerts."

In August, in advance of the tour, Springsteen released a four-song live EP titled *Chimes of Freedom* that included that Dylan cover, versions of "Tougher Than The Rest" and "Be True," and the live acoustic version of "Born To Run" that dominated the Tunnel of Love tour.

"When we come to your town," Springsteen said, introducing the title track, "come on out, support the tour, support human rights for everyone now and let freedom ring."

HUMAN TOUCH & LUCKY TOWN

1992

"FOR ME IT WAS DEEPLY ENJOYABLE TO PLAY WITH THOSE MUSICIANS—SOME VERY GOOD PLAYERS WHO BROUGHT SOME INTERESTING THINGS."

BRUCE SPRINGSTEEN, 2011

1989

March 1: Finalization of Springsteen's divorce from Julianne Phillips.

September 23: The E Street Band plays at Springsteen's fortieth birthday party; their next performance would not be until 1995.

October 18: Springsteen breaks up the E Street Band.

c. November: Recording of *Human Touch* starts, and continues throughout 1990 at various Los Angeles studios.

1990

February 12: Springsteen performs as part of a one-off all-stars group also featuring (among others) Sting, Paul Simon, Bruce Hornsby, Don Henley, and Herbie Hancock, at a benefit dinner for the Rainforest Alliance.

April 14: Duets with Tom Waits at the Santa Monica wedding reception of producer/engineer Chuck Plotkin.

July 24: Birth of Evan James Springsteen, Springsteen and Patti Scialfa's first child.

November 16–17: Springsteen plays a solo acoustic set at two benefit shows for the Christic Institute, a public-interest law firm, at the Shrine Auditorium in Los Angeles.

1991

March: End of the *Human Touch* recording sessions.

June 8: Springsteen and Scialfa get married at their home in Los Angeles.

c. July: Recording of *Lucky Town* starts at Thrill Hill West (Springsteen's Los Angeles home studio) and moves on to the nearby A&M Studios.

December 30: Birth of Jessica Rae Springsteen, Springsteen and Scialfa's second child.

1992

January: End of the *Lucky Town* recording sessions.

March 31: Release of *Human Touch* (US 2, UK 1) and *Lucky Town* (US 3, UK 2).

Right: "A bunch of leaders playing sidemen and butchering each others' tunes" was how Bruce Hornsby described this all-star fundraiser in aid of the Rainforest Alliance, February 12, 1990.

Page 145: Backstage at the Brendan Byrne Arena, East Rutherford, New Jersey, July 28, 1992.

"This comes from a record people generally consider my weakest album," Springsteen said on stage in 2005. "Whenever I'm paging through magazines and there's a compendium of your records, you know, the 'Bruce to buy' and the 'Bruce not to buy,' this is always sort of star-challenged, this record. Perhaps unfairly."

He chuckled, comfortably. The crowd followed his lead. Earlier in the day, a guy from Norway—Springsteen was pretty sure it was Norway—had requested "I Wish I Were Blind," from the album in question, *Human Touch*. Out on the road playing solo, bouncing between guitars, piano, and organ, Springsteen was happy to oblige, wishing the guy better days, because that tune meant one thing: "You just took one over the head *bad*," Springsteen joked.

By 1989, Springsteen had been taking—or administering—his own beating for going on two relentless decades. The first two albums had given way to the desperation of *Born to Run*, which led to the lawsuits that fed into *Darkness on the Edge of Town*. *Darkness* marked the start of an almost unparalleled period of productivity. He filled the vaults and then *The River*, which not only picked up where its predecessor left off, but foreshadowed the tumult of *Nebraska* and the joyful noise of *Born in the U.S.A.* He played to the point of exhaustion, his and everyone else's. Not because he could, but because it was the only way to quiet his inner turmoil.

"I couldn't stop until I felt burnt," he told *Rolling Stone*'s James Henke in 1992. "Thoroughly burnt." He stepped back. He got married. But rather than bringing some version of domestic bliss, married life just led Springsteen down the new maze of dark hallways from which *Tunnel of Love* was born. So another tour, and then another still, this one to the far corners of the world on behalf of Amnesty International. That came to an end in late 1988 and then … "I just got lost," he told Henke.

Two years later, he walked alone on stage at the Shrine Auditorium in Los Angeles for the first of two benefits for the Christic Institute, a law firm dedicated to social justice and civil rights. "This sounds a little funny, but it's been a while since I've done this," he said. "So if you're moved to clap along, please don't. It's going to mix me up."

Featuring stripped-down versions of old favorites, each night's set began with "Brilliant Disguise" and ended with Springsteen joined on stage by Jackson Browne and Bonnie Raitt for covers of Bob Dylan's "Highway 61 Revisited" and Ry Cooder's "Across The Borderline." Both nights, just before that finale, Springsteen unwound his narrative in one stunning three-song arc: "Thunder Road" to "My Hometown"

"EVEN THOUGH SOME PART OF US YEARNS FOR A MORALLY CERTAIN WORLD, THAT WORLD DOESN'T EXIST. THAT'S NOT PART OF THE REAL WORLD."

Bruce Springsteen, 1992

to "Real World," one of six new songs he debuted over the course of the two shows.

Performed alone at the piano, with Springsteen's voice a powerful mix of anguish and resolve, "Real World" is a reckoning. "Year gone by feels like one long day," he sings. "But I'm alive, and I'm feelin' all right." The obstacles have been numerous, the "roadside carnival" built of "hurt and self-pity," the shrine in his heart constructed of "fool's gold, memory, and tears cried." He strips away the illusions of happiness, the "church bells ringing," the "flags unfurled." What is left then is a man, a woman, and "the hope we're bringing into the real world."

After coming off the road in 1988, he and Patti Scialfa attempted to settle in New Jersey, but that didn't feel right. They tried New York City, but that didn't work. Finally, Springsteen suggested they pack up and head for Los Angeles. In the sunshine and relative anonymity Hollywood provides he began to work himself out of another dark hole. He returned to therapy ("I wanna find some answers, I wanna ask for some help," he sang in "Real World") and attacked it with the same energy he'd put into learning to play guitar, into building his career and his band. Now he was trying to build his life.

In March 1989, Springsteen's divorce became final. That summer, back in New Jersey, he popped up in bars to jam. On September 23, backed by the E Street Band (Steve Van Zandt included), he celebrated his fortieth birthday at McLoone's Rum Runner in Sea

Bonnie Raitt and Jackson Browne joining Springsteen for the encore at the first Christic Institute benefit, Shrine Auditorium, Los Angeles, November 16, 1990.

Bright, New Jersey, playing a set of rock and soul classics like "Twist And Shout" and "Having A Party." They fell into a perfect-for-the-occasion pass at "Glory Days." Less than a month later, Springsteen, determined to do something other than relive the past, sat down and called each member of the band to tell them he was moving on without them.

"I never looked at it as the band being done or kaput or finished," Springsteen said in 2011. How the E Street Band looked at it depended on the individual. There was plenty of hurt, but to some it was hardly unexpected. They'd felt the distance building toward the end of the Born in the U.S.A. tour, and seen Springsteen's interest in change play out in the way he recorded *Tunnel of Love*, and on the road after the release of that record. Clarence Clemons was on tour in Japan with Ringo Starr when he got the call. Starr, who'd been through it himself with the Beatles, managed to calm the Big Man down. Roy Bittan had been convinced enough of coming change that he made one of his own. He moved to Los Angeles, too. Not far from Springsteen, who would eventually move from the cozy little house he'd bought in the early 1980s to a $14 million estate.

A month after breaking up the band, he called up Bittan and the two went to dinner. (It was also around this time that Springsteen and Scialfa learned she was pregnant.) After dinner, Bittan showed off the recording setup he'd installed in his garage, and played Springsteen some of the songs he'd written, including a built-for-the-E Street Band rocker called "Roll Of The Dice." When Springsteen had made the phone calls to the band, he didn't know what would happen next. "I didn't have a plan, y'know," he said. Without a plan, he was having a hard time coming up with songs. Springsteen took Bittan's compositions home on cassette and spent the night adding lyrics. Bittan awoke the next day to his phone ringing. It was his old boss, about to become his new boss, calling to say he'd written a hit. Inspired by Bittan, Springsteen's workbooks began to fill. They'd record as a two-man band, and then bring in musicians like Toto drummer Jeff Porcaro, and future *American Idol* judge Randy Jackson on bass. David Sancious played organ on a couple of songs. Sam Moore, of Sam & Dave fame, added vocals.

The process was somewhat new, the players were mostly new, recording exclusively in Los Angeles was entirely new, but one thing was the same: The songs piled up as the months passed. Springsteen had

"I KNEW IT WAS GOING TO BE CHALLENGING FOR ME BECAUSE I HAD SO MUCH PERSONAL LICENSE. I DIDN'T KNOW BASIC BEHAVIORS, OF, LIKE, IF YOU'RE OUT AND GONE, IT'S NICE TO CALL."

Bruce Springsteen, on family life, 2011

good reasons not to rush an album. In July 1990, Evan James Springsteen was born. Springsteen and Scialfa married in June 1991. Diapers were changed. Family life took hold.

Meanwhile, rock 'n' roll marched on. Since their 1987 debut, *Appetite for Destruction*, had introduced a much-needed element of danger into the cartoon world of pop metal, Guns N' Roses had grown into the next World's Biggest Band. So big that on September 17, 1991, they released two albums, *Use Your Illusion I* and *Use Your Illusion II*. A week earlier, Nirvana released "Smells Like Teen Spirit," the lead single from *Nevermind*. The song and the album would usher in an even louder and angrier sound. And hip-hop was establishing itself as another outlet for young frustration and a powerful commercial force.

In December 1991, the Springsteens welcomed a daughter, Jessica Rae. Springsteen was now forty-two and hadn't released an album in four years. The good news for those who were waiting was that one was finished. The better news was that a second was nearly complete.

Opposite: The proud parents show off Evan James Springsteen, born in July 1990.

Left: Having broken up the E Street Band, Springsteen worked with a new group of musicians, including Toto drummer Jeff Porcaro.

Overleaf: Second Christic Institute benefit, November 17, 1990.

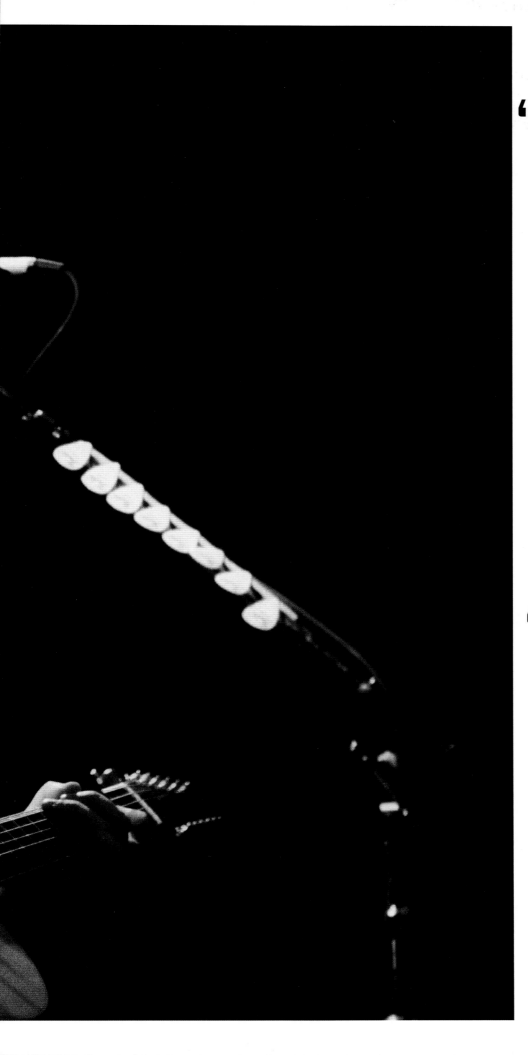

"NOW I SEE THAT THE TWO BEST DAYS OF MY LIFE WERE THE DAY I PICKED UP THE GUITAR AND THE DAY THAT I LEARNED HOW TO PUT IT DOWN. SOMEBODY SAID, 'MAN, HOW DID YOU PLAY FOR SO LONG?' I SAID: 'THAT'S THE EASY PART. IT'S THE STOPPING THAT'S HARD.'"

Bruce Springsteen, 1992

"Human Touch was definitely something I struggled to put together," he told Henke. "It was a job." Everyday work he eventually molded into his post–Tunnel of Love story. Then he put it away to think about and in a matter of weeks wrote a new record, Lucky Town. If Guns N' Roses could do it, why not Bruce Springsteen? Either way, no one was in the position to tell him "no." On March 31, 1992, both records arrived in stores.

Human Touch stars a middle-aged man trying to act his age and accept ambiguity in a world he can't control. "At some point you've got to make that realization, you make your choices, and do the best you can," he told Bill Flanagan for a November 1992 piece in Musician.

You recognize the dark places, the "black river of doubt" in "Real World," the "black sky pourin' snakes, frogs, and a love in vain" in "Soul Driver." You appreciate the rivers crossed, as Springsteen does on "With Every Wish," but you know that "on the far banks there's always another forest where a man can get lost." What you don't do is duck the challenges. It's a gamble, sure, that's "Roll Of The Dice." There are losers (see: "I Wish I Were Blind" and "Gloria's Eyes"), but it's a gamble for everyone. "So you've been broken and you've been hurt, show me somebody who ain't," Springsteen sings on "Human Touch."

"Man's Job" and "Real Man" both recast the muscle-bound hero of Born in the U.S.A. as a stone-cold romantic, a guy whose manliness has nothing to do with his bench press and everything to do with his ability to commit. "All Or Nothin' At All," as that song says. "Cross My Heart," a song based on a Sonny Boy Williamson piece (earning the long-dead bluesman a co-write) professes a similar commitment.

"57 Channels (And Nothin' On)" puts Springsteen in his "bourgeois house in the Hollywood hills," but proves money can't buy everything. There still isn't a thing on TV. "The Long Goodbye" tackles the move West ("Well, I went to leave twenty years ago, since then I guess I been packin' kinda slow") with optimism ("kiss me baby and we're gonna fly"). The album's final track, "Pony Boy," is based on a traditional song Springsteen's grandmother used to sing to him, and which he sang to his son before he was born.

One reason Human Touch has proven "star-challenged" over the years may be that it doesn't sound particularly human. It's studio slick, and that's made especially obvious when you listen to the performances of "Real World" and "Soul Driver" from the Christic shows. Both raw and powerful on stage, they've had the dents banged out and been given happy paint jobs. When Van Zandt heard the album,

"WE ALL LIVE WITH OUR ILLUSIONS AND OUR SELF-IMAGE, AND THERE'S A GOOD PERCENTAGE OF THAT THAT'S A PIPE DREAM."

Bruce Springsteen, 1992

he suggested re-recording it with the E Street Band. "And he might have been right!" Springsteen said. But that was the last thing Springsteen was going to do.

Another of Human Touch's problems: Lucky Town. Written fast, the companion album captures Springsteen after he's been pulled from the struggle and put himself back together. All the hard work put into the first album, he benefits from on the second. Down in "Lucky Town," the "sky's been cleared by a good hard rain," and Springsteen's got "dirt on my hands, but I'm building me a new home." That dirt is not insignificant; it gives the record a little texture.

"Better Days" rides a gospel chorus to the realization that "it's a sad funny ending when you find yourself pretending, a rich man in a poor man's shirt." In that bout of self-awareness he finds strength and a new beginning. To that end, the wedding scene at the heart of "Book Of Dreams" is a setting for self-forgiveness.

"Local Hero" tells the sad but true story of Springsteen coming across a black velvet painting of himself in his old hometown—on sale for $19.99. "The worst part was on one side Bruce Lee looked like he was about to kick me in the head," Springsteen told an MTV crowd in 1992. "On the other side there was a dog who wasn't even looking my way." Perhaps anticipating what was coming (or reacting to pieces like John Lombardi's 1988 polemic in Esquire), Springsteen took three lines to deconstruct the celebrity's circle of life: "First they made me the king, then they made me pope, then they brought the rope."

At the Rock and Roll Hall of Fame annual awards in January 1989, Springsteen performed "Crying" as a tribute to Roy Orbison, who had died the previous month.

"Leap Of Faith" takes the same consequences-be-damned approach to love as *Human Touch* but gives it a better beat and one possibly blasphemous metaphor: "You were the Red Sea, I was Moses."

"If I Should Fall Behind" is a quiet little prayer for patience and understanding that's likely Springsteen's biggest wedding hit.

The "one clear moment of love and truth" Springsteen went looking for in "Real World," he found when his son was born. "You shot through my anger and rage," he sings on "Living Proof," "to show me my prison was just an open cage."

It's not all pretty. "Souls Of The Departed" takes images of violence in the Middle East and on the streets of Los Angeles and juxtaposes them with the fears of a father tucking his son in at night—only to juxtapose those with the father's admission of a job where he plies his trade "in the land of king dollar, where you get paid and your silence passes as honor."

The father in "Souls Of The Departed" isn't any more innocent than the characters in "The Big Muddy" wrestling with their own moral obligations. That song took its title (and chorus) from Pete Seeger's 1967 anti-Vietnam song "Waist Deep In The Big Muddy."

Lucky Town ends far from darkness as the voice in "My Beautiful Reward" takes flight as a bird, "high over gray fields" and "down along the river's silent edge."

"Both *Human Touch* and *Lucky Town* came out of a moment in which to find what I needed, I was going to have to let things go, change, try new things, make mistakes—just live," Springsteen wrote in *Songs*.

Human Touch rose to number two on the *Billboard* album chart; *Lucky Town* made it to number three. By the time Henke's story arrived in August 1992, each had sold more than 1.5 million copies. Those are good numbers, especially when added together. But Springsteen had gotten rid of the E Street Band and hit the road with a new group of musicians and he lived in Los Angeles. There was a lot for reporters and longtime fans to pick apart if they wanted. The tour sold well where he was strong, not as well in other markets. Where once there were multi-night stands, sometimes there was only a single night booked.

From the outside, Springsteen's career looked troubled. In important ways, it was refreshed. "In retrospect, it was an important transitional period for him," Bittan said. It had to be done. Springsteen had to see what he could do, and what he learned was he could do anything he wanted.

Above: You can look, but you better not touch. Lingering by the lingerie on the Hollywood Walk of Fame, 1992.

Opposite: Rounding off the European leg of the 1992 World Tour with a five-night stand at London's Wembley Arena, July 1992.

AND THE AWARD GOES TO ...

Then suddenly Bruce Springsteen was an Academy Award–winning hero in the gay community. Director Jonathan Demme put the events in motion with a phone call and a request. He was making a movie called *Philadelphia* about an AIDS-infected lawyer fired from his firm who responds by filing a discrimination suit. Tom Hanks had the lead. Demme was hoping Springsteen might write a song.

With the memory of a friend who'd recently died of cancer fresh in his mind, Springsteen wrote "Streets Of Philadelphia." He programmed the drum machine then slowed the beat down. He sat down at a synthesizer and built a lonely canvas of minor chords. "I was bruised and battered, I couldn't tell what I felt," he sang.

"You caught a particular isolation that many gay AIDS patients experience," the *Advocate*'s Judy Wieder told him during a 1996 interview.

"That's all anybody's asking for—basically some sort of acceptance and to not be left alone," Springsteen replied. Earlier in the interview, he said he thought Demme had hoped to make the subject less threatening by using him, and Hanks, and Neil Young, who also contributed a song. The film was released late in 1993, and all three were nominated for Oscars. Hanks won Best Actor, and Springsteen beat Young to the award for Best Original Song. Released as a single, "Streets Of Philadelphia" reached number nine, Springsteen's first top-ten hit since "Tunnel Of Love."

Two years later, Springsteen was again nominated for a song of desperate isolation. "Dead Man Walkin'," from the Tim Robbins–directed film of the same name, captured the voice of a condemned man who, in one of Springsteen's most devastating lyrics, says he won't ask for forgiveness, "my sins are all I have."

Asked by Wieder if he was going to win again, Springsteen said, "When those Disney pictures are out there, you don't stand a chance." He was right. A song from *Pocahontas* picked up the prize.

Main photo: Still from the "Streets Of Philadelphia" video, 1993.

Inset: With fellow Oscar winners Tom Hanks and Steven Spielberg, March 21, 1994. Elton John (left) would win in 1995, with a song from one of "those Disney pictures," *The Lion King*.

THE GHOST OF TOM JOAD

1995

"IT'S A BIG STORY. IT'S THE STORY OF
WHAT THIS COUNTRY IS GOING TO BE:
A BIG, MULTICULTURAL PLACE."

BRUCE SPRINGSTEEN, 1996

1992

May 6: First performance by Springsteen's new band, at a special show for record-company executives at the Bottom Line, New York City.

May 9: Springsteen appears for the first time on NBC's *Saturday Night Live*.

June 15: First night of World Tour 1992, at the Globe Arena, Stockholm.

July 13: End of the European leg of the tour, at Wembley Arena, London.

July 23: The US leg of the tour kicks off with an eleven-night stand at the Brendan Byrne Arena, East Rutherford, New Jersey.

September 22: Recording of the *MTV Plugged* live performance at the Warner Hollywood Studios, Los Angeles.

December 17: End of World Tour 1992, at the Rupp Arena, Lexington, Kentucky.

1993

January 13: Springsteen gives the speech to induct Creedence Clearwater Revival into the Rock and Roll Hall of Fame.

March 31: First night of World Tour 1993, at the SECC, Glasgow.

April 12: Release of *In Concert/MTV Plugged* (US 189, UK 4).

May 20: The tour's stop at the RDS Arena in Dublin features guest appearances by Joe Ely and Jerry Lee Lewis.

June 1: End of World Tour 1993, at the Valle Hovin Stadion, Oslo.

June 24: Springsteen performs at the Concert to Fight Hunger, at the Brendan Byrne Arena, East Rutherford, New Jersey.

June 25: Appears for the first time on NBC's *Late Night with David Letterman*.

Fall: Records material for a new album that has not been released to date.

December 23: Release of the Jonathan Demme movie *Philadelphia*, which features Springsteen's theme song, "Streets Of Philadelphia."

1994

January 5: Birth of Samuel Ryan Springsteen, Springsteen and Scialfa's third child.

January 22: Springsteen wins a Golden Globe for Best Original Song for "Streets Of Philadelphia."

March 21: "Streets Of Philadelphia" also receives the Academy Award for Best Original Song.

March: Springsteen records more songs for his "lost" album.

September–October: Main recording phase of the Springsteen-produced *American Babylon* album for Joe Grushecky and the Houserockers.

October–December: Final sessions for Springsteen's "lost" album.

1995

January: Springsteen reconvenes the E Street Band in New York to record some new songs for inclusion on his first greatest-hits compilation.

February 27: Release of *Greatest Hits* (US 1, UK 1).

March 1: Springsteen wins Grammys for Song of the Year, Best Male Rock Vocal Performance, Best Rock Song, and Best Song Written Specifically for a Motion Picture or TV—all for "Streets Of Philadelphia."

March: Recording of *The Ghost of Tom Joad* starts at Thrill Hill West.

September 2: Springsteen and the E Street Band back Chuck Berry and Jerry Lee Lewis at the Rock and Roll Hall of Fame inauguration concert at the Cleveland Municipal Stadium.

September: Final *Ghost of Tom Joad* recording sessions.

October 17–24: Springsteen plays lead guitar on Joe Grushecky and the Houserockers' October Assault mini-tour.

November 19: Participates in Frank Sinatra's eightieth-birthday tribute concert, at the Shrine Auditorium, Los Angeles.

November 21: Release of *The Ghost of Tom Joad* (US 11, UK 16).

November 22: First night of the Solo Acoustic tour, at the Count Basie Theater, Red Bank, New Jersey.

December 29: World premiere, in Los Angeles, of the Tim Robbins movie *Dead Man Walking*, featuring Springsteen's theme song, "Dead Man Walkin'."

1996

January 28: End of the first US leg of the Solo Acoustic tour, at the Fox Theater, Atlanta.

February 12: Start of the first European leg of the tour, at the Alte Oper, Frankfurt.

February 13: "Dead Man Walkin'" receives an Oscar nomination for Best Original Song (but loses out to "Colors Of The Wind" from *Pocahontas*).

February 20: Springsteen opens the prestigious Sanremo Music Festival in Italy.

May 8: End of the first European leg of the tour, at the Palacio de Congresos y Exposiciones, Madrid.

September 16: The Solo Acoustic tour resumes back in the US, at the Benedum Center, Pittsburgh.

October 26: Springsteen receives the first annual John Steinbeck Award, designed to recognize writers, artists, thinkers, and activists whose work captures the spirit of Steinbeck.

November 8: Having moved his family from Los Angeles back to New Jersey earlier in the year, Springsteen performs a fundraiser at his elementary school, the St. Rose of Lima, Freehold.

December 14: End of the second US leg of the Solo Acoustic tour, at the Ovens Auditorium, Charlotte, North Carolina.

1997

January 27: Start of the Japan/Australia leg of the Solo Acoustic tour, at the Kokusai Forum Hall, Tokyo.

February 17: End of the Japan/Australia leg of the tour, at the Palais Theatre, Melbourne.

February 26: Springsteen wins a Grammy for Best Contemporary Folk Album for *The Ghost of Tom Joad*.

May 5: Receives the Polar Music Prize from King Carl XVI Gustaf of Sweden, at the Grand Hotel, Stockholm.

May 6: Start of the final leg of the Solo Acoustic tour, at the Austria Center, Vienna.

May 26: After 127 shows spanning eighteen months, the Solo Acoustic tour finally comes to an end, at the Palais des Congrès in Paris.
November 2: First "Seeger Session," at Thrill Hill East.

1998

April 4: Springsteen performs "The Ghost Of Tom Joad" at a tribute to theater director Elaine Steinbeck (widow of John Steinbeck), at the Bay Street Theater, Sag Harbor, New York.
April 26: Death of Doug Springsteen, aged seventy-three.
November 10: Release of the *Tracks* box set (US 27, UK 50).
December 5: Broadcast of the BBC TV documentary *Bruce Springsteen: A Secret History*.

1999

March 15: Springsteen enters the Rock and Roll Hall of Fame in his first year of eligibility.
April 9: Start of the Reunion tour, at the Palau Sant Jordi, Barcelona.
April 13: Release of *18 Tracks* (US 64, UK 23).
June 9: Springsteen is inducted into the Songwriters Hall of Fame.
June 27: End of the European leg of the Reunion tour, at the Valle Hovin Stadion, Oslo.
July 15: Start of the first US leg of the Reunion tour, a fifteen-show run at the Continental Airlines Arena, East Rutherford, New Jersey.
September 4: New Zealand astronomer I. P. Griffin discovers minor planet 23990 and officially names it Springsteen.
November 29: The first US leg of the tour ends at the Target Center, Minneapolis, Minnesota.

2000

February 28: The Reunion tour resumes at the Bryce Jordan Center, Penn State University, Pennsylvania.
March 28: Premiere of *High Fidelity*, which includes Springsteen as himself in a short dream sequence—his first ever appearance in a feature film.
June 4: The first public performance of "American Skin (41 Shots)" at the Philips Arena in Atlanta provokes strong reactions.
July 1: The Reunion tour ends in style, with a ten-night run at Madison Square Garden, New York City.

Right: Down time at Thrill Hill West, Springsteen's home studio in Beverly Hills, where *The Ghost of Tom Joad* was recorded.

Page 161: Portrait by Neal Preston, 1995.

Springsteen was in Europe playing big, loud, euphoric rock shows with what became known as the "Other Band" on April 3, 1993 when the *Los Angeles Times* ran a piece headlined "Children of the Border." Writer Sebastian Rotella journeyed into San Diego's 1,200-acre Balboa Park, home to the renowned San Diego Zoo, museums, theaters, and a hidden community of children who would cross over from Mexico to set up camp under a bridge, huff a gasoline additive, and hustle drugs and sex to men trawling the grounds in high-end automobiles.

Desperate, hungry, and strung out, they had nicknames like Squirrel and Little Dracula. One, asked if he worried about AIDS, said, "Of course. But the money comes first." They were, Rotella wrote, "nomads in the limbo between societies."

Living in Los Angeles afforded Springsteen a certain privacy. The city is vast, dense, and heavily populated with both famous people and people trying to look like famous people. The city also offered Springsteen an easy route of escape on his motorcycle, alone or with friends, out to Joshua Tree National Park, or Angeles National Forest, up into the San Gabriel Mountains, or farther still into the Mojave Desert and the sparsely populated areas of Arizona, New Mexico, Colorado, and Nevada.

At an old motel in a Four Corners town one night, Springsteen and a pal struck up a conversation with a Mexican whose brother had been killed in an accident after joining a motorcycle gang in the San Fernando Valley. Stories like that blew in with the dust and the tumbleweeds out there. Springsteen would pass migrant workers on the roadside; the stories of the border boys and Mexican drug cartels would land in print on his doorstep.

That same shot at a second chance, at a better life, that had led folks west since the country's earliest days—that had led Springsteen's parents to California, and later Springsteen himself—pulled men, women, children north from Mexico. No matter the risk of crossing deserts and borders, whatever the complications waiting on the other side. "It wasn't any big secret, but California was what the rest of the country was going to be," Springsteen said in 2012.

Having spent much of the last decade turned inward, Springsteen was again interested in exploring life beyond his walls. What he saw took him back to *Darkness on the Edge of Town* and to one of its influences—John Ford's 1940 film adaptation of *The Grapes of Wrath*, John Steinbeck's 1939 novel about another westward

"JOHN HAMMOND WOULD BE LAUGHING RIGHT NOW, BECAUSE HE WAS ALWAYS SAYING TO ME, 'YOU SHOULD MAKE AN ALBUM WITH JUST A GUITAR.'"

Bruce Springsteen, 1996

migration. "Their skin was darker and their language had changed, but these were people trapped by the same brutal circumstances," Springsteen wrote in *Songs*.

Conjuring the spirit of Steinbeck's justice-for-all protagonist, Springsteen wrote "The Ghost Of Tom Joad." Steinbeck set the Joads against the Dust Bowl heartbreak scattered along Route 66 from Oklahoma to California. Springsteen populated his song with modern refugees sleeping in cars and under overpasses and bridges "on a pillow of solid rock." The song ends with Springsteen putting to verse Tom Joad's promise that "wherever somebody's strugglin' to be free, look in their eyes, Mom, you'll see me."

"I don't think there is such a thing as an innocent man," Springsteen told David Corn in a 1996 interview for *Mother Jones*. "There is a collective responsibility. That's the song's line: 'Where it's headed everybody knows.'" Once again "it" was a highway, one that was "alive tonight," but only because it was populated with so many broken souls.

Springsteen had been busy in his Los Angeles home studio since he had finished touring in mid-1993. He'd recorded with various members of that touring band.

Opposite: In a move signaled by the Christic Institute benefits five years previously, Springsteen kept his Fender in its case. *Greatest Hits* recording session, January 1995.

Left: Springsteen's songwriting had been influenced by *The Grapes of Wrath* since *Darkness on the Edge of Town*, but with his new album he spelled out the link.

Overleaf: The E Street Band back on stage, briefly, to film a video for "Murder Incorporated" at Tramps nightclub in New York City, February 21, 1995.

He'd recorded solo. He'd made most of a record based on pulsating keyboards and drum loops. "That's a record that's going to come out sometime," Jon Landau said in 2011, but 1994, which passed without a new release, wasn't the right time. And while "Joad" would have seemed the perfect song to receive the *Nebraska* treatment, it wasn't written with that in mind. It was written for the E Street Band.

In January 1995, on short notice, Springsteen and the E Street Band gathered at the Hit Factory in New York, their first time together in a studio since they recorded *Born in the U.S.A.* more than a decade earlier. Over ten days they'd attack a new stack of songs, some of which would be tacked on to a greatest-hits package. Not quite a reunion, not necessarily a fleeting idea, not even Springsteen knew exactly what it was. "I don't know how I feel tonight ... if I've lost or I've gained sight," he wrote on the eve of the sessions. The many re-workings of that song, "Blood Brothers," framed a documentary of the sessions released in 2001. "Blood Brothers" ends up a better explanation of why ("we got our own roads to ride and chances we gotta take") than what next, and when *Greatest Hits* was released at the end of February 1995, Springsteen's handwritten note on the song was open-ended: "It was good to see the guys."

The record debuted at number one on *Billboard*'s album chart, and surely the return of the E Street Band contributed to that. Another of the new recordings, "Secret Garden," a tender ode to the mysteries of romance (with some not-so-mysterious sexual images), featured the first Clarence Clemons solo since *Born in the U.S.A.* Recorded for that landmark album, but previously unreleased, was the paranoid, heat-packing rocker "Murder Incorporated." The collection closed dusty and sunbaked "way down south of the Rio Grande," Springsteen using "This Hard Land," yet another *Born in the U.S.A.*–era work, as a call to arms: "stay hard, stay hungry, stay alive ... and meet me in a dream of this hard land."

Two weeks after *Greatest Hits* hit the shelves, the *Los Angeles Times* ran another story that found its way to Springsteen. Written and reported by Mark Arax and Tom Gorman, "California's Illicit Farm Belt Export" shined a light on the growing influence of Mexican drug cartels in the state's Central Valley, where they'd set up labs to produce millions of dollars worth of methamphetamine—leaving a path of death and destruction in their wake. Nicknamed "Sinaloa cowboys" after the west Mexican state from which most of them came, the traffickers had labs that were so hard to detect authorities were alerted to their presence only "after a shed or house explodes."

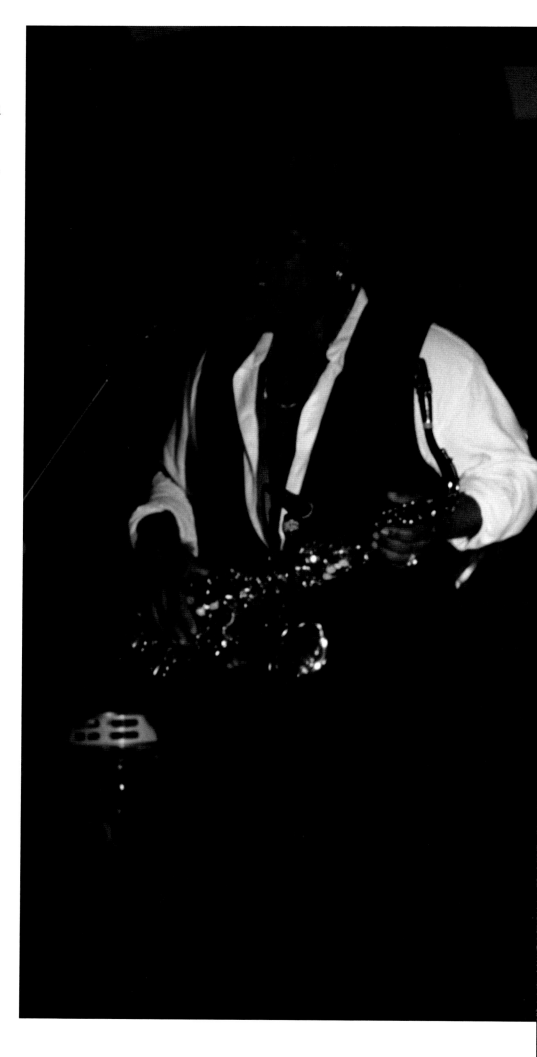

Reminded of the man he'd met on his motorcycle trip, the one whose brother had been killed while riding with a gang, Springsteen took the details that filled the news story—the way the hydriodic acid used in production would burn through skin while its fumes inflicted similar damage on the lungs— and wrote a song about two brothers, Miguel and Luis, who wander into a job cooking meth because "you could spend a year in the orchards or make half as much in one ten-hour shift." When the shack blows, Miguel's left to dig up $10,000 ("all that they'd saved") and bury Luis where the money had been. The listener is left to consider the exchange rate.

The tale of the border boys became "Balboa Park," Springsteen giving the kids nicknames like Little Spider, X-man, and Cochise. They smuggle drugs; they climb into some rich guy's Mercedes to do whatever for however much is offered. When a car speeding away from a border-patrol sweep hits Spider, the price of business is again made clear.

"I was interested in reconnecting with the things I'd written well about," Springsteen said, "but in a different setting and in a different way." The kids in the park, the brothers Miguel and Luis, they were "others." They were on the fringes of society, and so they were easy for most people to ignore. It didn't matter that Springsteen had an Academy Award and those houses end to end across the country, he could see his story in their stories. *The Ghost of Tom Joad*, released on November 21, 1995, took shape. "What you are being drawn into is scenarios of hell," Mikal Gilmore wrote in his 1997 book *Night Beat: A Shadow History of Rock & Roll*. "American hell."

"Straight Time" traces an ex-con from prison to the altar to man in the kitchen "tossin' my little babies high," a success story but for the sideways looks he gets even from his wife. "Seems you can't get any more than half free," he says. He earns the skepticism in the basement as he sips a beer and saws off a shotgun. The same restlessness infects the shoe salesman in "Highway 29." That guy goes from helping a woman try on a shoe to fugitive on the run to dying with her in a wreck on the highway in four taut verses.

In the 1980s, writer Dale Maharidge and photographer Michael Williamson traveled the United States, often hopping freight trains, to document the poor and the disenfranchised. The result was *Journey to Nowhere: The Saga of the New Underclass*. A copy of the book sat on a shelf in Springsteen's living room. One night, unable to sleep, he pulled

it down and read it in one sitting. "I lay awake that night thinking: What if the craft I'd learned was suddenly obsolete, no longer needed?" he wrote in the foreword to an edition of the book published in 1996. "What would I do to take care of my family? What wouldn't I do?"

Springsteen pulled two songs from Maharidge and Williamson's reporting: "Youngstown," which asks those questions in the context of the abandoned steel mills of northeast Ohio, and "The New Timer," the story of two hobos, one new, one who had been riding the rails since the Great Depression. The Old Timer, a man known as No Thumbs in the book, is killed one night. "Nothin' taken nothin' stolen, somebody killin' just to kill."

The narrators in "The Line" and "Dry Lightning" are both searching for someone. One is former military, discharged and living near San Diego. He goes to work for the Immigration and Naturalization Service, patrolling "the line" with a ten-year veteran whose family comes from Mexico. "So the job it was different for him." The two go to Tijuana for a drink "alongside the same people we'd sent back the day before." The narrator meets a woman, Louisa.

He helps her and her brother across the border and then things really get complicated. The brother's moving drugs, and the narrator's partner has just pulled up on his right. He pulls over and stares down both his colleague and the possibility of having to shoot him, of *needing* to shoot him to be with Louisa.

Above: Solo Acoustic tour, Beacon Theater, New York City, December 13, 1995.

Left: Dale Maharidge and Michael Williamson's *Journey to Nowhere* was another key influence on the album.

Opposite: Portrait by Neal Preston, 1995.

He doesn't. Six months later he's left the job to go town to town, bar to bar, looking for her.

"Dry Lightning" is a lonely memory on a morning when "there's a low thunder rolling 'cross the mesquite plain." The beautifully compact image of a screen door slamming, so full of power and potential in "Thunder Road," here is just an annoyance that keeps you up all night. And the hurt doesn't go away. "Well you get so sick of the fightin' you lose your fear of the end."

"Who hasn't lain awake in bed and debated the day's decisions," Springsteen said. "Or the year's decisions, or their life's decisions?"

"Galveston Bay" presents another decision, and one of the album's few bright moments. Rather than continue a cycle of violence that began with the locals who brought in the "Texas Klan" to "burn the Vietnamese boats into the sea," Billy Sutter puts away his knife and walks away from Le Bin Son, an immigrant who'd been cleared, on grounds of self-defense, of murdering two of those Texans.

"Across The Border" is a prayer the night before the journey. "I know love and fortune will be mine, somewhere across the border." The album closes with "My Best Was Never Good Enough," a purposely cliché-filled poke at the nightly news and the way it's built to "strip away the dignity of human events," Springsteen wrote in *Songs*.

The Ghost of Tom Joad is a whisper. Very little happens musically. The smallest details matter, the narrator in "Dry Lightning" watching "the ring on the stove turn red," Little Spider's shoes "covered in river mud," Youngstown's "beautiful sky of soot and clay." It won a Grammy Award for Best Contemporary Folk Album, but folk albums don't get much radio play, and the record didn't. It worked its way to number eleven on *Billboard*'s album chart, and that was fine. Springsteen knew it wasn't going to be a hit. He didn't need a hit. He'd made peace with his options and figured out how to do it all, how to play with the band and make the record that fit the voice he was most comfortable writing in at any moment. The album also allowed him to do something he'd considered since *Nebraska*—tour solo playing theaters the size of which he hadn't worked since the 1970s. Each night he'd ask for quiet. Most nights he'd get it.

On January 13, 1996, the day after he played in front of a sold-out crowd of 2,600 at the Stambaugh Auditorium in Youngstown, Ohio, Springsteen met up with Maharidge and Williamson. They'd come to town because *CBS Morning News* was doing a story on their book. They hadn't expected Springsteen to still be there. Together, they quite illegally sneaked into the abandoned steel mill that was home to

"THE BOTTOM LINE IS THAT, THROUGH THE NINETIES, THE VOICE I'VE FOUND, THE VOICE THAT'S FELT THE MOST PRESENT AND VITAL FOR ME, HAD BASICALLY BEEN THE FOLK VOICE. IT REALLY HASN'T BEEN MY ROCK VOICE."

Bruce Springsteen, 1996

a blast furnace named Jeanette—the "Jenny" of Springsteen's song. Later, when he realized the camera crew was there to profile the book, Springsteen went outside and gave an interview that had earlier been denied by his people.

In 2011, Maharidge and Williamson revisited their earlier work—and the story of trespassing with Springsteen—in *Someplace Like America: Tales From the New Great Depression*. The question Springsteen faced time and again on the tour was why? Why write these stories? Or how? How could a guy with so much money and fame relate to a kid sneaking across the border to get high under a bridge? As if getting lost in celebrity would make the problems go away. He wrote a new foreword, for the new book. Too often, the issues of labor are told only by statistics. By presenting the people behind those numbers in their "full humanity," it allowed for a connection, maybe even some empathy. With that, "some optimism that we may still find our way back to higher ground as a country and as a people," Springsteen wrote.

Laying down the haunting vocals which characterize *The Ghost of Tom Joad*.

TRACKS

Released in November 1998, *Tracks* was, Springsteen wrote, an "alternate route to some of the destinations I traveled." The artwork—an old boardwalk carousel, hubcap art, an American flag backlit by the sun, the side mirror of a car rolling down a desert highway—was familiar. The eponymous tracks, sixty-six spread across four discs, were (for the most part) not. They were the orphans and the alternate takes, the songs that, for whatever reason, didn't fit. No matter how good they were.

For years, Steve Van Zandt has said the second disc, made up largely of songs tossed from *The River*, was his favorite Springsteen record. "Thundercrack," the showstopper of years gone by, got a release. Soul and R&B mingle with broken hearts and fractured lives. After so many songs about his father, "The Wish," debuted at the Christic Institute shows in 1990, was a sweet one for his mother.

Why not "Loose Ends" or "Bring On The Night" for *The River*? Could "No Surrender" have been "Brothers Under The Bridge"? What if the tormented and broken "Wages Of Sin" had replaced "My Hometown"? What if they'd found room for sixty-eight songs and gotten "The Promise" and "The Fever" in the box set? (They did add both those songs to a single-disc sampler, *18 Tracks*, released in April 1999.)

"I tried to have a very hard focus on my records," Springsteen told talk-show host Charlie Rose in 1998. "It was part of the way I protected myself at the time … And so I made a lot of tough decisions and left off a lot of music that was actually very enjoyable that I'm glad I can get out now."

Explaining this 1978 portrait, photographer Frank Stefanko said he "imagined what it would be like to be Bruce, cruising that Vette up the Pike … thinking up song ideas." Many of those songs were discarded, but *Tracks* steered Springsteen back to them.

THE BAND GETS BACK TOGETHER

Near the end of a 1998 appearance on the *Charlie Rose* talk show, the host prodded Springsteen to just go ahead already and announce *something* with the E Street Band. No luck. He settled for an answer to this: What has the E Street Band meant to you? "Outside of my family," Springsteen said, "they're the most essential relationships of my life."

Four months later, in March 1999, Springsteen jumped on stage with the band to celebrate his induction into the Rock and Roll Hall of Fame. By then they'd already been at work preparing for a tour that would begin in Spain in April. At a pre-tour rehearsal show at Asbury Park's Convention Hall, Springsteen declared "a rededication of our band."

Steve Van Zandt was back, making for a three-guitar attack. *Tracks* gave Springsteen an abundance of new material to work from and, inspired by the moment, he'd rediscovered his rock voice. Springsteen wrote "Land Of Hope And Dreams" to close the shows, a mission statement for a new era. By the end of the tour, he'd added "Further On (Up The Road)," a couple of songs he'd co-written with Pittsburgh pal Joe Grushecky, and, finally, "American Skin (41 Shots)."

A response to the killing of Amadou Diallo, a twenty-three-year-old immigrant from Africa, by four New York City police officers (who fired forty-one shots), the song burned with purpose as it attempted to make sense of the violence that slashes at the American landscape. The song—as empathetic as angry—didn't assign blame, but that didn't stop it provoking an angry reaction from police union leaders and a pundit or two. Working direct from the headlines had returned Springsteen to a venue he hadn't played since *Born in the U.S.A.*—the political arena. Springsteen did what he'd always done: He let the song speak for him. A version was chosen to close the 2001 HBO special *Live in New York City*, which documented the E Street Band's tour-ending ten-show stand at Madison Square Garden in the summer of 2000.

Flanked by Nils Lofgren and Steve Van Zandt during the European leg of the Reunion tour, Palais Omnisports de Paris-Bercy, Paris, June 2, 1999.

THE RISING

2002

"THE RECORD NEEDED TO BE FILLED WITH A CERTAIN SORT OF HOPEFUL ENERGY BUT THE HOPE HAD TO BE EARNED, Y'KNOW? IT COULDN'T JUST BE PLATITUDES OR 'EVERYTHING'S GONNA BE ALL RIGHT' OR 'THINGS ARE GONNA BE BETTER.'"

BRUCE SPRINGSTEEN, 2002

2001

March 27: Release of the *Live in New York City* album (US 5, UK 12) and DVD.

September 21: Springsteen takes part in the *America: A Tribute to Heroes* telethon to raise money for the victims of September 11 and their families.

2002

January–March: Main recording sessions for *The Rising*, at Southern Tracks in Atlanta.

July 30: Release of *The Rising* (US 1, UK 1).

August 7: Start of the Rising tour, at the Continental Airlines Arena, East Rutherford, New Jersey.

December 17: End of the 2002 leg of the Rising tour, at the Conseco Fieldhouse, Indianapolis, Indiana.

2003

February 23: Springsteen wins Grammys for Best Rock Album (for *The Rising*) and Best Rock Song and Best Male Rock Vocal Performance (for "The Rising").

February 28: The Rising tour resumes at the Arena at Gwinnett Center, Duluth, Georgia, the first of seven US shows before taking in Australia, New Zealand, and Canada in March and April.

May 6: Start of the main European leg of the tour, at the Stadion Feyenoord, Rotterdam.

June 28: Last European concert of the tour, at the Stadio Giuseppe Meazza, Milan.

July 15: Start of the final leg of the tour, a seven-show stand at Giants Stadium, East Rutherford, New Jersey (there would be another three Giants Stadium dates in August).

October 4: End of the Rising tour, at Shea Stadium, New York City.

November 11: Release of *The Essential Bruce Springsteen* (US 14, UK 28).

November 18: Release of the *Live in Barcelona* DVD.

2004

February 8: Springsteen and Warren Zevon share the Grammy for Best Rock Performance by a Duo or Group with Vocal for "Disorder In The House."

March 15: Gives the speech for Jackson Browne's induction into the Rock and Roll Hall of Fame.

March–August: Main-phase recording sessions for *Devils & Dust*, at Thrill Hill East, Thrill Hill West, and Southern Tracks.

October 1–13: Springsteen and the E Street Band headline the Vote for Change tour in support of John Kerry's presidential candidacy.

October 28–November 1: Attends and performs at Kerry's Fresh Start for America rallies.

Right: Sydney Cricket Ground, March 22, 2003.

Page 177: Portrait by Mitch Jenkins, 2002.

On September 21, 2001, televisions across the United States and around the world cut to a shot of New York Harbor. In the foreground, the Statue of Liberty, torch aglow. Behind her, the demolished New York skyline. On a nearby soundstage lit like a church, Springsteen stood with an acoustic guitar slung over his shoulder and a harmonica racked, ready to open the celebrity-filled benefit telethon *America: A Tribute to Heroes*. The shot faded to him, backed by a chorus featuring Patti Scialfa, Steve Van Zandt, and Clarence Clemons. "This is a prayer for our fallen brothers and sisters," he said. "There's a blood red circle, on the cold dark ground," he sang. "And the rain is falling down."

"My City Of Ruins" wasn't written for that night. It was written for Asbury Park. Decades of economic hardship had peeled the paint off the town, left it broken down, beaten up, and empty. The song crashes loneliness into hope, "Tell me how do I begin again?" set flush against the gospel chorus of "Come on, rise up!" It closes with prayers for strength, faith, and love—cornerstones of Springsteen's work. After September 11, "My City Of Ruins" became about far more than a struggling beach town.

Springsteen had worked through the tangle of emotions over those ten days like everyone else. There was the initial shock when the first two planes hit the World Trade Center's twin towers, when another crashed into the Pentagon in Washington, DC, and another still into a Pennsylvania field. He drove to the nearby Rumson–Sea Bright Bridge, where on any other day there would have been a perfect view of the towers. They were gone.

Everywhere people wrestled with fear, and anger. All over people were looking for solace in the familiarity of family and old, trusted friends. And so the story goes that Springsteen was pulling out of a parking space at the beach a few days after the attacks when a passerby rolled down a window and shouted, "We need you, man!"

Springsteen had returned to New Jersey from Los Angeles. He lived on a four-hundred-acre farm and worked there in a renovated three-hundred-year-old farmhouse. He wasn't far from Freehold, where he'd grown up, or from Asbury Park, where he'd begun to build his legend. He was even closer to the house where he'd recorded *Nebraska* and cut deep into the darkness of the American psychic landscape. He was again working with the E Street Band. He was home, and home was where every story he'd ever tried to tell began.

"If you roll out of bed in the morning, even if you're the deepest pessimist or cynic, you just took a step into the next day," Springsteen told *Time* in 2002.

"EVERYTHING I WROTE AFTER SEPTEMBER 11 WAS CONTEXTUALIZED IN SOME WAY BY THAT EVENT. I TRIED TO FIND SOME EMOTIONAL CENTER THAT JUST FELT RIGHT. THE FUNNY THING IS, WHAT YOU DO FOR OTHER PEOPLE COMES OUT OF WHAT YOU'RE TRYING TO DO FOR YOURSELF."

Bruce Springsteen, 2002

On September 11, thousands of people took that step and found their lives changed forever. They got up and went to work, and didn't come home. There was a moment that changed *everything*. That moment, and the hard, haunted ones that followed were Springsteen's trade. As the *New York Times* began profiling the victims in its "Portraits of Grief" series, Springsteen time and again saw his name associated with the lives of the dead. There were ticket stubs and photos from tailgates and memories of his music blasting from car stereos. Steven B. Lillianthal's story read, "Besides his family, he loved golf, the Jets, and Bruce Springsteen, not necessarily in that order."

When he could, Springsteen phoned survivors with words of support and to learn more about their loved ones.

"The difference was that on this record you're writing about something that everyone saw and had some experience with," Springsteen told *Time*, "and obviously some people experienced it much more intimately."

In the stories of courage and grief, Springsteen found the album he'd been looking for since he got off the road with the E Street Band in 2000. For the first time since Jon Landau stepped in to help finish *Born to Run*, a new face appeared in the control room. Brendan O'Brien, whose credits included Pearl Jam and Rage Against the Machine, produced the album with most of the work being done at Southern Tracks in Atlanta. They never discussed making an album about September 11. It was only when Springsteen brought the title track, which gives voice to a firefighter "wearin' the cross of my calling," charging up into the smoke and then into the afterlife, that O'Brien realized just what Springsteen was doing. O'Brien wrestled with the enormity of the task for a moment, but then "it occurred to me, Hold on, this is Bruce," he said in 2011. "And I think it's working. Working strong."

"Into The Fire" takes the story of that firefighter charging up the stairs and tells it from the point of view of his widow. "I need your kiss," Springsteen sings, "but love and duty called you someplace higher." Like "My City Of Ruins," it also ends in a prayer, this time that we all might find strength, faith, hope, and love in the strength, faith, hope, and love displayed by those who sacrificed their lives. Time and again on the album Springsteen comes back to these bedrock concepts. "Countin' On A Miracle," which Springsteen wrote in 2000, turns on the possibility of faith, hope, and love in a world stripped to its harshest realities. There's no "storybook story," there's no "never-ending song." As for happily ever after, it's "forever come and gone." Whatever magic is left is between two people, and even that might take divine intervention.

Above: Springsteen opened the *America: A Tribute to Heroes* telethon with a performance of "My City Of Ruins."

Left: Firefighters make their way through the rubble of the World Trade Center, September 11, 2001.

"THE BAND'S PLAYING AS GOOD—AS COMMITTED AND INTENSE—AS AT ANY TIME IN ITS HISTORY, AND MAKING A RECORD THAT CARRIED ON THOSE VALUES AND IDEALS WAS VERY IMPORTANT."

Bruce Springsteen, 2003

"You're Missing" is a sad, dazed inventory of life's little details, things you never notice until they're all you see: the clothes left behind in the closet, the coffee cup on the counter, the pictures on the nightstand. Everything's the way it was before. "But you're missing," says a narrator struggling to reconcile the loss of a partner with having to comfort children and keep life moving. Of course there'd be anger, too. "Empty Sky" introduces revenge ("I want an eye for an eye"), but doesn't go for easy answers or high-decibel jingoism. "Lonesome Day" cautions to "ask questions before you shoot."

"Worlds Apart" is about two people who are exactly that, presented in a way to shade black and white distinctions between good and bad. "'Neath Allah's blessed rain, we remain worlds apart," and if the lyrics didn't make it clear enough, Springsteen drove the point home by adding to the E Street Band the sounds of Pakistani singer Asif Ali Khan and his group.

"Paradise" begins with a suicide bomber scanning faces in a crowd before the song's focus moves to the Pentagon where "the Virginia hills have gone to brown," and where the bereaved are left yearning for that familiar touch and smell and taste. "Loss is about what you miss," Springsteen told *Time*. Those things you revisit over and over in your mind.

Final performance of the Rising tour, Shea Stadium, New York City, October 4, 2003.

"THIS WAS ONE OF THOSE MOMENTS WHEN THE YEARS THAT I'VE PUT IN AND THE RELATIONSHIPS THAT I'VE DEVELOPED AND NURTURED WITH MY AUDIENCE—THIS WAS ONE OF THOSE TIMES WHEN PEOPLE WANT TO SEE YOU."

Bruce Springsteen, 2002

"That's your dream at night," he told the *New York Times*'s Jon Pareles. You can drown in that grief, which nearly happens, until the narrator of the second part of the song breaks "above the waves" and feels the sun. Paradise is empty; there's warmth in the world of the living.

"Nothing Man" presents a local hero, someone who got out and maybe helped a few others along the way, struggling with survivor's guilt. "Around here, everybody acts like nothing's changed," while at home, all he can do is stare at the gun on the nightstand. It's there in the dark unknown of what's next that Springsteen does his best work.

"Further On (Up The Road)," which Springsteen and the band played on the Reunion tour, takes a sense of purpose ("a song to sing") and a "fever burnin' in my soul" as fuel for the journey through good times and bad. "Waitin' On A Sunny Day" gave Springsteen a sing-along about the purposelessness that can accompany loss, a drift that can make a person feel as useless as "an ice-cream truck on a deserted street." A pure pop song, Springsteen told the VH1 *Storytellers* crowd it's the type of song he usually writes and throws away. But then, "Mr. Landau usually steps in and says, '*Nope*, not that one,'" Springsteen said.

Call "Let's Be Friends (Skin To Skin)" and "The Fuse" stories about love in the time of terrorism, when there's

no reason not to give it a shot, because who knows when things might end. "Let's Be Friends" plays like a light-hearted sidewalk pick-up line on a sunny afternoon. In "The Fuse," a sultry afternoon tryst is juxtaposed against the "long black line in front of Holy Cross."

Across *The Rising*, the E Street Band stretched its sound in ways it had never been asked to before. "Didn't want to be sparse," O'Brien said. "He was into the idea of making it lush." Heavy on overdubs, it was a much different process from when they made the "loudest possible noise" on *Born in the U.S.A.*, their last full album together. But "Mary's Place" was where they got to be the E Street Band, the house band playing the house party on a Saturday night, Springsteen "pullin' all the faith I can see." Once again he turned to music to heal what ailed him and listener alike. Knowing nothing soothes quite like an old soul song, he borrowed the chorus from Sam Cooke's 1964 album track "Meet Me At Mary's Place."

At fifteen songs spanning well over an hour, it was the longest Springsteen album since *The River*. "I was trying to help him make an eleven- or twelve-song record," O'Brien said. "And his take was, 'Hey, man, I don't know when I'll ever do this again.' So I said, 'OK,' and on they all went."

Released on July 30, 2002, *The Rising* arrived with the full weight of Springsteen's authority. "Most pop stars

Left and opposite: To mark their first album together since *Born in the U.S.A.*, Springsteen and the E Street Band staged this release-day special for NBC's *Today* show live from the Asbury Park Convention Hall.

seemed irrelevant immediately after September 11," Pareles wrote in a feature for the *New York Times*. "... Mr. Springsteen did not." *Time* called *The Rising*, "the first significant piece of pop art to respond to the events [of September 11]." For *Slate*, critic A. O. Scott wrote, "If any American artist could summon up an adequate, inclusive response to the events of that day, it would have to be Springsteen."

He'd been prepping for the job and filling out his résumé since *Born to Run*. The songs on *The Rising* weren't all written in the aftermath of the attacks, but the finished product took measure of the country on September 12, and didn't shy from the weight of the task. Even the cover, Springsteen a blur, the album title rising orange like a burning tower, suggested the moment things changed and new challenges arose. Springsteen avoided the mawkishness that defined other September 11 works, songs like Alan Jackson's "Where Were You (When The World Stopped Turning)," by understanding that the world didn't stop turning. Springsteen also avoided the hawkishness of Toby Keith's "Courtesy Of The Red, White And Blue (The Angry American)" and its fist-shaking, bomb-dropping, ass-kicking Statue of Liberty.

"The secret of the songwriting was to get personal first, and then you can sort of shade in universal feelings," Springsteen told *Uncut*'s Adam Sweeting in 2002.

But in 2002, with the music industry at the dawn of the digital age and with the consolidation of radio stations (and their playlists) under fewer and fewer corporate roofs, could Springsteen be assured that would be enough to get people to listen to the record? To make certain, he and Landau set out the most ambitious publicity plan of Springsteen's career— a delicate task given the subject.

He did David Letterman's late-night show, including a sit-down interview on the host's couch. Letterman asked if Springsteen worked on songs in the car. "Do you do comedy bits when you're driving in?" Springsteen countered. Introduced by actor James Gandolfini and with New York's Hayden Planetarium as a backdrop, Springsteen and the band opened MTV's Video Music Awards playing "The Rising" in a driving rain.

He was back on the cover of *Time*, under the headline "Reborn in the U.S.A." and once again on the cover of *Rolling Stone*, where he was shown at his farm standing in a wild-grass meadow, but it might as well have been the amber waves of grain that inspired "America The Beautiful" itself. That headline: "Bruce Springsteen's American Gospel."

ABC's newsman Ted Koppel visited the farm and an E Street Band rehearsal for a two-part *Nightline*

feature. Reporters from the biggest publications slipped into Springsteen's world, sitting down for a chat in the farmhouse and noting how comfortable he seemed and how easily he'd laugh. "He can sound incongruously like Dick Dastardly's dog, Muttley," Sweeting wrote in *Uncut*.

On the morning of the album's release, NBC's *Today* show went live from Asbury Park to interview fans, Springsteen, the band, and broadcast a special performance of some of the songs at the town's Convention Hall. For the first time since *Born in the U.S.A.* nearly two decades previously, Springsteen was everywhere. *The Rising* debuted at number one and stayed there for three weeks. He hit the road, barnstorming the United States and into Europe. A portion of a show in Barcelona was later broadcast on CBS; the full show was eventually released on DVD, the first time a complete Springsteen concert had been made officially available.

By the summer of 2003, the tour was back in stadiums, including ten sold-out nights in New Jersey at Giants Stadium where tailgates fired up in view of a massive banner featuring Springsteen and Clemons in silhouette. By then, Springsteen had shifted his attention to the one thing *The Rising* had avoided: politics. War in Afghanistan had turned to war in Iraq. "I think the administration took September 11 and used it as a blank check," Springsteen said to Ken Tucker in a 2003 interview with *Entertainment Weekly*. You need a certain amount of skepticism in the modern world, he observed later in the interview. The trick is changing whatever insight comes from that into something creative. "Tommy Morello, the guitarist from Rage Against the Machine, said in an interview that history is made in people's kitchens, in living rooms, at night," Springsteen continued. "It's made by people talking and thinking things through. That, I think, is true: You should throw your two cents in as best you can."

Above: Stadion Feyenoord, Rotterdam, Netherlands, May 8, 2003.

Opposite: "Let it rain, let it rain ..." MTV Video Music Awards, Hayden Planetarium, New York City, August 29, 2002.

VOTE FOR CHANGE

Writing in the *New York Times* on August 5, 2004, op-ed contributor Bruce Springsteen set a clear goal: "to change the direction of the government and change the current administration come November."

He'd have help. The purpose of the piece was to announce an October tour that would include the Dave Matthews Band, Pearl Jam, R.E.M., Bonnie Raitt, Keb' Mo', Jackson Browne, John Fogerty, and plenty of others. Under the banner Vote for Change, they'd spread out and flood some of the most important electoral states with energy. On October 1, for example, there were five shows throughout Pennsylvania. Springsteen headlined the biggest— in his old stronghold of Philadelphia.

The war in Iraq, tax cuts for the richest ("well-to-do guitar players" included) coupled with too many cuts to too many programs essential in supporting the country's most vulnerable had pushed Springsteen into the noisy fray of partisan politics. In response, the fray wondered why he didn't just shut up and play the guitar that bought him that big house. "This is an interesting question that seems to only be asked of musicians and artists, for some reason," Springsteen told Ted Koppel on *Nightline*. Lobbyists get to influence government every day and no one says a word. "Artists write, and sing, and think."

And anyway, Springsteen *could* just play and sing and he'd say the same thing he wrote in the *New York Times*. He had the songs to do it, and, after the tour, he took a couple of them out to rallies alongside the Democratic presidential candidate, Senator John Kerry, who still lost the election to George W. Bush.

With John Kerry, Fresh Start
for America rally at Ohio
State University, Columbus,
October 28, 2004.

DEVILS & DUST

2005

"WHATEVER DIVINITY WE CAN LAY
CLAIM TO, IS HIDDEN IN THE CORE OF
OUR HUMANITY. AND WHEN WE LET OUR
COMPASSION GO, WE LET GO OF WHAT
LITTLE CLAIM WE HAVE TO THE DIVINE.
SO IT'S SPOOKY OUT THERE SOMETIMES."

BRUCE SPRINGSTEEN, 2005

2005

February 13: Springsteen wins a Grammy for Best Solo Rock Vocal Performance for "Code Of Silence."

March 19: Second "Seeger Session," at Thrill Hill East.

April 4: Recording of Springsteen's performance for VH1's *Storytellers* (broadcast on April 23).

April 25: Release of *Devils & Dust* (US 1, UK 1) and start of the Devils & Dust tour, at the Fox Theater, Detroit.

May 20: End of the first US leg of the tour, at the Orpheum Theater, Boston.

May 24: Start of the European leg of the tour, at the Point Theatre, Dublin.

June 29: End of the European leg of the tour, at ICC Berlin.

July 13: Start of the tour's final leg, at the Corel Center, Ottawa.

September 6: Release of the *VH1 Storytellers* DVD.

November 15: Release of *Born to Run: 30th Anniversary Edition* (US 18, UK 63).

November 22: End of the Devils & Dust tour, at the Sovereign Bank Arena, Trenton, New Jersey.

Above: Rehearsing for the Devils & Dust tour, April 2005.

Right: Royal Albert Hall, London, May 27, 2005.

Page 191: Portrait by Danny Clinch, 2005.

Collect a critical mass of pop stars inside a cavernous basketball arena and there will be bright lights and bombast, bad fashion, and the kind of racket that gets made only when popular culture celebrates itself. Properly harnessed, the swagger displayed at a single Grammy Awards show could light the western United States. Take, for example, the Forty-Eighth Grammy Awards, held at the Staples Center in Los Angeles on February 8, 2006.

Gorillaz, animated in 3-D for the occasion, opened and were joined first by De La Soul, and then by Madonna, who began on video and then arrived live on stage with the requisite number of background dancers and just enough grind for prime-time television. A tribute to Sly and the Family Stone featured (among many) Joss Stone, Maroon 5, will.i.am of the Black Eyed Peas, John Legend, Aerosmith's Steven Tyler and Joe Perry, and, finally, Sly Stone his own bad self—not only appearing on stage for the first time since 1987, but doing so in a silver suit and rocking a fantastic white mohawk. He looked like the first cockatoo of funk.

Linkin Park paired up with Jay-Z (wearing a John Lennon t-shirt). Paul McCartney then strolled out to assist them all with "Yesterday." Kanye West and Jamie Foxx performed "Gold Digger," West's ode to financially ambitious girlfriends, with the help of the Florida A&M University Marching 100.

Between those high-wattage moments, Springsteen, wearing jeans and a black jacket, performed alone.

"I got my finger on the trigger," he began, "but I don't know who to trust." Standing half in the darkness and half in the light, everything about the performance suggested high stakes. In that opening lyric alone life and death and confusion swirl. "What if what you do to survive kills the things you love? Fear's a powerful thing." Relative to the rest of the night, "Devils & Dust" was a deadly serious whisper Springsteen built to a raging finish and punctuated with the show's only political exclamation: "Bring 'em home!"

Like most of the 48.05 percent of 2004 voters who cast ballots for Senator John F. Kerry, Springsteen spent the days after the reelection of President George W. Bush in a state best described as seriously bummed. Springsteen had stood shoulder to shoulder with Kerry in the campaign's final days, lending a little of the credibility he had earned with decades of careful artistic decisions. Kerry lost and

"YOU'RE ALWAYS TRYING TO COME UP WITH A VOICE YOU HAVEN'T SUNG FROM YET, AND IT MAKES THE CHARACTERS SOUND VERY ALIVE."

Bruce Springsteen, 2005

so, in a sense, had Springsteen. But what are you going to do? A new day dawns and everyone, regardless of party affiliation, gets back to work.

Having established a pattern since *Nebraska*, it was time again for Springsteen to go it (mostly) alone. The tumult of the 1990s behind him and buoyed by the success of recent tours, there was no need to worry about the E Street Band. There was no breakup, just a shifting of gears. Springsteen made only one phone call—to Brendan O'Brien in Atlanta. "I'll play you some songs, you tell me what you think, and we'll take it from there," Springsteen said.

A year earlier, in November 2003, *The Essential Bruce Springsteen* hit stores with two discs of old favorites and a third featuring a dozen songs pulled from the vault. "From Small Things (Big Things One Day Come)," was a 1979 *River*-era outtake, a breakneck shuffle about the seeds we sow and the choices we make. "County Fair," a post-*Nebraska* home recording, set a sweet scene on a summer's night—complete with crickets chirping. The sweeping "None But The Brave" was put down in New York during sessions for *Born in the U.S.A.* but walks 1970s Asbury Park restless with a memory and looking for answers: "Now who's the man who thinks he can decide, whose dreams will live and whose shall be pushed aside?"

The death-row sketch "Dead Man Walkin'" was one of three soundtrack works included

Left: Backstage with Paul McCartney at the Grammy Awards, February 8, 2006.

Opposite: Springsteen's intense, austere performance of "Devils & Dust" stood out from the bright lights and bombast of the rest of the ceremony.

"AS A CHILD I FELT BOTH THE CRUSHING HAND OF FATE AND FORTUNE, AND THEY DON'T QUITE CANCEL EACH OTHER OUT."

Bruce Springsteen, 2005

on *Essential*. Sean Penn used "Missing" in *Crossing Guard*, and John Sayles—who'd directed the videos for "Born In The U.S.A.," "I'm On Fire," and "Glory Days"—used "Lift Me Up" in his film *Limbo*. "Lift Me Up" features Springsteen singing in a soft falsetto, the same touch he applied to an acoustic take of "Countin' On A Miracle" recorded in the lounge at Southern Tracks while recording *The Rising*.

"He had different voices, and he'd say, 'I could be this guy,' and sing it one way. 'Or I could be this guy,' and sing it a whole other way," O'Brien said in 2011. "So he'd go through voices, trying to figure out how much he believed it."

Released on April 25, 2005, *Devils & Dust* conjured from the archives more voices for more characters set against more precarious circumstances. "These are all songs about people whose souls are in danger or at risk," Springsteen said. In the *New York Times*, Jon Pareles tagged it Springsteen's "family-values album, filled with reflections on God, motherhood, and the meaning of home." They're both right. Like Springsteen at the Grammys, *Devils & Dust* walks that line between the light and the dark, between salvation and damnation.

"We all carry around the seeds of our destruction," Springsteen said in Detroit on the opening night of the solo tour in support of the album. "The other seeds, too." He was introducing "Leah," where he'd set a man optimistically walking the road toward a new life with a house "on higher ground." In one hand, the narrator carries a hammer. In the other, "a fiery lantern." With one hand he has built, and with the other he has burned. He's one of the lucky ones. He's figured out "how to tip the scales *just* this

All the way home—well, almost. Theater at Continental Airlines Arena, East Rutherford, New Jersey, May 19, 2005.

much in the right direction," Springsteen said. So too the trucker racing back toward the warmth and comfort of "Maria's Bed" and doing so with the same high and happy falsetto as the singer of "All I'm Thinkin' About."

In a hotel room in "Reno," Springsteen presents the other side of the story, the what-could-have-been, or the what-might-still-be. There a man settles in with a prostitute, trying to lose himself in flesh for sale. Through the window, he sees the sun has "bloodied" the sky. It "slices" through the blinds. As his companion gets to work, he closes his eyes and drifts into a memory of what was. In his head, the sunlight streams through his lover's hair while the air smells of "mock orange." In his head he's content. But, "Somehow all you ever need's, never really quite enough you know. You and I, Maria, we learned it's so." There the scene moves back into the hotel room where they finish, share a drink, and his woman for the moment offers a toast to the "best you've ever had." In one of the album's most heartbreaking moments, the guy thinks, "It wasn't the best I've ever had, not even close."

Springsteen's scene setting (which includes pricing options for various sex acts) managed to get *Devils & Dust* a label proclaiming "some adult imagery," and caused the record to be banned from Starbucks—no small accomplishment for a fifty-five-year-old icon. Patti Scialfa said she used it as license to write "Bad For You," a lustful number from her 2007 solo album *Play It as It Lays*. And Springsteen had to answer for the song to NBC's Matt Lauer.

"Actually, it's a love song," Springsteen said.

"It's a *graphic* love song," Lauer said.

"It just comes from a different point of view."

A more commonplace perspective on love, one that splits the difference between "Leah" and "Reno," is found in the hopes and fears of the father at the center of "Long Time Comin'." Again we meet a familiar partner—"It's me and you, Rosie, cracklin' like crossed wires." Like in "Reno," Springsteen again puts us out west. The difference this time is that the open landscape, the vastness of the stars above and the mesquite on the wind, suggests potential. "If I had one wish in this god forsaken world, kids, it'd be that your mistakes would be your own," Springsteen sings. Later, reaching under his wife's shirt to feel the kicks of a third kid on the way, he announces "I ain't gonna fuck it up this time."

When the tour rolled through Portland, Oregon, it was his son Evan who delivered Springsteen his guitar before "Long Time Comin'." "That just cost me $100," Springsteen joked, adding his son had been quick to note the correct phrasing should have been "I'm not gonna fuck it up *too bad* this time."

Taping VH1's *Storytellers* earlier in the year, Springsteen said he'd once worried about his kids growing up amid wealth, and not having to struggle like he had. Don't, a friend told him. "If you're a parent, you give them the best, because the world's going to take care of the rest," Springsteen said. "That's true. The world awaits us all."

In "Black Cowboys," the world crashes down around a boy in the Bronx named Rainey Williams. Inspired by Jonathan Kozol's book *Amazing Grace*, the song describes Rainey watching helplessly as his mother gives in to the street and to drugs until "the smile Rainey depended on dusted away." He grabs the money her dealer boyfriend keeps under the sink and heads for Oklahoma. "Silver Palomino" was written for a friend who'd died of cancer, and for her two sons. "The Hitter" recounts the story of a boy who gets in trouble and whose mother ships him to New Orleans to keep him from the police. He becomes a pretty good fighter. Then he takes some dives. He makes his money. Those days past, he's fighting anyone, anywhere, for cash, and telling his story to his mother through a locked door. "Just let me lie down for a while and I'll be on my way," he requests.

Above: Patti Scialfa coming on stage for "Brilliant Disguise" at the *VH1 Storytellers* taping, Two River Theater, Red Bank, New Jersey, April 4, 2005.

Opposite and overleaf: Portraits by Danny Clinch, 2005.

"THE POINT OF IT WAS YOUR OWN VOICE IS SUPPOSED TO ... DISAPPEAR INTO THE VOICE OF THE PERSON YOU'RE SINGING ABOUT— WHAT WOULD THEY DO, WHAT WOULDN'T THEY DO ... THE RHYTHM OF THEIR SPEECH."

Bruce Springsteen, 2005

"They say your desire to protect your children is the first thing that deeply shocks you when the kids come along," Springsteen said one night in Philadelphia. "How bottomless that feeling is." And it is. You'll do anything. Imagine then Mary, following as her boy Jesus made that march up Calvary Hill. "That's his proving ground," Springsteen said on *Storytellers*. "That's his darkness on the edge of town." Imagine Jesus, and what must have been going through his mind. Springsteen did throughout the tour, each time he performed "Jesus Was An Only Son," figuring the guy must have been thinking about that little bar in Galilee. He could manage the place. Mary Magdalene could tend bar. They could have some kids and watch them grow up.

"I always figured, our choices, they gain their value by the things we sacrifice," Springsteen said. "You choose something, and you give up other things. And that's what gives our choices value, and meaning."

"Matamoros Banks" begins at the bottom of the ledger sheet. Springsteen gives you the cost of one man's shot at the other side of the border. There's no hiding the consequence of his choices. "For two days, the river keeps you down," Springsteen sings softly.

"The people that are interesting are the people that have something eating at them," Springsteen said, "and they're not exactly sure what that thing is." You'd have thought what was bothering Springsteen most was that election. He followed "Devils & Dust" with "All The Way Home," which begins with an admission of knowing what it's like to fail with the whole world watching—but he'd written that song in 1991. Many of the others date to the time of *The Ghost of Tom Joad*. O'Brien and Springsteen took them and sharpened them up musically. Most critics kicked the tires on the album and arranged it alongside *Nebraska* and *Joad*. Roy Bittan had a different idea. "*Devils* is closer to *Human Touch* in concept. Just realized better," he said in 2011.

Like the Tom Joad tour, the Devils & Dust shows began with Springsteen asking for quiet, but they were livelier events with Springsteen bouncing from guitar to piano to electric piano to pump organ to banjo. He returned "Real World" to its rightful arrangement. He howled a distorted "Reason To Believe" through a bullet mic. Introducing "Part Man, Part Monkey," he poked at the president and conservative skepticism about evolution. He joked about his kids and his career and his life. Taking a

"I STILL KIND OF KEEP TABS ON HOW THE OLD TEAM IS DOING. IT'S LIKE A BALL CLUB. THEY MAKE THOSE BIG HIGH-END TRADES WHERE THE NEW POPE COMES IN AND YOU'RE HOPING FOR A BETTER SEASON."

Bruce Springsteen, on his lapsed Catholicism, 2005

wedding request for "Book Of Dreams" in St. Paul, Minnesota, he said, "I had a couple of weddings." When the audience snickered, he added, "A couple's not bad. Clarence is still out there swinging away." In Florida, Clarence joined him on stage, as did Steve Van Zandt. Springsteen took to ending the shows with a hypnotic take on Suicide's "Dream Baby Dream" that he'd begin on pump organ and

then loop so as to be able to wander the stage repeating the song's few simple phrases time and again. "It's so purely musical," Springsteen told *Mojo* in 2006. "That's what's beautiful about it. It's so simple and so purely musical." It's joyful and hopeful and timeless. It fit the show as well as the songs on *Devils & Dust* fit the moment, regardless of when they were written. Addressing that question with Pareles, Springsteen made it sound easy: "It's both not connected to the chronology," he said, "and yet it always is."

Opposite: Springsteen's *Storytellers* show combined electrifying solo acoustic performances and warmly revealing commentaries and anecdotes.

Left: Guitars lined up ready for the *Storytellers* taping, although Springsteen had to restart "Waitin' On A Sunny Day" because he forgot his harmonica.

WE SHALL OVERCOME:
THE SEEGER SESSIONS

2006

"THERE'S A THING CALLED THE FOLK PROCESS
THAT HAS BEEN GOING ON FOR THOUSANDS
OF YEARS, BY WHICH YOU REARRANGE
SOME OLDER FORM, YOU REARRANGE
AN OLD MELODY, TO FIT NEW EARS."

PETE SEEGER, 2006

2006

January 21: Final "Seeger Session," at Thrill Hill East.

February 8: Springsteen wins his second consecutive Grammy for Best Solo Rock Vocal Performance, this time for "Devils & Dust."

February 28: Release of *Hammersmith Odeon London '75* (US 93, UK 33).

April 24: Release of *We Shall Overcome: The Seeger Sessions* (US 3, UK 3).

April 30: Start of the "Seeger Sessions" tour, at the New Orleans Fairgrounds.

May 27: After a short European leg, the tour returns to the US, at the Tweeter Center, Mansfield, Massachusetts.

June 25: End of the US leg of the tour, at the PNC Arts Center, Holmdel, New Jersey.

October 1: Start of the main European leg of the tour, at the Palamalaguti, Bologna.

November 21: End of the "Seeger Sessions" tour, at the Odyssey Arena, Belfast.

Above: Tweeter Center, Camden, New Jersey, June 20, 2006.

Right: The Sessions Band at Thrill Hill East.

Page 205: Final adjustments during tour rehearsals, April 2006.

MR. TAVENNER: *What is your profession or occupation?*

MR. SEEGER: Well, I have worked at many things, and my main profession is a student of American folklore, and I make my living as a banjo picker—sort of damning, in some people's opinion.

It was the summer of 1955 and Pete Seeger had been called to New York to appear before the House Un-American Activities Committee and explain himself. A congressional investigative panel, HUAC's mission was to weed out the country's disloyal, those who might be sympathetic to, or engaged in, communist plots to overthrow The American Way of Life. Representative Francis E. Walter, a Democrat from Pennsylvania and the committee's chair, presided over the hearing. Two other members were on hand, as well as lawyer Frank Tavenner, two investigators, and a clerk.

The transcript crackles like black-and-white newsreel, Seeger as righteously stubborn as his interrogators were exasperated. It was their contention he should answer for his name appearing regularly in the communist newspaper the *Daily Worker* and for performances at various rallies and meetings. It was Seeger's position that no American should be asked to answer for religious, political, or philosophical beliefs. "Any of these private affairs," he said.

Believing it would cloak him in guilt were he to seek protection under the Fifth Amendment, he refused to do that as well. Instead, Seeger ran the committee in circles, offering time and again to talk about his songs and his life while refusing to talk about where, when, and for whom he had performed. "Mr. Chairman, the answer is the same as before," Seeger said, referencing his belief that the questions themselves were illegitimate. "We don't accept this answer," they said. "Sir, my answer is always the same."

"YOUR JOB IS PUTTING ON SOMEBODY ELSE'S CLOTHES. THE ACT OF MAKING MUSIC AND MAKING ART, A VERY LARGE PART OF IT IS AN ACT OF IMAGINATION. IT'S ALSO A TREMENDOUS ACT OF EMPATHY."

Bruce Springsteen, 2006

Not *always*. Asked whether he was or was not in a photo taken at a May Day parade in 1952, Seeger said, "It is like Jesus Christ, when asked by Pontius Pilate, 'Are you king of the Jews?'"

"Stop it," Walter said.

Eventually, Seeger hit the committee with "my answer is the same as before" nine straight times. "The witness is dismissed," Walter said. Though not noted on the transcript, he *had* to have sighed.

Fifty-four years and two subway stops from where Seeger sat that day, Springsteen stood on stage at Madison Square Garden adding his voice to the many who had turned out to celebrate Seeger's ninetieth birthday.

"At some point," Springsteen said, "Pete Seeger decided he'd be a walking, singing reminder of all of America's history. He'd be a living archive of America's music and conscience."

Opposite: Backstage with Pete Seeger at the Clearwater Concert to celebrate Seeger's ninetieth birthday. Madison Square Garden, May 3, 2009.

This page: Seeger appears before the House Un-American Activities Committee, August 1955 (left); and back in New York performing with Bob Dylan at the Woody Guthrie Memorial Concert, Carnegie Hall, January 20, 1968 (right).

Seeger learned from Lead Belly himself and sang with Woody Guthrie in the Almanacs. In 1963, Bob Dylan appeared at a civil-rights gathering in Greenwood, Mississippi. Seeger did, too, and had been there for days when Dylan arrived. Later that year, Dylan played the Newport Folk Festival for the first time. Seeger was a founding board member and the festival closed with Dylan, Seeger, Joan Baez, and more performing "We Shall Overcome" and "Blowin' In The Wind." At the famous March on Washington in August that year, Peter, Paul and Mary sang Seeger's "If I Had A Hammer." In 1965, when Dylan went electric at Newport, Seeger got so furious about the distorted sound he threatened to find an ax and cut the power.

Seeger had stood on that hill in fights for civil rights, for labor and migrant workers, for the environment, and against war. Seeger traveled state to state, town to town to deliver his songs, to ask that people sing along, to do his part to move the folk tradition forward. He was unrelenting, and uncompromising. A 2006 *New Yorker* profile ended with the sight of Seeger, in his eighties, alone on the side of the road in the cold and the slush, holding a cardboard sign upon which he'd written one word: Peace.

"That spirit, the very ghost of Tom Joad is with us in the flesh tonight," Springsteen told the crowd at Madison Square Garden. "He'll be on this stage momentarily. He's going to look an awful lot like your granddad who wears flannel shirts and funny hats. He's going to look like your granddad, if your granddad could kick your ass."

Of course the rock star who had become increasingly explicit with his own political beliefs would be enamored with Seeger, but Springsteen knew very little of the story in 1997 when he wrapped his solo tour in support of *The Ghost of Tom Joad*. As he settled back into home, among the items on his musical to-do list was a song for an upcoming album honoring Seeger. Springsteen's first move was to hit the record store, buy up all the Pete Seeger on the shelves, and begin to absorb his story.

Springsteen also needed to find a band—for a party at his place in New Jersey. At the suggestion of Soozie Tyrell (who would join the E Street Band with the Rising tour), he hired the Gotham Playboys, who specialized in Cajun, zydeco, and acoustic revelry. "This was the sound I was looking for, for the [Seeger] project," Springsteen wrote in 2006. A one-day session was booked at his farmhouse in November 1997, the band in the main room, horns in the hallway, and they let loose. From that, a version of "We Shall Overcome"—which began as a labor anthem and with the help of Seeger went on to

"THOSE ARE THE TRUE FOLK INSTRUMENTS. THE ONES THAT DIDN'T HAVE TO BE PLUGGED IN. THEY WERE MEANT TO TRAVEL ... THEY WERE MEANT TO BE PLAYED IN HOMES, AND BARS, AND UNION HALLS. THOSE ARE INSTRUMENTS THAT STILL COME TO LIFE IN THAT SETTING."

Bruce Springsteen, 2006

become an integral part of the civil-rights struggle— was given to the 1998 tribute *Where Have All the Flowers Gone: The Songs of Pete Seeger*.

Then the E Street Band roared back to life. Late in 2004, after the Vote for Change tour, Springsteen and Jon Landau revisited the 1997 session with an eye toward a second *Tracks* collection. They found the guts of a stand-alone project and a second one-day session was booked in March 2005, just before the Devils & Dust tour. After those shows, in early 2006, a third session filled the farmhouse for one more day.

"We are brothers and sisters, all." Warming up before the final pre-tour public rehearsal, Asbury Park Convention Hall, April 26, 2006.

On April 24—only 364 days after *Devils & Dust*—Springsteen released *We Shall Overcome: The Seeger Sessions*, his first (and only) album of non-original material. It is filled with, in Springsteen's words, the sound of music being *made* as opposed to *played*. "There's an energy to that, when no one knows it, and you're just playing," Springsteen says on a making-of DVD. "When you're fumbling around, that's the moment opportunity and disaster are close at hand. If you can push it to opportunity, you get something really special."

He'd shout out solos and key changes on the fly. Laughter and commotion and mistakes made it to tape. "Anybody need another beer or anything?" Springsteen says. "Loosen you up for those vocals? We need a *wild* sound. I want a beer-drunk, whiskey-drinking sound!"

Seeger didn't write the songs on the album, but he had carried them with him on his journey, led the sing-alongs they starred in, found and shared comfort and strength in them. "We Shall Overcome," a Baptist hymn that became a labor-movement standard before becoming a civil-rights rallying cry, stands proud on its history. It's declarative: "We shall overcome," and "we'll walk hand in hand," and "we are not afraid." It's as unstoppable as "Eyes On The Prize": "Freedom's name is mighty sweet, and soon we're gonna meet." That's a promise, one you can sing then, now, and forever. You can sing those songs on picket lines. You can sing them at marches. You can sing them in churches right alongside the record's two spirituals, "O Mary Don't You Weep" and "Jacob's Ladder." "Shenandoah" isn't church music, but it is prayerful, a heartfelt sketch of home from the memory of a westward-bound pioneer.

The oldest song, the charming, anthropomorphic "Froggie Went A Courtin'," dates at least to Scotland in the mid-1500s. The newest, "My Oklahoma Home," was written in 1961 by Sis Cunningham and her brother Bill. It tells the story of a poor soul who settles down in Oklahoma only to have his entire life—his crops, his wife, his house—blown away by the Dust Bowl winds. "Everything except my mortgage blown away," he says.

"Old Dan Tucker" washes his face with a frying pan, combs his hair with a wagon wheel, and had a toothache in his heel when he died. Go figure. He's a good drunk, a fun drunk, and as Springsteen told Dave Marsh in a satellite-radio interview, the kind of drunk who could have fit on *Greetings*. At the opposite end of the mood spectrum is "Mrs. McGrath," a booming antiwar tune in which a son returns home after more than seven years, his legs having been blown away by cannon fire. "All foreign wars I do proclaim, live on blood and a mother's

pain," Mrs. McGrath says. Marsh, who did the research for the album's liner notes, traces the song back to 1815, but Springsteen snaps it into the present day with one small change: "I'd rather have my son as he used to be, than the King of America and his whole Navy!"

"John Henry" and "Jesse James" bring back to life classic American folk heroes. While both end up dead—James by the hand of one of his own gang members, Henry after his symbolic battle with the railroad baron's steam hammer—their stories don't end. Jesse has a wife and kids. John Henry's wife picks up his hammer and gets to work, as hard as anyone on the record.

You spend "forty days and nights at sea" working—a job of biblical proportions—and you're going to expect the guy who hired you to pay you, so you can see where the voice of "Pay Me My Money Down" is coming from. The guy in "Erie Canal" doesn't have a job, but he's got experience and a mule in possession of a rugged disposition. Never anger an animal with an "iron toe" capable of kicking a man "back to Buffalo."

"I heard a hundred voices in those old folk songs, and stories from across the span of American history—parlor music, church music, tavern music, street and gutter music," Springsteen told the *New Yorker*. "He had a real sense of the musician as historical entity … At the same time, Pete always maintained a tremendous sense of fun and lightness, which is where his grace manifested itself."

Six days after the album's release, Springsteen, backed by seventeen musicians who looked like they'd taken the first stagecoach from New Jersey, closed out the first weekend of the first New Orleans Jazz and Heritage Festival since Hurricane Katrina. It had been eight months since floodwaters swamped the city, drowning citizens, turning the Louisiana Superdome into a refugee camp, and wiping out neighborhoods that had given birth to the music Springsteen was bringing to town.

The day before his performance, he visited the destruction, and talked with volunteers. The New Orleans *Times-Picayune* music critic Keith Spera, in his book *Groove Interrupted: Loss, Renewal, and the Music of New Orleans*, reported that Springsteen donated $80,000 to the New Orleans Musicians Clinic.

In front of the city that perfected music as a healing agent, Springsteen and the Sessions Band went to work, opening with "O Mary Don't You Weep," and its apocalyptic promise from God to Noah of "no more water but fire next time." In the heart of the set, he paused to address what he'd witnessed

Above: The emotional tour-opening show at the New Orleans Jazz and Heritage Festival, April 30, 2006.

Opposite: A break during rehearsals for the Grammy Awards show, February 8, 2006. Springsteen won his second consecutive award for Best Solo Rock Vocal Performance, for "Devils & Dust."

"IT'S MUSIC WHERE YOU GET TO SING OUT. IT ROCKS, BUT IT'S NOT QUITE ROCK MUSIC. YOU'RE NOT CONFINED TO THIS PARTICULAR BEAT, OR THOSE TEMPOS. IT'S AMAZING, CONSIDERING HOW QUICKLY WE ARRANGED THE THING, HOW WELL THE ARRANGEMENTS HELD TOGETHER."

Bruce Springsteen, 2006

the day before. "I think I saw sights I never thought I'd see in an American city," Springsteen said. "… It's what happens when people play political games with other people's lives."

With that, he introduced "How Can A Poor Man Stand Such Times And Live," a song written by "Blind" Alfred Reed shortly after the 1929 stock-market crash. Springsteen kept the first verse, wrote three new ones that specifically addressed New Orleans, and dedicated the song to "President Bystander." Springsteen thrashed at his guitar (hiked to his chest, far more Woody Guthrie than star of E Street) until it finally popped a string. He ripped it out of the way and kept charging. Next, "Jacob's Ladder" and then into "We Shall Overcome." In three songs, he'd carried the mood from anger over what was, to hope for what will be. Springsteen closed the main set with "My City Of Ruins," and the encore with the most familiar song in town, "When The Saints Go Marching In." But with a band built for second-line horn jams, Springsteen played it as a vow, and dug into its history to restore the final verse: "Now some say this world of trouble is the only world we'll ever see. But I'm waiting for that morning when the new world is revealed."

"I was sitting there crying like a third-grader," Dave Malone, singer and guitarist for the New Orleans group the Radiators, told Spera.

The tour moved from New Orleans to Europe. Old Springsteen songs were given new life. "Open All Night" became big-band barroom swing. "If I Should Fall Behind" turned into a waltz. "Blinded By The Light" was put through the time machine and came out sounding something like Dust Bowl funk.

Working off the declaration he'd made at the end of his Grammy Awards performance of "Devils & Dust," Springsteen added new lyrics to Seeger's anti–Vietnam War song "Bring Them Home" and dropped the "Th" from the title. Inspired by "He Lies In The American Land," a poem by Andrew Kovaly that Seeger set to music, Springsteen wrote "American Land." In the key of just about every Celtic sing-along, the song presents the immigrant's fantasy of the country ("there's diamonds in the sidewalk," "gold comes rushing out the river") against the reality ("the hands that built the country, we're always trying to keep down"). Those made it onto an expanded edition of *We Shall Overcome* (along with "How Can A Poor Man …"). A live album and DVD of a show from Dublin were also released.

Seeger told *Billboard* he'd have been happy to attend a show—if he could have found a disguise. He was honored, and hopeful Springsteen's attention might bring more people to the music, but "good heavens, I don't need the publicity," he said.

Springsteen, on the other hand: "You can feel the freshness in the sound of surprise in the applause," he told NPR. "Over a long period of years, the element of ritual creeps into different parts of your show. But to have everything come fresh out of the box, every song is a step into slightly uncharted territory."

On the charge at the Heineken Music Hall, Amsterdam, May 16, 2006.

MAGIC

2007

"I REMEMBER READING SOME OF THE REVIEWS WHERE THE CRITICS SAID, 'HE'S OVERINDULGENT,' AND I FIGURED, SCREW THEM."

BRENDAN O'BRIEN, 2011

2007

February 11: Springsteen wins Grammys for Best Traditional Folk Album (for *We Shall Overcome: The Seeger Sessions*) and Best Long-Form Music Video (for *Wings for Wheels: The Making of Born to Run*).
February–May: Recording sessions for *Magic* at Southern Tracks. The *Working on a Dream* sessions follow straight on and are interspersed between legs of the Magic tour through 2007 and 2008.
June 5: Release of the *Live in Dublin* album (US 23, UK 21) and DVD.
July 30: Death of Terry Magovern, Springsteen's longtime friend and assistant, aged sixty-seven.
August 2: Springsteen performs "Terry's Song" at Magovern's funeral in Red Bank, New Jersey.
October 2: Release of *Magic* (US 1, UK 1) and start of the Magic tour, at the Hartford Civic Center, Hartford, Connecticut.
November 19: End of the first US leg of the tour, at the TD Banknorth Garden, Boston; Danny Federici's last full performance.
November 25: Start of the first European leg, at the Palacio de Deportes, Madrid; Charles Giordano replaces Federici.
December 19: End of the first European leg of the tour, at the O$_2$ Arena, London.

2008

February 10: Springsteen wins Grammys for Best Rock Song and Best Solo Rock Vocal Performance (for "Radio Nowhere") and Best Rock Instrumental Performance (for "Once Upon A Time In The West" from the *We All Love Ennio Morricone* tribute album).
February 28: The Magic tour resumes where it started, at the Hartford Civic Center.
March 20: Federici makes a final appearance with the E Street Band, at the Conseco Fieldhouse, Indianapolis.
April 16: Springsteen endorses Barack Obama's presidential bid.
April 17: Death of Danny Federici, aged fifty-eight.
April 21: Springsteen sings three songs and gives a eulogy at Federici's funeral in Red Bank, New Jersey.
May 2: End of the second US leg of the tour, at the Bankatlantic Center, Sunrise, Florida.
May 7: Performance of the entire *Darkness on the Edge of Town* and *Born to Run* albums in order at a fundraiser for the venue, the Count Basie Theater, Red Bank, New Jersey.
May 22: Start of the last European leg, at the RDS Arena, Dublin.
July 20: Final European show of the tour, at the Camp Nou, Barcelona.
July 27: The final leg of the tour starts at Giants Stadium, East Rutherford, New Jersey.
August 24: End of the Magic tour, at the Sprint Center, Kansas City.
September 5: World premiere, at the Venice Film Festival, of the Darren Aronofsky movie *The Wrestler*, featuring a theme song by Springsteen.

Right: Datch Forum, Milan, November 28, 2007.

Page 217: Light and shades, 2007.

The Dixie Chicks were a warning. In March 2003, during a show in London, singer Natalie Maines made clear the band's opposition to impending war in Iraq. For good measure, she declared that she was ashamed President George W. Bush was from Texas, her home state. And then people went nuts. Records were smashed. They were run off the radio. Concerts were protested. They were called un-American and unpatriotic. Shut up and sing, they were told. Battle lines were drawn. Springsteen, busy with the Rising tour, took to his website to offer support. "To me," he wrote, "they're terrific American artists expressing American values by using their American right to free speech." Seven months later, his bags barely unpacked, he sat down and wrote a song called "Livin' In The Future." Time passed.

"Rock star Bruce Springsteen is a liberal guy," conservative Bill O'Reilly said during his October 3, 2007 Fox News show. "He's currently promoting a new album. And doing that, he appeared on the *Today* show last Friday." O'Reilly cut to tape of Springsteen speaking in Rockefeller Plaza outside NBC's New York headquarters: "In the past six years, we've had to add to the American picture rendition, illegal wiretapping, voter suppression, no habeas corpus, the neglect of our great city of New Orleans and her people, an attack on the Constitution, and a loss of our best men and women in a tragic war. So this is a song about things that shouldn't be happening here."

Being a magnanimous guy, O'Reilly granted that Springsteen's speech was "legitimate dissent." However, it would only truly be *respected* once Springsteen agreed to come on O'Reilly's show and defend his positions. "Pop stars, as you know, are rarely held accountable," O'Reilly said. Five days later, O'Reilly offered $25,000 to charity if Springsteen would come on the show. Two days after that, comedian Stephen Colbert, whose character on the *Colbert Report* parodies O'Reilly, wagged his finger at Springsteen and his new album "packed with antiwar, Bush-hating propaganda." The only way for Springsteen to redeem himself? Come on Colbert's show and apologize. "You know what?" Colbert said. "I'll be big about it. You don't even have to apologize. Just come on my show."

Springsteen's response was to do what everyone who had been so angry with the Dixie Chicks had wanted *them* to do. The world was coming unstitched and the E Street Band was going to do something about it. "We plan to *sing* about it," Springsteen said. With that, he cued Max Weinberg, who snapped the band into "Livin' In The Future," its ominous imagery dancing to the sound of Clarence Clemons's saxophone and a "Tenth Avenue Freeze-Out"–like groove.

"IT HAS TO BE POLITICAL TO HAVE RESONANCE. ALONG WITH THAT, IT SHOULD BE A GOOD BREAKUP SONG ... THAT'S THE WAY I LIKE TO DO IT. IT KEEPS YOU OFF THE SOAPBOX."

Bruce Springsteen, 2011

Springsteen's opening lyric sets the mood: "A letter come blowin' in, on an ill wind." The sky is "gunpowder and shades of gray." The horizon is "bloody red." A kiss comes with the "taste of blood on your tongue." Wild dogs have been set on the loose. The seas are rising and the earth is crumbling. A woman comes walking through town, her "boot heels clickin' like the barrel of a pistol spinnin' round." It's bad news in every direction. Is that thunder in the distance? Or is it "the sinkin' sound of somethin' righteous goin' under?"

"Livin' In The Future" was the "genesis, the little starting point of the record," Springsteen said in 2011. Released on October 2, 2007, *Magic* has an uneasiness drifting through it the way freedom moves "like a ghost amongst the trees" in the title song. Across the dozen tracks, blood falls and spills and colors the sky. That blood is the price

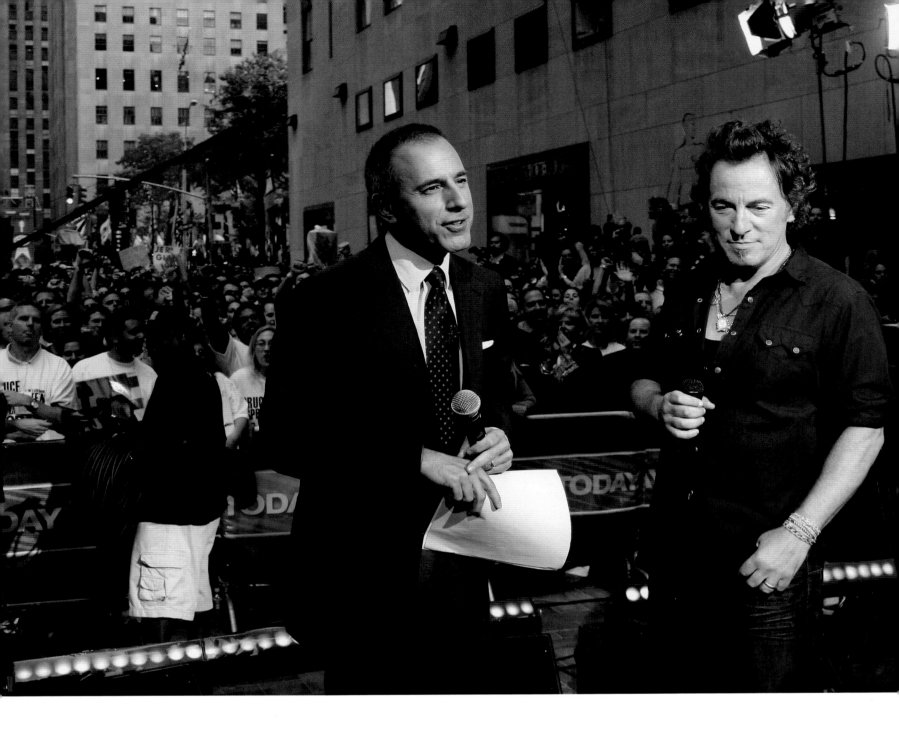

of deceit, of falling for the trick and giving in to the illusion. "I'll cut you in half, while you're smiling ear to ear," Springsteen sings, playing the part of the creepiest carnival barker.

He knew he was releasing the album on the eve of an election year. He knew he'd become something of a barometer, each release an update on the current weather conditions in the American Dream. As such, *Magic* was going to be batted about by the right and the left as they yelled at each other for fun and profit. The rabid snarling of the discourse, the reliance on blunt-force opinion, wasn't news to Springsteen. When it came time to promote the album, he even sat down with a news show. It was the reliably calm *60 Minutes*, but it was a news show nonetheless. At fifty-eight, he gladly charged into the fray. "That's

the soup we're in, and it's not going anywhere," he told *Spin* in December 2007. "You just have to keep pressing and remain committed to your ideas and the small part you can play. Bill O'Reilly's gonna curse me? God bless him."

Working in Atlanta with producer Brendan O'Brien and the E Street Band, Springsteen built his most musically ambitious record since *Born to Run*, far more *Pet Sounds* than punk assault. Cellos and violins flesh out pop melodies. The spacious arrangements are Springsteen's own sleight of hand. *Magic* sounds like everything's OK. It's not. Taken one way, "I'll Work For Your Love" is a hummable number about exactly what the title implies. But in her eyes are "the pages of Revelation"—the apocalypse itself. The "city of peace has crumbled,

Opposite: With their criticisms of George W. Bush, the Dixie Chicks exposed themselves to conservative vitriol.

Above: Springsteen also put himself in the firing line with his comments on the *Today* show, September 28, 2007.

"IT'S THE LONGING, THE UNREQUITED LONGING FOR THAT PERFECT WORLD. POP IS FUNNY. IT'S A TEASE. IT'S AN IMPORTANT ONE, BUT IT'S A TEASE, AND THEREIN RESIDES ITS BEAUTY AND ITS JOKE."

Bruce Springsteen, 2007

our book of faith's been tossed." Faith, love, peace, and hope ... everything that had kept *The Rising* from turning into a dirge has gone missing in the years since. "The record is a tallying of cost and of loss," Springsteen told *New York Times* critic A. O. Scott.

A tally most weren't that interested in taking. Far easier to argue about which side might be winning a political war than to focus on the toll of either of the actual wars being fought. "We don't measure the blood we've drawn anymore," Springsteen rages on "Last To Die." "We just stack the bodies outside the door." The song takes its chorus—"Who'll be the last to die for a mistake?"—from the 1971 speech John Kerry, having recently returned from Vietnam, gave before the Senate Foreign Relations Committee. "How do you ask a man to be the last man to die in Vietnam?" Kerry said. Only the names of the wars change.

Dropping in on a pre-tour rehearsal in Asbury Park, Scott watched Springsteen and the band work to perfect a transition from "The Rising" to "Last To Die." "It's not much of an exaggeration to say that Mr. Springsteen's take on the post-9/11 history

Above: John Kerry testifies before the Senate Foreign Relations Committee, April 1971.

Right: Tour rehearsals back at the Asbury Park Convention Hall, September 2007.

"IT'S ALWAYS MY THINKING THAT IF YOU CAN PRESENT A TOUGH LYRIC WITH A BRIGHTNESS TO IT, IT KEEPS IT FROM GETTING TOO ONE-DIMENSIONAL. AND HE WAS LETTING IT GO. LET 'EM ALL BE FILLED WITH CANDY AND SUGAR. AND I WAS ONLY TOO HAPPY TO OBLIGE."

Brendan O'Brien, 2011

of the United States can be measured in the space between the choruses of those two songs," Scott wrote. From any point in those two songs, really. In 2002: "dream of life." In 2007: the sun is setting "in flames as the city burns."

In "Gypsy Biker," the mother of a dead soldier takes the sheets from his bed, the first step to packing away his life. His sister sits quietly. His brother is drunk. "This whole town's been rousted, which side are you on?" What difference does it make? "To the dead it don't matter much, 'bout who's wrong or right." It's a sad song punctuated by wailing, grief-stricken guitar solos, but it's angry, too. It's angry from its very first line: "Speculators made their money on the blood you shed."

In "Devil's Arcade," the soldier makes it home alive, but certainly not in one piece. Wounded in body and soul, he wakes each day with "the thick desert dust" on his skin. "Somebody made a bet, somebody paid." They're different somebodies, to be sure. They always are.

"You'll Be Comin' Down" and "Your Own Worst Enemy" play as warnings. "Easy street, a quick buck and true lies," Springsteen sings on the former, setting up a scenario that's bound to fall apart. The latter is marked by a willful lack of self-reflection. When faced with too clear a picture of the times, "you removed all the mirrors."

For years Springsteen had employed the question "Is there anybody alive out there?" as a piece of stagecraft. In "Radio Nowhere," it holds together

the search for meaningful human connection in a world of satellites where too often one feels like "another lost number in a file."

"Girls In Their Summer Clothes" looks like a Beach Boys song, and sounds like a Beach Boys song, but there's a hint of autumn in the story of a guy on the wrong side of a breakup and out on the town. There's enough melancholy and creeping nostalgia to make you think the best days are behind him, especially when the girls pass him by.

When Springsteen released *The Rising*, he could still see those days immediately following the September 11 terrorist attacks when the country came together and anything seemed possible. The path to *Magic*, a path marked for Springsteen by that checklist of violations to the nation's civil liberties he rattled off on *Today*, was a long one. Getting back was going to take a lot of work. To make the point, he again turned to the flag, knowing full well the power of the image. In "Long Walk Home," it's flying over the courthouse in a memory of something the narrator's father said. The flag's a promise. It "means certain things are set in stone: who we are, what we'll do, and what we won't." Springsteen saw a betrayal of the flag, and figured it was time to go to work. "When it gets dark, you're supposed to be singing," Springsteen told Scott Pelley on *60 Minutes*. "It's dark right now."

Magic was finished when, on July 30, 2007, Springsteen's longtime friend and assistant Terry Magovern died of cancer. Magovern's singular

Portrait by Todd Heisler, 2007.

role was best described in the Devils & Dust tour program, where his job title was "Terry Magovern." "Encountering Terry was like coming across a huge rock formation in the desert," Springsteen wrote on his website. "You could go around it, ignore it, climb over it, though that would be ill advised, but you had to deal with its presence, its permanence." Springsteen wrote "Terry's Song," played it at Magovern's funeral, and added it to the end of the album.

On tour, the songs on *Magic* fit easily alongside the best of Springsteen's catalogue. "Gypsy Biker" turned into a ferocious guitar duel between Springsteen and Steve Van Zandt. The sequence Scott noted, "The Rising" into "Last To Die," continued into "Long Walk Home" and from that to "Badlands." "Devil's Arcade" featured Max Weinberg pounding like a beating heart, Springsteen backlit with his Fender stretched toward the sky. In Anaheim, California, Springsteen called up Rage Against the Machine guitarist Tom Morello for an intense new electric version of "The Ghost Of Tom Joad." "Reason To Believe" was rearranged into a roadhouse stomp. "Livin' In The Future" kept some form of a public-service announcement from Springsteen, and, as the tour moved through election season and toward the end of the Bush presidency, "Magic" came with a toast: "Here's to the final curtain on eight years of magic tricks."

In November 2007, at the end of the first US run of dates, Danny Federici left the tour to focus on his own battle with cancer. Charles Giordano, of the Seeger Sessions band, stepped in as they headed to Europe. Four months later, on March 20, 2008, back in the United States, Federici stepped onstage for a handful of songs. "C'mon brother," Springsteen said, smiling at Federici and his accordion. "Ready? We'll start it, just Danny and I." Springsteen began "4th Of July, Asbury Park (Sandy)" and for a brief moment, things were as they always had been. Federici died on April 17.

When the tour resumed on April 22 in Tampa, Florida, the show opened with a video tribute set to "Blood Brothers." A spotlight shone on Federici's empty seat as Springsteen led the band through an organ-less "Backstreets." Roy Bittan took up the accordion for "Sandy," Springsteen saying, "Roy, you better get this one right." Opening the encore, they picked "I'll Fly Away." A little New Jersey bluegrass, Springsteen joked.

By that time, Springsteen had also made his endorsement for president, putting whatever weight he pulled behind Barack Obama, who would eventually win the Democratic nomination over Hillary Clinton. "He speaks to the America I've envisioned in my music for the past thirty-five

years," Springsteen wrote on his website, "a generous nation with a citizenry willing to tackle nuanced and complex problems, a country that's interested in its collective destiny and in the potential of its gathered spirit." Quoting "Long Walk Home," Springsteen added, "a place where '… nobody crowds you, and nobody goes it alone.'"

As he'd done for John Kerry, Springsteen hit the road on behalf of Obama, playing acoustic sets featuring "This Land Is Your Land," "The Rising," "No Surrender," "The Promised Land," and "The Ghost Of Tom Joad." In Ohio, he threw in the Byrds' "Mr. Spaceman," for former astronaut and senator John Glenn. In Michigan, down the road from Detroit, he pulled "Used Cars" from the bin of the rarely played.

On November 2, two days before the election, Springsteen and Patti Scialfa appeared with Obama at a rally in Cleveland, Ohio. Springsteen gave a speech about dreams, determination, and the hard work required to build a more equitable country. "And whatever grace God has decided to impart to us," he said, "it resides in our connection with one another … that's where we make our small claim upon heaven." Then, to his catalogue of songs perfectly suited for such an occasion, Springsteen added a new one, "Working On A Dream." Love and hope, it seemed, had returned.

Above: Danny Federici's last full show with the E Street Band, TD Banknorth Garden, Boston, November 19, 2007.

Opposite: "Yes we can!" On the campaign trail with soon-to-be-president Barack Obama, Cleveland, November 2, 2008.

DANNY FEDERICI
(1950–2008)

Danny Federici was an "intuitive" musician. Time and again you heard that description after he died on April 17, 2008. "His style was slippery and fluid, drawn to the spaces the other musicians in the E Street Band left," Springsteen said at Federici's funeral. He couldn't play a song the same way twice if you asked him. And if you asked him, he definitely wouldn't do it, because he was his own character. He was the Phantom, the guy who knocked the speakers over on the cops then disappeared into the ether in the middle of the Great Clearwater Swim Club Disturbance of 1970—and for weeks avoided a warrant for his arrest.

"My pal, quiet, shy Dan Federici, was a one-man creator of some of the hairiest circumstances of our forty-year career," Springsteen said. Like the time Federici parked a car in a tow-away zone. There was a marijuana plant on the seat. "The car was promptly towed," Springsteen said. "He said, 'Bruce, I'm going to go down and report it was stolen.' I said, 'I'm not sure that's a good idea.'" It wasn't. "He was my homeboy, and great," Springsteen said, "and for that you make considerations."

They went back to the days before E Street, to the Upstage when Federici and Vini "Mad Dog" Lopez talked Springsteen into *their* band. It was Child then, and then it was Steel Mill, and then eventually it was world domination. From his B3 organ Federici could pull the carnival sound of the boardwalk, or the dread of a coming storm. He played, in Springsteen's words, miracles. "Of course we all grow up and we know 'it's only rock 'n' roll' … but it's not," Springsteen said. "After a lifetime of watching a man perform his miracle for you, night after night, it feels an awful lot like love."

Danny Federici during rehearsals
for the Magic tour at the
Asbury Park Convention Hall,
September 2007.

WORKING ON A DREAM

2009

"I REALIZED, I DO LOVE THOSE
BIG SWEEPING MELODIES AND THE
ROMANTICISM, AND I HAVEN'T ALLOWED
MYSELF MUCH OF IT IN THE PAST.
WHEN YOU HAVE A LITTLE VEIN YOU
HAVEN'T TOUCHED, IT'S FULL."

BRUCE SPRINGSTEEN, 2009

2009

January 11: Springsteen wins a Golden Globe for Best Original Song for "The Wrestler."

January 13: Release of second *Greatest Hits* (US 43, UK 3).

January 18: Springsteen performs at We Are One: The Obama Inaugural Celebration at the Lincoln Memorial in Washington, DC.

January 27: Release of *Working on a Dream* (US 1, UK 1).

February 1: Springsteen and the E Street Band give the halftime show at Super Bowl XLIII.

February 8: Wins a Grammy for Best Rock Song for "Girls In Their Summer Clothes."

April 1: Start of the Working on a Dream tour, at the HP Pavilion, San Jose, California.

May 3: Springsteen performs at the Clearwater Concert at Madison Square Garden, a celebration for Pete Seeger's ninetieth birthday.

May 23: End of the first US leg of the tour, at the Izod Center, East Rutherford, New Jersey.

May 30: Start of the European leg of the tour, at the Pinkpop Festival at Megaland, Landgraaf, the Netherlands.

June 27: Headline slot at the Glastonbury festival, UK.

August 2: End of the European leg of the tour, at the Auditorio Monte do Gozo, Santiago de Compostela, Spain.

August 19: Start of the final leg of the tour, at the Comcast Theater, Hartford, Connecticut.

September 20: The tour's first full live performance of *Born to Run*, at the United Center, Chicago.

September 25: Recording of a show at the Apollo Theater, New York City for Elvis Costello's *Spectacle* TV series (and a DVD release).

October 2: The tour's first full live performance of *Darkness on the Edge of Town*, at Giants Stadium, East Rutherford, New Jersey.

October 9: First ever full live performance of *Born in the U.S.A.*, at the last concert at Giants Stadium before its demolition.

October 29–30: Springsteen performs at the 25th Anniversary Rock and Roll Hall of Fame Concerts, Madison Square Garden.

November 7: First ever full live performance of *The Wild, the Innocent & the E Street Shuffle*, at Madison Square Garden.

November 8: First ever full live performance of *The River*, at Madison Square Garden.

November 22: End of the Working on a Dream tour, at the HSBC Arena, Buffalo, New York (includes first full live performance of *Greetings from Asbury Park, N.J.*).

December 5–6: Springsteen receives one of the 2009 Kennedy Center Honors.

December 13: Filming of a live performance of *Darkness on the Edge of Town* at the Paramount Theater, Asbury Park for inclusion on *The Promise: The Darkness on the Edge of Town Story*.

2010

January 31: Wins a Grammy for Best Solo Rock Vocal Performance for "Working On A Dream."

June 22: Release of the *London Calling: Live in Hyde Park* DVD.

November 16: Release of *The Promise* double album (US 16, UK 7) and box set *The Promise: The Darkness on the Edge of Town Story*.

December 7: Clarence Clemons plays with the E Street Band for the last time, at the Carousel House, Asbury Park.

2011

c. February: Recording of *Wrecking Ball* starts.

June 18: Death of Clarence Clemons, aged sixty-nine.

June 21: Springsteen sings two songs and gives a eulogy at Clemons's funeral in Palm Beach, Florida.

c. October: Final *Wrecking Ball* sessions.

Top: Set list, Madison Square Garden, November 7, 2009.

Bottom: Italian premiere of *The Promise*, Rome, November 1, 2010.

Center: Hyde Park, London, June 28, 2009.

Page 231 and far right: Portraits by Danny Clinch, 2010.

Springsteen was standing next to Pete Seeger in Washington, DC. "It was *freezing*," Springsteen recalled. "It was like fifteen degrees." Seeger, four months from his ninetieth birthday, had a banjo, but a banjo won't keep you warm. "I said, 'Man, you better wear something besides that flannel shirt,'" Springsteen said. Seeger looked at him. "Yeah, I got my long johns on under this thing," he said. Then they set about the task at hand: perfecting their performance of "This Land Is Your Land" that would close We Are One, a concert to mark the presidential inauguration of Barack Obama.

The next day, January 18, 2009, a bundled-up Springsteen took his place on the steps of the Lincoln Memorial. In front of him, hundreds of thousands filled the National Mall. To his right, Obama and his family watched. Behind him, a gospel choir in bright red robes lined the steps between the rock star and Lincoln. The Joyce Garrett Singers lifted the chorus of "The Rising" toward the heavens. Springsteen grinned and strummed his way into a song of salvation that, at that moment, seemed like it might actually be within reach. So much of what he'd seen in recent years seemed opposite to what he imagined the country should be. "Then, suddenly, election night," Springsteen told *Rolling Stone*'s David Fricke. "Suddenly the place you've been singing about all these years, it shows itself."

Near the end of the show, Springsteen met Seeger and his grandson at center stage to sing *all* the verses of "This Land Is Your Land"—even the ones about the relief office and private property that often get left behind. They did it the way Woody Guthrie would have, the only way Seeger ever has. Seeger, in his flannel shirt and stocking cap, shouted out the words so all could sing along. He pumped his fists in the air. It was beautiful.

"It was a good warm-up for this," Springsteen said eleven days later in Tampa, Florida. "We'll have a lot of crazy football fans, but you won't have Lincoln staring over your shoulder."

While the Pittsburgh Steelers and the Arizona Cardinals were putting the finishing touches on their Super Bowl XLIII game prep, Springsteen and the E Street Band were fine-tuning the halftime spectacular. Having agreed to the gig, he also agreed to what was announced as his first press conference since the 1988 Amnesty International tour. He was surprised he'd done one that recently. "If there's gonna be a lot of questions about football, this is gonna be the shortest press conference," Springsteen, a baseball guy, said. "Because I don't know anything about it." He pointed toward Clarence Clemons. "Clarence actually played football," Springsteen said. "Which is why he has the cane."

If the inaugural ceremonies were a chance for thoughtful reflection, the Super Bowl was an opportunity to blow stuff up. The National Football League has so perfectly packaged the event that each year the cry gets slightly louder to designate it a national holiday. In 2009, a thirty-second ad spot during the game cost $3 million. Ninety million people watched the event in the United States. "The NFL threw us an anniversary party the likes of which we'd never throw for ourselves, with fireworks and everything," Springsteen said in a behind-the-scenes documentary that begins with him sitting in a trailer, contemplating a set list of "Nebraska," "The Ghost Of Tom Joad," *The Communist Manifesto*, and "Badlands."

"Uh, *no*," he finally says.

Thirty-four years since the release of *Born to Run*, Springsteen opened his four-song set in silhouette with Clemons, recreating that album's cover. They kicked into "Tenth Avenue Freeze-Out," then into "Born To Run." The Joyce Garrett Singers returned to assist with "Working On A Dream." And finally "Glory Days." From the band's story, to Springsteen's story, to everyone's story, to the end of the story is how he summarized the narrative. It was big and bright and a little campy—a referee ran on stage to flag them for delay of game as Springsteen and Steve Van Zandt joked around at the end of "Glory Days." It was the pink Cadillac on display for the world. "If somebody wanted to take twelve minutes and

Above: Performing with Pete Seeger and his grandson Tao Rodriguez-Seeger (top) and with the Joyce Garrett Singers (bottom) at the Obama inaugural celebration. Lincoln Memorial, Washington, DC, January 18, 2009.

Opposite: Blowing stuff up during the halftime show at Super Bowl XLIII, Raymond James Stadium, Tampa, February 1, 2009.

see a good deal of what we were about, that's a pretty good piece of film to check out," Springsteen said in 2011.

The NFL had been after Springsteen for years to play the Super Bowl. They got him because longevity was powerful enough to make him realize he didn't have to be so fussy. "You're less caught up into being fooled that you've got something to protect," he said. (Watching Tom Petty play the year before didn't hurt.) Also, *Working on a Dream* had been released five days before the game. "So we have our mercenary reasons, of course," he said at the press conference. Toss in the Golden Globe award Springsteen won on January 11 for the title track to the Mickey Rourke film *The Wrestler*, and 2009 was off to a pretty good start.

He never would have imagined playing "The Rising" at the inauguration of the country's first African-American president. "But eight years go by, and that's where you find yourself," Springsteen told *New York Times* critic Jon Pareles. "You're swimming in the current of history and so is your music."

History in a different sense flows through *Working on a Dream*. The relationships that define the album are long ones. They're trusted, treasured, and proven. Having lost Terry Magovern and Danny Federici, Springsteen released a record that focused not so much on death, as time. "And at certain moments time is obliterated in the presence of somebody you love," he told the *Guardian*'s Mark Hagen. "There seems to be a transcendence of time in love."

Specifically, Springsteen was talking about "Kingdom Of Days," where the seasons pass unnoticed but for "a subtle change of light on your face," and where "we laugh beneath the covers and count the wrinkles and the grays."

"I thought, Geez, that's just perfect," Garry Tallent said in 2011. "One of the best songs he's ever written."

"This Life" likens love to the Big Bang itself, the very creation of the universe. "A billion years or just this night," Springsteen sings sweetly. "Tomorrow Never Knows" chimes with happy memories and a future that, while unknown, *sounds* nice. The whole album *sounds* nice.

The gift for pure pop writing Springsteen had for so long ignored (to the eternal frustration of Van Zandt), he now finally and fully acknowledged. He fell into the warm embrace of the Beach Boys, the Byrds, and Roy Orbison. *Magic* arrived with a sepia-toned Springsteen staring from the cover—a picture of stone-cold seriousness. *Working on a Dream* is awash in soft colors, faded light, and comforting nostalgia. The moon and the stars are high in the sky behind Springsteen, who's grinning as he looks away.

"I'LL PUT *THE RISING, MAGIC,* AND THE NEW ONE AGAINST ANY OTHER THREE RECORDS WE'VE MADE IN A ROW, AS FAR AS SOUND, DEPTH OF AND PURPOSE OF WHAT THEY'RE SAYING AND CONVEYING. IT'S VERY SATISFYING TO BE ABLE TO DO THAT AT THIS POINT IN THE ROAD."

Bruce Springsteen, 2009

He and Brendan O'Brien began recording the album while *Magic* was still being mixed. Roy Bittan, Max Weinberg, and Garry Tallent did the basic tracks. The rest of the E Street Band—including Federici—piled on the overdubs. "We need a bed of sound in the voices," Springsteen said in the studio, listening to a playback of "This Life." "We need the sound lusher."

Standing in front of his microphone in the middle of the studio, explaining "Life Itself," Springsteen says, "This thing is based around its retaining tension, so you've got to be careful. It's all sort of a taut wire, you know?" It's one of the few songs on the record where anything is at risk.

Guesting with U2 at the second of two concerts at Madison Square Garden to celebrate the twenty-fifth anniversary of the Rock and Roll Hall of Fame, October 30, 2009.

"I'M NOT WORRIED NOW ABOUT WHO I AM. MY IDENTITY, WHAT PEOPLE ARE CONNECTING WITH— THOSE THINGS ARE SET PRETTY FIRMLY ... I ALSO HAVE A WORLD OF CHARACTERS AND IDEAS I HAVE ADDRESSED FOR A LONG TIME. BY NOW, AT MY AGE, THOSE THINGS AREN'T SUPPOSED TO INHIBIT YOU. THEY ARE SUPPOSED TO FREE YOU."

Bruce Springsteen, 2009

"Outlaw Pete," the eight-minute western that opens the album, presents the past as something that can't be ignored and must be reckoned with. When bounty hunter Dan tracks down a changed Pete, only to be killed in the fight, he whispers, "We cannot undo these things we've done" and declares "You're Outlaw Pete." Whether Pete wants that or not. But that song's a fairytale, an ode to a bedtime story called *Brave Cowboy Bill* which Springsteen's mother read to him every night. He told *Rolling Stone* he wanted something cartoonish, like the Beatles' "Rocky Raccoon." Pete, we're told, had spent three months in jail by the time he was six months old. He robbed a bank in his diapers. To make it even more cartoonish, Springsteen seems to borrow a melody from Kiss's "I Was Made For Lovin' You."

"Life Itself," on the other hand, presents a couple falling apart. Most often, Springsteen has presented romantic conflict from the point of view of the narrator—we're in his head, and he's wrestling with commitment. "Good Eye" is a typical example, a howling blues number which turns fast from "you were the only one" to "but I had my good eye to the dark and my blind eye to the sun." "Life Itself" comes at the story from the other side, from the perspective of someone who "left the rest for

the others" and settled in. Only now, "I knew you were in trouble, anyone could tell ... Like you had no further use for, for life itself."

Discussing the crash-bang opening of "My Lucky Day," Springsteen said to Weinberg, "It's gotta be reckless coming in. Anything that sounds like you're almost gonna lose it. Wild. Sloppy. But not sloppy." Weinberg's ability to translate that is a testament to the longevity of *that* relationship. "My Lucky Day," "What Love Can Do," and "Surprise, Surprise" are reasons why reviewers like Noel Murray in the *Onion*'s AV Club loved the sound of the record but suggested no one "look too hard at the lyric sheet." They're about love. The strength of love. The wonder of love. Love, love, love.

And then there's "Queen Of The Supermarket." On the Devils & Dust tour, Springsteen joked about visiting Roy Orbison. "I got this new song about windsurfing," Orbison said. "Uh-huh," Springsteen thought. But Orbison had the voice to pull anything off. "Next record came out, and there was a beautiful song called 'Windsurfer.' I remember it almost made me want to go windsurfing, but not quite," Springsteen said.

"Queen Of The Supermarket" is a beautifully orchestrated and arranged song about a grocery store, about the abundance of riches held therein,

"He was born a little baby on the Appalachian Trail." Outlaw Bruce fills the ten gallon, Wachovia Spectrum, Philadelphia, April 28, 2009.

and one particularly lovely woman who works there. "A dream awaits in aisle number two," Springsteen sings, pushing his shopping cart and admiring her hair, though it's hidden by the "company cap." "It's kind of a song about finding beauty where it's ignored or where it's passed by," Springsteen told Hagen, who, in reply, suggested that sometimes a grocery store is just a grocery store.

"The Wrestler," the story of a man wearing his wounds as the only badge he's got, was added as a bonus track, and gives the album some weight. The highlight, however, was written for Federici. "The Last Carnival" revisits Wild Billy, his circus story having come to an end. With Federici's son, Jason, on accordion, Springsteen revisits the boardwalk sounds of the band's earliest days. "We'll be riding the train without you tonight," he sings. "The train that keeps on movin', its black smoke scorching the evening sky."

Onward they rolled. On the road, the songs from the album quickly faded from the set list. Eventually, the title track was all that remained. Springsteen was excited about the album, but it was released into a world where the bottom had fallen out of the economy, unemployment was spiking, and the misery index was redlining. More than any other popular artist, Springsteen's tone had always been current and correct. It had been right on albums, it had been right in speeches. He understood the moment, and worked to meet it. Always. No matter how gorgeous the music, this was no time for watercolor pop from "the Rock Laureate" (as the *New York Times* called him).

Old reliables like "Johnny 99" and "Badlands" took over the set. Springsteen worked Stephen Foster's "Hard Times Come Again No More" into a chill-inducing prayer. They began playing complete albums in order—most often *Born to Run* or *Darkness on the Edge of Town*. In New York, they took on all twenty songs from *The River*. To mark the final shows at New Jersey's Giants Stadium before its demolition, Springsteen wrote a song called "Wrecking Ball" that managed to be about both a stadium and standing tough in tough times.

On the tour's final night, November 22, 2009, in Buffalo, New York, Springsteen ordered up a complete performance of *Greetings from Asbury Park, N.J.* as part of a thirty-four-song set. With Mike Appel on hand to watch, Springsteen, having turned sixty that September, pulled out an old trick during "Growin' Up."

"There we were …" Springsteen said, going into the story of that fabled night at the Student Prince, he and Van Zandt playing on stage, a storm howling outside down Kingsley. "Suddenly the door

lifted open and blew off down the street," Springsteen said. "And a large shadow of a man stepped in …"

In 2009, that man was stepping slower than ever. Clarence Clemons needed more than a cane. With new hips and new knees and in a lot of pain, he needed an elevator to get to the stage each night. But he worked his way to Springsteen, playing his part in their story.

"I wanna play witchoo," Clemons said.

"What could I say? I said, 'Sure.'"

Clemons began to play. "Something cool as a river," Springsteen said, urging Clemons to keep going. "At the end of the night," Springsteen said, "We just looked at each other and …" nodded. They again struck their pose from the cover of *Born to Run*. The arena went nuts.

"Got in the car, a big long Cadillac. Drove through the woods on the outskirts of town. And we got very sleepy, and we fell into this long, long, long, long dream. And when we woke up …"

Two weeks later, Springsteen was at the White House. This time he was the one being celebrated, receiving Kennedy Center Honors along with Robert De Niro, Mel Brooks, Dave Brubeck, and Grace Bumbry. "I'm the president," Obama said, "but he's the Boss."

"WHEN YOU LISTEN TO BRUCE'S MUSIC, YOU AREN'T A LOSER. YOU ARE A CHARACTER IN AN EPIC POEM ... ABOUT LOSERS."

Comedian Jon Stewart,
Kennedy Center Honors, 2009

Above: With his fellow Kennedy Center honorees, December 2009.

Opposite, top: Borrowing a fan's beanie for the last show at Giants Stadium, October 9, 2009.

Opposite, bottom: Where the heart is—Thrill Hill East, June 2010.

CLARENCE CLEMONS (1942–2011)

He was the Big Man. Throughout history there have been rock stars. There have been legends and myths and figures larger than life. There has been only one Big Man. And so it almost didn't seem real when Clarence Clemons died on June 18, 2011, a week after suffering a stroke at his home in Florida.

"Standing next to Clarence was like standing next to the baddest ass on the planet," Springsteen said at Clemons's funeral. With Clemons, all things seemed possible. When Springsteen would call out a solo—"Big Man!"—he wasn't summoning music. He was summoning nature. "Losing Clarence is like losing something elemental," Springsteen said. "It's like losing the rain, or air." For four decades, Clemons had been Springsteen's foil: comedic, dramatic, and joyous—the only member of the E Street Band to ever appear on an album front cover. And the cover of *Born to Run* was more than just Springsteen and Clemons, it was Springsteen *leaning* on Clemons. "I leaned on Clarence a lot," he said. "I made a career out of it in some ways."

Without Clemons, "Jungleland" loses some of the mystery in its night, "Badlands" is a little less fortified, "Ramrod" and "Working On The Highway" lack some barroom rowdiness. The soaring hopefulness that punctuated "Thunder Road"? That came from Clemons's saxophone. Clemons was essential. Clemons was undeniable. "How big was the Big Man?" Springsteen said. "*Too fucking big to die*. And that's just the facts … Clarence doesn't leave the E Street Band when *he* dies. He leaves when *we* die."

Clarence Clemons observes a
minute's silence for Japanese
earthquake victims before the
Florida Marlins' season opener,
Sun Life Stadium, Miami,
April 1, 2011.

WRECKING BALL

2012

"YOU CAN NEVER GO WRONG
PISSED OFF IN ROCK 'N' ROLL."

BRUCE SPRINGSTEEN, 2012

2012

March 6: Release of *Wrecking Ball* (US 1, UK 1).

March 9: Springsteen and the E Street Band play the Apollo Theater in Harlem.

March 15: Gives the keynote speech at the SXSW music festival in Austin.

March 18: Start of the Wrecking Ball tour, at the Philips Arena, Atlanta.

May 2: End of the first US leg of the tour, at the Prudential Center, Newark, New Jersey.

May 13: Start of the first European leg, at the Estadio Olímpico de la Cartuja, Seville, Spain.

July 31: Springsteen ends the first European leg of the tour at the Olympic Stadium, Helsinki with the longest show of his career to date—four hours and six minutes.

August 14: Start of the final North American leg of the tour, at Fenway Park, Boston.

October–November: Joins Barack Obama on the campaign trail, which culminates in the president's November 6 reelection.

November 2: Springsteen and the band take part in NBC's *Hurricane Sandy: Coming Together* fundraising telethon.

December 5: *Wrecking Ball* tops *Rolling Stone*'s list of the fifty best albums of 2012.

December 10: End of the 2012 leg of the tour, at the Palacio de los Deportes, Mexico City.

December 12: Springsteen and the band perform at 12-12-12: The Concert for Sandy Relief, at Madison Square Garden.

2013

February 8: Springsteen receives the MusiCares Person of the Year award.

March 8: Release of *Collection 1973–2012* (Australian tour limited edition) (US not released, UK did not chart).

March 14: Start of the Australian leg of the tour, at the Brisbane Entertainment Centre, Brisbane.

March 31: End of the Australian leg, at Hanging Rock, Macedon.

April 29: Start of the second European leg of the tour, at the Telenor Arena, Oslo.

June 14: Springsteen plays an acoustic version of "The Promised Land" in London for agit8, a music-based anti-poverty campaign.

June 20: Dedicates a full performance of *Born to Run* at the Ricoh Arena, Coventry, UK, to Steve Van Zandt's *Sopranos* colleague James Gandolfini, who died the previous day.

July 22: Global premiere of *Springsteen & I*, a feature-length "user-generated" documentary.

July 28: End of the second European leg of the tour, at Nowlan Park, Kilkenny, Ireland.

September 12: Start of the South American leg of the tour, at the Movistar Arena, Santiago.

September 21: End of the Wrecking Ball tour, at the Cidade do Rock, Rio de Janeiro.

October 12: Springsteen is inducted into the American Academy of Arts and Sciences.

Top: Keynote speech at the SXSW festival, March 15, 2012.

Above: *Hurricane Sandy: Coming Together* telethon, November 2, 2012.

Left: Receiving the MusiCares Person of the Year award, February 8, 2013.

Far left: Fenway Park, Boston, August 14, 2012.

Page 245: Oslo, April 29, 2013.

On January 19, 2012, at the beginning of a year that promised another contentious presidential election and a still grumpy electorate, the details of Bruce Springsteen's seventeenth studio album, *Wrecking Ball*, were announced.

The title was instantly recognizable as the song Springsteen debuted in 2009 during the final months of the Working on a Dream tour, but the mood of the first single was decidedly different. "We Take Care Of Our Own" arrived equally anthemic, but angry. After Springsteen and the E Street Band opened the Grammy Awards on February 12 with the song, the *New York Times* wrote that it "mistakes jingoism for empathy."

"Whoever said that, they need a smarter pop writer," Springsteen told comedian Jon Stewart in *Rolling Stone*. Not only does "We Take Care Of Our Own" emphatically lack the rah-rah quality necessary for a good jingoistic romp, it's almost cynical. Having been through this kind of misunderstanding with "Born In The U.S.A.," you wonder if Springsteen was picking this fight, drawing people in only to hit them with the rest of the record.

Taken as a preface, "We Take Care Of Our Own" portends seething stadium rock. The New Orleans Superdome referenced (alongside shotgun shacks) isn't the one the world sees during a global sporting event like the Super Bowl; it's the refugee camp of Hurricane Katrina, a horrible place seeming to lack the most necessary human element: hope.

"The road of good intentions has gone dry as a bone," Springsteen sings. Where are the hearts? Where's the mercy? The love, the work, the spirit, the *promise* "from sea to shining sea."

"Do we take care of our own?" Springsteen mused before a theater full of reporters in Paris on February 16 in advance of the record's March 6 release. That's the album's premise. "Then there are scenarios where you meet the characters who have been impacted by the failure of those ideas and values."

Wrecking Ball is about loss. The characters have lost homes, jobs, and pensions. Gone is a basic sense of fairness and decency, the bedrock of the American core Springsteen had been mining since the 1970s. As with *The Rising* and *Magic*, it was as if the moment demanded Springsteen. The time for lushly arranged pop songs about love was over.

Since 2010, Springsteen had been collaborating with producer Ron Aniello, who had previously worked on Patti Scialfa's 2007

album *Play It as It Lays*, on just such a set of more orchestrated songs, a more likely sonic follow-up to *Working on a Dream*. In February 2011, Springsteen arrived to work with "Easy Money," which would end up as the second song on *Wrecking Ball*. "Easy Money" takes the bankers who had so ruthlessly, recklessly, and without consequence crashed economies and equates them to simple street thugs. Or vice versa. Either way, well-dressed thugs. The next day, he moved on to "We Take Care Of Our Own." In the two weeks after that, the rest of the album was written.

"Shackled And Drawn" casts an angry glare from the unemployed below up toward the partying bankers in the mansion on the hill. In "Jack Of All Trades," the banker gets fat, while the working man stays thin. "Death To My Hometown" is close to open rebellion, an Irish stomp punctuated with the sound of an AK-47, Springsteen spitting "Send the robber barons straight to hell."

The Occupy protests, a pushback against growing corporate power and wealth disparity, which began in New York on Wall Street in September 2011 and spread around the country and the world for much of that fall, might have beaten Springsteen to press, but he'd tapped their rage months earlier.

"IT'S A LITTLE BIT LIKE THE SESSIONS BAND HAD MADE A RECORD OF ORIGINAL MUSIC AND I TOOK IT A STEP FURTHER THAN I TOOK IT ON STAGE."

Bruce Springsteen, 2011

Opposite: Getting *Wrecking Ball* swinging with a premiere of "We Take Care Of Our Own" at the Grammy Awards, February 12, 2012.

Left: "From the shotgun shack to the Superdome, there ain't no help, the cavalry stayed home."

He augmented it, even, with passionate Occupy supporter and Rage Against the Machine guitarist Tom Morello, who plays on two of the record's more somber tracks, "Jack Of All Trades" and "This Depression." The latter marks the moment when politics turns explicitly personal. It's not economic depression. This time, it's the darkness-closing-in-all-around kind. The kind that brings to mind the image of Doug Springsteen alone in the dark in the kitchen, beer on the table, a glowing cigarette in his mouth.

Wrecking Ball turns on its title track, a eulogy of sorts. Written as Springsteen was preparing to play the final shows in New Jersey's soon-to-be-demolished Giants Stadium, it had all the reason to be a one-off novelty for the locals. Instead, Springsteen found strength in the passage of time, in the way everything crumbles, but people persevere. "Hard times come, and hard times go, yeah just to come again," he sings. "Bring on your wrecking ball." At that moment, the album digs in its heels. It finds a determination, and these characters start to reassemble their lives, even finding time for a little romance on "You've Got It."

"The lack of work creates a lack of self," Springsteen told the reporters in Paris. He'd seen it growing up, the way unemployment tore at his father while employment buoyed his mother. That dynamic, those formative years, were what he would reference when he once again was asked how a guy with more bankers than some banks can get so upset about bankers.

The fundamental injustices Springsteen sensed as a child, he wrote about explicitly now, maybe as explicitly as at any time since *Darkness on the Edge of Town*—the record he'd most recently revisited in box-set form. Bruce Springsteen was mad. But there has to be more than anger, he said in Paris. You have to advance the story. To move forward, Springsteen looked back. "Shackled And Drawn" pulls from 1972 and Lyn Collins's James Brown–produced "Me And My Baby Got Our Own Thing Going."

"Death To My Hometown" includes an excerpt from "The Last Words Of Copernicus," recorded by archivist Alan Lomax at the Alabama Sacred Harp Convention on September 12, 1959—less than two weeks before Springsteen's tenth birthday, and in the midst of the American civil-rights movement.

"Rocky Ground" samples "I'm A Soldier In The Army Of The

"IF YOU LOOK AT THE CHARACTER IN 'JACK OF ALL TRADES' OR WHEN YOU MOVE TO 'ROCKY GROUND' AND THOSE VOICES, THEY'RE RESILIENT VOICES, AND THE VOICES GO THROUGH TO THE NEXT GENERATION."

Bruce Springsteen, 2012

Lord," a 1942 recording Lomax made at a church in Clarksdale, Mississippi. The Lomax recordings sound like strength and spirit. "Rocky Ground" is an especially masterful mashup, featuring a gospel foundation and a hip-hop break (provided by singer Michelle Moore after Springsteen decided he didn't have the flow for the job). It is heavy with religious imagery: flocks wandering, angels shouting, money changers in the temple, and a new day coming.

In the same way he has refused to surrender the flag, Springsteen stakes out a position on the political left with religious language commonly appropriated by the right. Springsteen connects the modern struggle to the past. None of this is new, and if you don't believe him, listen to the voices in the album's final track, "We Are Alive." They're of the dead, speaking to the living. They've seen this all before. We're all in this together, they're saying, echoing the album's penultimate song.

Left: Musicologist Alan Lomax, whose archives Springsteen drew upon for two of the songs on the album.

Opposite: Another pair of tracks featured present-day collaborator Tom Morello, who also filled in for Steve Van Zandt on tour in Australia in March 2013.

"WE'RE HERE TO PLAY ONE MORE SHOW THAT FEELS LIKE TONIGHT WAS THE GREATEST NIGHT WE EVER PLAYED. THAT'S JUST A ROAD-DOG CODE OF HONOR. WE'RE NOT OUT HERE TO PASS THE TIME."

Bruce Springsteen, 2013

The latest greatest night ever, at Harlem's legendary Apollo Theater, March 9, 2012.

"Land Of Hope And Dreams" was an old song by the time *Wrecking Ball* was released. Written during the Reunion tour in 1999, it predates the Bush administration, the September 11 attacks, two wars, debates about torture and wiretapping, Katrina, the financial crash, the hope that surrounded the election of the country's first African-American president, and all the many loud, acrimonious cultural clashes that followed.

Elements date back farther. You can hear Curtis Mayfield's civil-rights anthem "People Get Ready" in the song. You can hear "This Train Is Bound For Glory," made most famous by Woody Guthrie, but also performed memorably by Sister Rosetta Tharpe. In her work is rock 'n' roll's earliest rumbling.

Whereas admission on "This Train" is limited to the righteous, the "Land Of Hope And Dreams" is for everyone: saints, sinners, winners, losers, whores, gamblers, the lost, and the broken-hearted. "Faith will be rewarded," Springsteen promises. And because the song arrived with history, it meant Springsteen could get Clarence Clemons on the record. On an album about what's missing and gone, the Big Man was Springsteen's loss to reckon with.

Clemons's final appearance wasn't with the E Street Band—that had been in 2010 at the tiny Carousel House in Asbury Park—it was with Lady Gaga on *American Idol*. Clemons played on two songs that appeared on her album *Born This Way*, and was featured in the video for "The Edge Of Glory." But he hadn't yet been able to get into the studio with Springsteen. After Clemons died, Aniello spliced together his "Land Of Hope And Dreams" solos from existing live tapes.

As the March 6 release date approached, and Springsteen and the band retreated to an abandoned New Jersey military base to rehearse—a base he'd once played as a teenager—how Springsteen's live career would move forward without Clemons was a popular topic of discussion. The answer came on March 9.

"Ladies and gentlemen, are you ready for showtime!"

The E Street Band kicked in.

"Welcome to Harlem's legendary Apollo Theater!"

The band rose up higher.

In "the true temple of soul," as he called it, Bruce Springsteen was copping James Brown's iconic "Star Time" intro. Having once studied Brown's moves on tape, now Springsteen had the guy's stage.

"He was *Born in the U.S.A.*! Arrived here tonight in his "Pink Cadillac"! ... The man who paid the

"WE TALK, WE WRITE, WE THINK, AND EVEN AS LATE IN THE DAY AS I AM, WE EXPERIENCE SO MUCH THROUGH THE VEIL OF THE FORMATIVE YEARS OF OUR LIFE. THAT NEVER GOES AWAY."

Bruce Springsteen, 2012

cost to be the boss! The hardest working *white* man in show business!"

Max Weinberg launched "We Take Care Of Our Own" and the band was off, Springsteen taking time that night to recognize the band's losses alongside all the nation had lost in recent years.

Unemployment was high, but not on E Street, where the band now had seventeen musicians. It took a five-piece horn section to replace Clemons, though all eyes were on his nephew Jake, who'd brought his saxophone aboard.

"If you're here, and we're here, then they're here," Springsteen said of Clemons and Federici during "My City Of Ruins." In "Tenth Avenue Freeze-Out," just before the change was made uptown and the Big Man joined the band, the music stopped cold, letting Springsteen take the lyric. The crowd took over—until finally the band punctuated the noise, and the moment, with the full collection of horns playing Clemons's part.

Left: By headlining the Apollo, Springsteen emulated childhood hero James Brown.

Opposite: With Clarence Clemons's nephew Jake, Cidade do Rock, Rio de Janeiro, September 21, 2013.

A week later, in Austin, Texas, they were at the 2,750-seat Moody Theater. The day before, *Wrecking Ball* had landed at the number-one spot on *Billboard*'s Top 200 chart, making Springsteen only the fourth artist with at least ten US chart-topping albums. He was tied with Elvis, one behind Jay-Z, and nine behind The Beatles.

Thousands of bands had packed Austin for the annual SXSW (South by Southwest) music conference, and by ten thirty on the morning of March 15, a line of people snaked around the corners of the top floor of the Austin Convention Center, everyone waiting for the doors of a massive ballroom to open so seats for Springsteen's keynote speech could be secured. "How important can this speech be if we're giving it at noon," Springsteen said.

If the Apollo was about Springsteen as showman, SXSW was about Springsteen as activist. In Harlem, it was "Star Time." In Austin, he led the band on stage and, with Woody Guthrie's centenary being celebrated that year, offered a simple, "Happy Birthday, Woody."

They opened with Guthrie's "I Ain't Got No Home": "Oh, the gamblin' man is rich an' the workin' man is poor," is how Guthrie wrote it in 1938. "Gambling man rolls the dice, working man pays the bill," is what Springsteen did with it seventy-four years later on "Shackled And Drawn."

The tour rolled out—around the United States and then through Europe where, in Finland, he actually did play a four-hour show. His first, mythology notwithstanding. For the first time since 1987, Springsteen cooperated with a biographer, Peter Ames Carlin, and he admitted to battling depression. Springsteen spent time with David Remnick for a career-spanning profile in the *New Yorker*.

Throughout the year, the depth of Springsteen's songbook came alive in the headlines. They played Florida shortly after a young unarmed African-American had been shot dead on his way back from the store. The neighborhood-watch captain who shot him said it was, in part, a hooded sweatshirt that had raised suspicions. Without referencing the tragedy directly, Springsteen ordered up "American Skin (41 Shots)," his eyes blazing as he cried out, "You can get killed just for living in …"

In late October, as a second American tour was underway, a massive storm coming off the Atlantic Ocean smacked the East Coast causing serious flooding in New York and New Jersey. Overnight, "My City Of Ruins," which had been written about Asbury Park, and became about America after September 11, was again about Asbury Park.

"Land Of Hope And Dreams" was all-purpose. Major League Baseball used it to soundtrack the playoffs, and Springsteen played it to close his concerts, and on behalf of President Barack Obama, who, oddly, had put "We Take Care Of Our Own" to work at rallies.

Having initially said he'd be sitting out the election cycle, Springsteen was back as campaigns charged toward November 6 and election day. He appeared three times with the president on the final day of the campaign, in Madison, Wisconsin, Columbus, Ohio, and Des Moines, Iowa. In Columbus, they were joined by Jay-Z.

At the final stop in Des Moines, it was frosty. The crowd was bundled. Springsteen had his shirt sleeves rolled up. "What I do for a living, is I imagine America," he said. The good and the bad. *Wrecking Ball* had both—the damage we inflict on ourselves through greed and avarice, and the power to redeem through community. What's true on the record is what's been true throughout Springsteen's career: The bad doesn't mean you quit. It means you work harder.

"So this is the night before the day," Springsteen said in Iowa. We'll "go to work the day after that and the day after that, when the work really counts."

> ## "PESSIMISM AND OPTIMISM ARE SLAMMED UP AGAINST EACH OTHER IN MY RECORDS, THE TENSION BETWEEN THEM IS WHERE IT'S ALL AT, IT'S WHAT LIGHTS THE FIRE."
>
> Bruce Springsteen, 2012

Above: Springsteen again campaigned for Barack Obama, and the president won a second term.

Opposite: Hard Rock Calling festival, Hyde Park, London, July 14, 2012. Paul McCartney joined Springsteen for the encore, but the sound was abruptly cut off as soon as the 10.30 p.m. curfew was reached.

HIGH HOPES

2014

"WHEN I GO INTO MY STUDIO, I'M SURROUNDED BY ALL MY MUSIC THAT I HAVEN'T RELEASED. I WAIT TO SEE WHAT'S GOING TO SPEAK TO ME."

BRUCE SPRINGSTEEN, 2013

2014

January 13: Release of *High Hopes* (US 1, UK 1).

January 16: *Rolling Stone* publishes a list of the "hundred greatest Bruce Springsteen songs of all time."

January 26: Start of the High Hopes tour, at the Bellville Velodrome, Cape Town—Springsteen's first show in South Africa.

January 28: Springsteen performs "We Shall Overcome" in honor of Pete Seeger, who died the previous day, aged ninety-four.

March 2: End of the South Africa/Australia/New Zealand leg of the tour, at Mt. Smart Stadium, Auckland, New Zealand.

March 25: Release of *A MusiCares Tribute to Bruce Springsteen* DVD.

April 4: Broadcast of the HBO "making of" documentary *Bruce Springsteen's High Hopes*.

April 6: Start of the US leg of the tour, at Reunion Park, Dallas.

April 10: Springsteen inducts the E Street Band into the Rock and Roll Hall of Fame, fifteen years after his own induction.

May 18: End of the US leg of the tour, at the Mohegan Sun Arena, Uncasville, Connecticut.

June: Launch of Springsteen web museum, blindedbythelight.com.

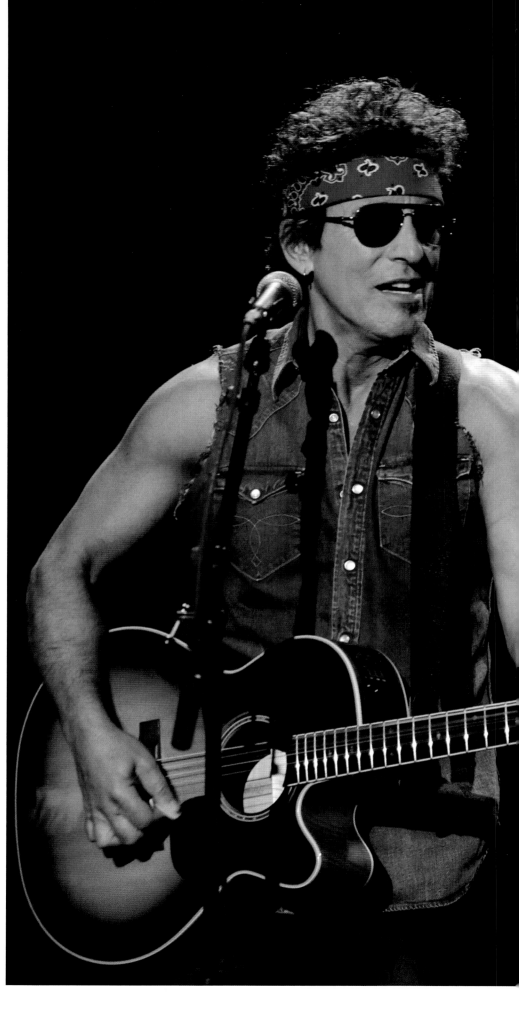

Above: Light of Day benefit concert in aid of Parkinson's research, Paramount Theater, Asbury Park, January 18, 2014.

Page 259: Appearing before the media in Perth, Australia, February 5, 2014.

Right: Springsteen and talk-show host Jimmy Fallon "Bruce" themselves up for a pastiche of "Born To Run" that mocks New Jersey governor Chris Christie for a recent traffic scandal. *Late Night with Jimmy Fallon*, January 14, 2014.

Some things never change. Remember 1975? When engineer Jimmy Iovine delivered to Springsteen a test pressing of *Born to Run*? A crowd gathered around a record player in a hotel room in Pennsylvania and dropped the needle. Then Springsteen threw the record in the pool. It didn't sound right. "The stereo he bought was crappy," Iovine said in the 2005 documentary *Wings for Wheels*. "Nobody knew what they were doing."

In the summer of 2013, Springsteen was in another, presumably much nicer, hotel room—this one in Europe. He and *Wrecking Ball* producer Ron Aniello had been at work on a group of songs that had made their way to the top of a pile of unfinished material that had accumulated since the E Street Band got back together in the late 1990s. Springsteen was listening to the mixes. He wasn't thrilled with the sound. "I was like, 'What are you listening to them on?'" Aniello told *Rolling Stone*, recalling the conversation. Springsteen had a pair of Beats by Dr. Dre headphones from Beats Electronics—a company Iovine cofounded. "Well, you're probably hearing a lot of bass that isn't there," Aniello said. Aniello dispatched an engineer to Italy to set up a proper audio experience. Problem solved, the two continued the process of assembling Springsteen's eighteenth studio release, *High Hopes*. "The best way to describe this album would be to say it's a bit of an anomaly," Springsteen told *Rolling Stone*. "But not that much."

A collection of covers, studio versions of live favorites, and songs that didn't quite make it on to recent records, *High Hopes* isn't tied together so much by a message as it is by a musician—guitarist Tom Morello—and the anything-goes spirit that came to define the Wrecking Ball tour. The freewheelin' Bruce Springsteen. "On any given night you could come out and find yourself in the middle of some sort of epic crowd and performance that you hadn't expected," Springsteen told the staff of his satellite station, E Street Radio, in advance of the album's release. At the end of 2013, he released online a handful of live videos from the tour. From Leeds, UK, a horn-heavy roll through "Local Hero." From Leipzig, Germany, footage of Springsteen and Steve Van Zandt hilariously working to find the right key and horn arrangement for Chuck Berry's "You Never Can Tell."

There was a thank-you note to fans, a montage of footage from the tour set to a studio version of Suicide's "Dream Baby Dream," the song that had provided an emotional punctuation to so many shows on the Devils & Dust tour. The rules that had governed Springsteen's working life since

forever—"Over-thinkers are us, that was our specialty," he said—seemed to have been tossed out in favor of an if-it-feels-good-do-it ethos. Then, on November 18, Springsteen's Twitter account announced a new single, "High Hopes," was to be released the next week. The obvious questions for fans were "What?" and "What then?"

"High Hopes" was familiar as the song Springsteen recorded when he brought the E Street Band back together in 1995 to work on material for *Greatest Hits*. Singer-songwriter Tim Scott McConnell wrote it for the 1990 self-titled debut of his Los Angeles–based roots band, the Havalinas. With its opening line, "Monday morning runs to Sunday night," "High Hopes" evokes the never-ending working-class grind as well as any song Springsteen has written. A "fearless" night's sleep, the chance to look in the eyes of his children "and know they'll stand a chance," that's all the song's narrator wants. The day the single was released, the album was announced.

In December 2012, Morello was in his car in Los Angeles when Springsteen's earlier version of "High Hopes" came on E Street Radio. Morello dashed off a text message to Springsteen suggesting they add the song to the set in March, when the E Street Band headed to Australia with Morello subbing for Van Zandt, who would be filming his television show *Lilyhammer* (where he plays a New York mobster trying to start over—in Norway).

But if that's where the album *High Hopes* begins, then it really starts in 2008 when Springsteen invited Morello to join the E Street Band for a song in Anaheim. They settled on "The Ghost Of Tom Joad," and Springsteen told Morello to bring an acoustic guitar and an electric guitar. They'd figure the rest out at the sound check, which began at 4.30 p.m. Springsteen told Morello to be there at 5 p.m.

"THE E STREET BAND IS A BIG HOUSE, BUT WHEN TOM IS ON STAGE HE BUILDS ANOTHER ROOM."

Bruce Springsteen, on Tom Morello, 2013

During the *Fallon* appearance Springsteen also promoted *High Hopes*, released in the US that day. Tom Morello (right) was credited as a special guest on the album and his spontaneous musical approach was one of its defining features.

"I don't get nervous about too much," Morello said in 2011. "I was terrified." His terror turned to something like mortification when he arrived to discover they had taken the song up to a key he was convinced he'd never be able to pull off with his baritone. Van Zandt coached; Morello tried not to let the panic show; Springsteen said that was the key they were going to play in, period. "And so, kind of freed from choice, we ran through it and I got over my jitters," Morello said. At least temporarily, until his jitters crept backstage and sat with him as the moment approached.

But what a moment. On stage they transformed "The Ghost Of Tom Joad" into what Springsteen had originally intended it to be—a rock song. Springsteen and Morello traded verses and guitar solos, before everyone stepped back and Morello let rip with just about every trick he'd ever learned in Rage Against the Machine, which had turned the song into a maelstrom when the band recorded it in the late 1990s and released it on its 2000 covers album *Renegades*. In Anaheim, the result was immediate, and devastating. No longer was Tom Joad's speech a solemn promise. "Look in their eyes, ma, you'll see me" sounded, as Morello would say, like a threat.

Just before heading to Australia, Morello hit the studio with Max Weinberg and Aniello to lay down the new-old version of "Joad." When they got to Australia, the re-energized "High Hopes" and a cover of "Just Like Fire Would," written and recorded by the Australian punk band the Saints, worked so well Springsteen took the E Street Band into the studio to record—something he'd never before done on the road.

Springsteen traveled with a computer loaded with unreleased material. In quiet moments after shows and on off days he'd work through it, looking for what might be of the moment. This is how the anomaly was only kind of an anomaly. Songs that didn't make *Darkness* made *The River*. Stuff meant for *Nebraska* ended up on *Born in the U.S.A.* But *High Hopes* was explicitly a mashup, and Morello was its muse. He features on eight of the album's twelve songs. "He took that music and sort of jolted it into the now," Springsteen told *Rolling Stone*.

"Harry's Place" was written for *The Rising* and nearly made *Magic*. In 2003, Springsteen sat at his house and read the first verse to Ted Koppel for a *Nightline* piece. Harry's Place is a "shithole on the corner, no light, no sign," and Harry is a local gangster, the guy you go to see for "a taste of that one little weakness you allow yourself." It comes with a hint of Glenn Frey's "Smuggler's Blues," and features Clarence Clemons playing a kind of noir saxophone you usually only hear leaning on a lamppost on a rainy, foggy night in the wrong part of town. "Down In The Hole," one of the few tracks without Morello, also was

"RAGE AGAINST THE MACHINE SHOWS WERE CARDIOVASCULARLY EXHAUSTING, BUT THE BRUCE SHOWS ARE ORTHOPEDICALLY EXHAUSTING."

Tom Morello, 2014

bumped from *The Rising* (in favor of "Empty Sky") and is notable for the recorded chorus of Springsteen's children, and Danny Federici playing organ.

"Heaven's Wall" features a gospel chorus, and "This Is Your Sword" is highlighted with Celtic flourishes—two of Springsteen's more recent sound obsessions. "Frankie Fell In Love" includes Albert Einstein and William Shakespeare sitting down for a beer. The scientist is trying to figure out "the number that adds up to bliss." The poet says simply, "it all starts with a kiss." It's perfectly calibrated for Springsteen and Van Zandt to hammer (and ham up) live.

"Hunter Of Invisible Game" cuts through a post-apocalyptic landscape where "hope and faith and courage and trust can rise or vanish like dust into dust." The salvation, as it ever was and ever will be, is love.

Springsteen's old pal Joe Grushecky gets credit for the idea and the title of "The Wall," but the song belongs to Walter Cichon. Cichon was a member of the Motifs, the first rock band Springsteen encountered growing up that seemed to be full of rock stars. "He was someone we were all scared of, but electric and charismatic," Springsteen said on E Street Radio. "He wasn't of your Earth." He went missing in Vietnam in 1968. "This black stone

and these hard tears are all I got left now of you," Springsteen wrote after visiting the Vietnam Veterans Memorial in Washington, DC and finding Cichon's name etched in the wall.

"American Skin (41 Shots)" remains one of Springsteen's greatest moments, and sadly relevant as gun violence only ever seems to escalate. Like "The Ghost Of Tom Joad," nearly perfect live versions of the song had been recorded and released. "Very, very hard to top any E Street Band live recordings of any of these songs," Springsteen said. At the same time, he said a song lacked authority if it didn't have a proper studio release. They gave it one that doesn't quite punch at the gut the way the live version does, but it does okay.

Springsteen said he didn't feel like he quite got "Dream Baby Dream" to the level of the live performance either, but when he put it out with the video, fans liked it, and so he added it at the end of *High Hopes*. "I felt they all deserved a home and a hearing," Springsteen wrote in the album's liner notes. The reviews were mixed, but critical reception hardly seemed the point. He'd banked enough praise to last a dozen careers. Instead, he seemed most interested in getting as much music out as he could.

"It's the old story that the light from the oncoming train focuses the mind," he told *Rolling Stone*.

The record hadn't even officially landed in the world yet when Springsteen made it known Aniello was at work on the album Springsteen had been making before *Wrecking Ball* revealed itself. He also talked about that electronic-influenced record he recorded in 1993 and 1994. Jon Landau said they were at work on a box set that would cover *The River*. Plans to make live and archival material available online were kicked around in interviews, and then an "official bootleg" of the first night of the tour, Springsteen's first ever South African gig, arrived on his website for download. He opened the show with the Special AKA's "(Free) Nelson Mandela." Two nights later, the song again opened the set, and then, in the opening spot of the encore, there was a tribute to another man who'd spent his life stubbornly advocating for a more just world—Pete Seeger. Seeger had died the night before, at the age of ninety-four. Introducing "We Shall Overcome," Springsteen said, "Once you heard this song, you were prepared to march into hell's fire."

So Springsteen went back to work. Some things never change.

A comparatively relaxed moment with reporters before the High Hopes tour opener, Bellville Velodrome, Cape Town, January 26, 2014.

AFTERWORD

Perhaps the most prophetic comment I've heard over the past quarter century about rock music was made by Lester Bangs upon Elvis's death. In 1977, Lester Bangs said Elvis was probably the last thing we were all going to agree upon …

It was a hell of a speech Springsteen gave at South by Southwest. Musicians around town were talking about it for days, and kept talking once they left Austin. A few weeks later, kicking around the show Springsteen played the night of the speech, singer-songwriter Todd Snider laughed and said, "I might as well just quit."

Bangs wasn't wrong. After Elvis, we went our own ways. "The center of your world might be Iggy Pop, or Joni Mitchell, or maybe Dylan," Springsteen said. "Mine might be KISS, or Pearl Jam, but we would never see eye to eye again and be brought together by one music again." You can't say Springsteen didn't try. You can't say he isn't *still* trying. You can't say he doesn't believe he can. Every night. Every time he steps on the stage. "He empties the tank," Jon Stewart said at the Kennedy Center Honors in 2009.

In November 2012, Springsteen and the E Street Band made Portland, Oregon dance. That's harder than it sounds. Portland's more of a fold-your-arms-and-nod-your-head kind of town. Springsteen opened with "Land Of Hope And Dreams," hit the heavy themes that defined the Wrecking Ball tour, but the set was never more than a song away from another descent into goofy fun. Late in the show, during "Dancing In The Dark," Springsteen spied two women as they climbed atop a riser in the middle of the arena's floor, one he'd used earlier in the evening before crowd surfing back to the stage. He broke up laughing in the middle of "worrying about your little world falling apart." His security team, less amused, moved in to calm the situation. Springsteen saw that,

too. "Go on and dance," Springsteen shouted. "Keep going, kids. Don't pay no attention to that guy! *Fuck* him!" It wouldn't seem possible to have more fun than Springsteen was having at that moment.

Eight months later, a sweat-soaked Springsteen stood alone on a stage in Kilkenny, Ireland for the closing moment of another uproariously successful European tour. "The older you get, the more it means," he said, thanking the E Street Band, the crew, the fans that came out night after night after night, so many decades into his career. As of 2014, he noted, he'll have been playing music for fifty years. He was a local hero and the New Dylan. He was the future, and the past. He found his voice, got hold of a dream, put it in a car, put that car on the road, and drove it hard until he got where he needed to go, until he became the voice of his times, like Woody Guthrie, Curtis Mayfield, Bob Dylan, and Elvis before him.

That's what Bruce Springsteen became. How he did it was pretty simple. He gave a damn. "He had the balls to be cornball," Steve Van Zandt said in 2011, "to risk being sentimental." To believe the work mattered—more than anything in the world. And believe that because it mattered so much to him, it would matter to his fans—that by wrestling with the issues in his life, he could help others wrestle with theirs. "Fundamentally, we're repairmen," he told E Street Radio. "Everybody's broken somewhere. You can't get through life without it." The job we ask of our artists is to rummage through the parts and see if they can make something useful for us all.

"The older you get, the more it means," he said, repeating himself. He closed that show in Kilkenny with "This Hard Land," a message of ruggedness and resiliency. At the song's end, he raised his guitar, blew a kiss, and made one last turn to the microphone. "Be good to yourselves," he said.

DISCOGRAPHY

STUDIO ALBUMS

GREETINGS FROM ASBURY PARK, N.J. 1973
Recorded at 914 Sound Studios, Blauvelt, New York
Produced by Mike Appel and Jim Cretecos

Personnel
Bruce Springsteen – acoustic guitar, bass, congas, electric guitar, harmonica, keyboards, piano, clapping, lead vocals
Clarence Clemons – saxophone, background vocals, clapping
Vini Lopez – drums, background vocals, clapping
David Sancious – keyboards, organ, piano
Garry Tallent – bass

Additional musicians
Richard Davis – double bass ("The Angel")
Steve Van Zandt – sound effects ("Lost In The Flood")
Harold Wheeler – piano ("Blinded By The Light")

Cover art
John Berg – front cover design
Fred Lombardi – photography and back cover design

Side one
"Blinded By The Light"
"Growin' Up"
"Mary Queen Of Arkansas"
"Does This Bus Stop At 82nd Street?"
"Lost In The Flood"

Side two
"The Angel"
"For You"
"Spirit In The Night"
"It's Hard To Be A Saint In The City"

Release date
January 5, 1973

Label and catalogue numbers
US Columbia KC 31903, UK CBS S 65480

Highest chart position on release
US 60, UK 41

Notes
All songs written by Bruce Springsteen.
Reissued on vinyl in 1975 (PC 31903); and in 1979 in a gatefold sleeve (JC 31903).
Reissued on CD in 1990 (CK 31903).

THE WILD, THE INNOCENT & THE E STREET SHUFFLE 1973
Recorded at 914 Sound Studios, Blauvelt, New York
Produced by Mike Appel and Jim Cretecos

Personnel
Bruce Springsteen – lead vocals, guitars, harmonica, mandolin, recorder, maracas
Clarence Clemons – saxophone, background vocals
Danny Federici – accordion, background vocals (and second piano on "Incident on 57th Street" and organ on "Kitty's Back")
Vini Lopez – drums, background vocals (and cornet on "The E Street Shuffle")
David Sancious – piano, organ, electric piano, clavinet, background vocals (and soprano saxophone on "The E Street Shuffle" and string arrangement on "New York City Serenade")
Garry Tallent – bass, tuba, background vocals

Additional musicians
Richard Blackwell – conga, percussion
Suki Lahav – choir vocals (uncredited)
Albany "Al" Tellone – baritone saxophone ("The E Street Shuffle")

Cover art
Teresa Alfieri and John Berg – design
David Gahr – photography

Side one
"The E Street Shuffle"
"4th Of July, Asbury Park (Sandy)"
"Kitty's Back"
"Wild Billy's Circus Story"

Side two
"Incident On 57th Street"
"Rosalita (Come Out Tonight)"
"New York City Serenade"

Release date
November 5, 1973

Label and catalogue numbers
US Columbia KC 32432, UK CBS S 65780

Highest chart position on release
US 59, UK 33

Notes
All songs written by Bruce Springsteen.
On the first UK pressing, the "Asbury" in "4th of July, Asbury Park (Sandy)" is misspelled as "Ashbury."
Reissued on vinyl in 1975 (PC 32432); and in 1977 (JC 32432).
Reissued on CD in 1990 (CK 32432).

BORN TO RUN 1975
Recorded at the Record Plant, New York City
Additional recording at 914 Sound Studios, Blauvelt, New York
Produced by Bruce Springsteen, Jon Landau, and Mike Appel

Personnel
The E Street Band
Bruce Springsteen – lead vocals, guitars, harmonica, percussion
Roy Bittan – piano, Fender Rhodes, organ, harpsichord, background vocals
Clarence Clemons – saxophone, tambourine, background vocals
Danny Federici – organ (and glockenspiel on "Born To Run")
David Sancious – keyboards ("Born To Run")
Garry Tallent – bass, tuba, background vocals
Max Weinberg – drums

Additional musicians
Wayne Andre – trombone
Mike Appel – background vocals
Michael Brecker – tenor saxophone
Randy Brecker – trumpet, flugelhorn
Charles Calello – conductor and string arrangements ("Jungleland")
Ernest "Boom" Carter – drums ("Born To Run")
Richard Davis – double bass ("Meeting Across The River")
Suki Lahav – violin ("Jungleland")
David Sanborn – baritone saxophone
Steve Van Zandt – background vocals ("Thunder Road"), horn arrangements

Cover art
John Berg and Andy Engel – design
Eric Meola – photography

Side one
"Thunder Road"
"Tenth Avenue Freeze-Out"
"Night"
"Backstreets"

Side two
"Born To Run"
"She's The One"
"Meeting Across The River"
"Jungleland"

Release date
September 1, 1975

Label and catalogue numbers
US Columbia PC 33795, UK CBS S 69170

Highest chart position on release
US 3, UK 17

Notes
All songs written by Bruce Springsteen.
On an early US pressing, Jon Landau's first name is misspelled as "John."
Reissued on vinyl in 1977 in a gatefold sleeve (JC 33795); and in 1980 as a half-speed mastered edition (CBS MasterSound) (HC 33795).
Reissued on CD in 1993 on remastered gold disc in a limited-edition presentation case (CK 52859).
Thirtieth Anniversary Edition box set (C3K 94175) released in November 2005, containing: a remastered all-black CD of the original album; a documentary DVD, *Wings for Wheels: The Making of Born to Run* (with bonus feature of three songs recorded in 1973 at the Ahmanson Theater, Los Angeles: "Spirit In The Night," "Wild Billy's Circus Story," and "Thundercrack"); and a concert DVD recording the band live at the Hammersmith Odeon, London on November 18, 1975 (later released on CD as *Hammersmith Odeon London '75*). An exclusive edition of the box set, available only from retailer Best Buy, also included a CD replica of the original "Born To Run"/"Meeting Across The River" single.

DARKNESS ON THE EDGE OF TOWN 1978
Recorded at the Record Plant, New York City
Produced by Jon Landau and Bruce Springsteen

Personnel
The E Street Band
Bruce Springsteen – lead vocals, lead guitar, harmonica
Roy Bittan – piano
Clarence Clemons – saxophone, percussion
Danny Federici – organ
Garry Tallent – bass
Steve Van Zandt – guitar
Max Weinberg – drums

Cover art
Frank Stefanko – photography

Side one
"Badlands"
"Adam Raised A Cain"
"Something In The Night"
"Candy's Room"
"Racing In The Street"

Side two
"The Promised Land"
"Factory"
"Streets Of Fire"
"Prove It All Night"
"Darkness On The Edge Of Town"

Release date
June 2, 1978

Label and catalogue numbers
US Columbia JC 35318, UK CBS 32542

Highest chart position on release
US 5, UK 16

Notes
All songs written by Bruce Springsteen.
Also issued in 1978 as a promotional picture disc (35318).
Reissued on vinyl in 1982 as a half-speed mastered edition (CBS MasterSound) (HC 45318).
Reissued on CD in 1990 (CK 35318).

THE RIVER 1980
Recorded at the Power Station, New York City
Produced by Bruce Springsteen, Jon Landau, and Steve Van Zandt

Personnel
The E Street Band
Bruce Springsteen – lead vocals, lead guitar, harmonica (and piano on "Drive All Night")
Roy Bittan – piano, organ, background vocals
Clarence Clemons – saxophone, percussion, background vocals
Danny Federici – organ, glockenspiel
Garry Tallent – bass
Steve Van Zandt – guitars, harmony vocals, background vocals
Max Weinberg – drums

Additional musicians
Flo and Eddie (Howard Kaylan and Mark Volman) – harmony vocals ("Hungry Heart")

Cover art
Frank Stefanko – photography

Side one
"The Ties That Bind"
"Sherry Darling"
"Jackson Cage"
"Two Hearts"
"Independence Day"

Side two
"Hungry Heart"
"Out In The Street"
"Crush On You"
"You Can Look (But You Better Not Touch)"
"I Wanna Marry You"
"The River"

Side three
"Point Blank"
"Cadillac Ranch"
"I'm A Rocker"
"Fade Away"
"Stolen Car"

Side four
"Ramrod"
"The Price You Pay"
"Drive All Night"
"Wreck On The Highway"

Release date
October 17, 1980

Label and catalogue numbers
US Columbia PC2 36854, UK CBS 88510

Highest chart position on release
US 1, UK 2

Notes
All songs written by Bruce Springsteen.
Also issued in 1978 as a promotional picture disc (35318).
Reissued on CD in 1990 (C2K 36854).

NEBRASKA 1982
Recorded in New Jersey by Mike Batlan on a four-track cassette recorder
Produced by Bruce Springsteen

Personnel
Bruce Springsteen – vocals, guitar, harmonica, mandolin, glockenspiel, tambourine, organ

Cover art
David Kennedy – photography
Andrea Klein – design

Side one
"Nebraska"
"Atlantic City"
"Mansion On The Hill"
"Johnny 99"
"Highway Patrolman"
"State Trooper"

Side two
"Used Cars"
"Open All Night"
"My Father's House"
"Reason To Believe"

Release date
September 20, 1982

Label and catalogue numbers
US Columbia QC 38358, UK CBS 25100

Highest chart position on release
US 3, UK 3

Notes

All songs written by Bruce Springsteen.

First released on CD in 1985 in Japan (CBS/SONY 32DP 357). This rare version used a different master, which included a synthesizer coda on "My Father's House."

Reissued on CD in the US in 1990 (CK 38358).

BORN IN THE U.S.A. 1984

Recorded at the Power Station, New York City

Additional recording at the Hit Factory, New York City

Produced by Bruce Springsteen, Jon Landau, Chuck Plotkin, and Steve Van Zandt

Personnel

The E Street Band

Bruce Springsteen – lead vocals, lead guitar

Roy Bittan – synthesizer, piano, background vocals

Clarence Clemons – saxophone, percussion, background vocals

Danny Federici – organ, glockenspiel (and piano on "Born In The U.S.A.")

Garry Tallent – bass, background vocals

Steve Van Zandt – acoustic guitar, mandolin, harmony vocals

Max Weinberg – drums

Additional musicians

Ruth Jackson – background vocals ("My Hometown")

Richie "La Bamba" Rosenberg – background vocals ("Cover Me" and "No Surrender")

Cover art

Annie Leibovitz – photography

Side one

"Born In The U.S.A."

"Cover Me"

"Darlington County"

"Working On The Highway"

"Downbound Train"

"I'm On Fire"

Side two

"No Surrender"

"Bobby Jean"

"I'm Goin' Down"

"Glory Days"

"Dancing In The Dark"

"My Hometown"

Release date

June 4, 1984

Label and catalogue numbers

Vinyl: US Columbia QC 38653, UK CBS 86304

CD: US Columbia CK 38653, UK CDCBS 86304

Highest chart position on release

US 1, UK 1

Notes

All songs written by Bruce Springsteen.

The album was the first commercially released compact disc to be manufactured in the United States. Copies of the test pressing were given away to attendees of the factory's official opening in September 1984 and are now extremely rare.

A European vinyl reissue in 2007 misprinted "I'm On Fire" as "I'm Free" on the label on side one.

TUNNEL OF LOVE 1987

Recorded at Thrill Hill East (Springsteen's home studio in New Jersey)

Additional recording at A&M Studios, Los Angeles

Produced by Bruce Springsteen, Jon Landau, and Chuck Plotkin

Personnel

The E Street Band

Bruce Springsteen – lead vocals, guitar, bass, keyboards, sound effects, harmonica

Roy Bittan – piano ("Brilliant Disguise"), synthesizer ("Tunnel Of Love")

Clarence Clemons – background vocals ("When You're Alone")

Danny Federici – organ

Nils Lofgren – guitar ("Tunnel Of Love"), background vocals ("When You're Alone")

Patti Scialfa – background vocals

Garry Tallent – bass ("Spare Parts")

Max Weinberg – drums, percussion

Additional musicians

The Schiffer Family – roller coaster background vocals ("Tunnel Of Love")

James Wood – harmonica ("Spare Parts")

Cover art

Sandra Choron – art direction

Annie Leibovitz – photography

Side one

"Ain't Got You"

"Tougher Than The Rest"

"All That Heaven Will Allow"

"Spare Parts"

"Cautious Man"

"Walk Like A Man"

Side two

"Tunnel Of Love"

"Two Faces"

"Brilliant Disguise"

"One Step Up"

"When You're Alone"

"Valentine's Day"

Release date

October 9, 1987

Label and catalogue numbers

Vinyl: US Columbia C 40999, UK CBS 460270 1

CD: US Columbia CK 40999, UK CBS COL 460270 2

Highest chart position on release

US 1, UK 1

Notes

All songs written by Bruce Springsteen.

Reissued on CD in "enhanced packaging" in Europe in 2003 (COL 511304 2).

HUMAN TOUCH 1992

Recorded at A&M Studios, Los Angeles

Produced by Bruce Springsteen, Jon Landau, Chuck Plotkin, and Roy Bittan

Personnel

Bruce Springsteen – lead vocals, guitar (and bass on "57 Channels (And Nothin' On)")

Roy Bittan – keyboards

Randy Jackson – bass

Jeff Porcaro – drums, percussion

Additional musicians

Michael Fisher – percussion ("Soul Driver")

Bobby Hatfield – harmony vocals ("I Wish I Were Blind")

Mark Isham – trumpet ("With Every Wish")

Bobby King – background vocals ("Roll Of The Dice" and "Man's Job")

Douglas Lunn – bass ("With Every Wish")

Ian McLagan – piano ("Real Man")

Sam Moore – background vocals ("Soul Driver," "Roll Of The Dice," "Real World," and "Man's Job")

Tim Pierce – guitar ("Soul Driver" and "Roll Of The Dice")

David Sancious – Hammond organ ("Soul Driver" and "Real Man")

Patti Scialfa – harmony vocals ("Human Touch" and "Pony Boy")

Kurt Wortman – percussion ("With Every Wish")

Cover art

Sandra Choron – art direction

David Rose – photography

Side one

"Human Touch"

"Soul Driver"

"57 Channels (And Nothin' On)"

"Cross My Heart"

"Gloria's Eyes"

"With Every Wish"

"Roll Of The Dice"

Side two

"Real World"

"All Or Nothin' At All"

"Man's Job"

"I Wish I Were Blind"
"The Long Goodbye"
"Real Man"
"Pony Boy"

Release date
March 31, 1992

Label and catalogue numbers
Vinyl: US Columbia C 53000, UK CBS COL 471423 1
CD: US Columbia CK 53000, UK CBS COL 471423 2

Highest chart position on release
US 2, UK 1

Notes
All songs written by Bruce Springsteen except:
"Cross My Heart" (by Bruce Springsteen and Sonny
Boy Williamson); "Roll Of The Dice" and "Real World"
(by Bruce Springsteen and Roy Bittan); and "Pony Boy"
(traditional).
Issued in Europe in 1992 with *Lucky Town* in a limited-
edition mahogany casket (COL SAMPCD 1630).

LUCKY TOWN 1992
Recorded at Thrill Hill West (Springsteen's home studio
in Beverly Hills)
Additional recording at A&M Studios, Los Angeles
Produced by Bruce Springsteen, Jon Landau, and
Chuck Plotkin (Roy Bittan coproduced "Leap Of Faith,"
"The Big Muddy," and "Living Proof")

Personnel
Bruce Springsteen – lead vocals, guitar,
various instruments
Gary Mallaber – drums

Additional musicians
Roy Bittan – keyboards ("Leap Of Faith,"
"The Big Muddy," and "Living Proof")
Randy Jackson – bass ("Better Days")
Lisa Lowell – background vocals ("Better Days,"
"Local Hero," and "Leap Of Faith")
Ian McLagan – organ ("My Beautiful Reward")
Patti Scialfa – background vocals ("Better Days,"
"Local Hero," and "Leap Of Faith")
Soozie Tyrell – background vocals ("Better Days,"
"Local Hero," and "Leap Of Faith")

Cover art
Sandra Choron – art direction
David Rose – photography

Side one
"Better Days"
"Lucky Town"
"Local Hero"
"If I Should Fall Behind"
"Leap Of Faith"

Side two
"The Big Muddy"
"Living Proof"
"Book Of Dreams"
"Souls Of The Departed"
"My Beautiful Reward"

Release date
March 31, 1992

Label and catalogue numbers
Vinyl: US Columbia C 53001, UK CBS COL 471424 1
CD: US Columbia CK 53001, UK CBS COL 471424 2

Highest chart position on release
US 3, UK 2

Notes
All songs written by Bruce Springsteen.
Issued in Europe in 1992 with *Human Touch*
in a limited-edition mahogany casket
(COL SAMPCD 1630).

THE GHOST OF TOM JOAD 1995
Recorded at Thrill Hill West (Springsteen's home studio
in Beverly Hills)
Produced by Bruce Springsteen and Chuck Plotkin

Personnel
Bruce Springsteen – lead vocals, guitar,
keyboards, harmonica

Additional musicians
Jennifer Condos – bass ("Across The Border")
Danny Federici – accordion ("Across The Border"),
keyboard ("The Ghost Of Tom Joad," "Straight Time,"
"Dry Lightning," and "Across The Border")
Jim Hanson – bass ("Straight Time" and "Youngstown")
Lisa Lowell – background vocals ("Across The Border")
Gary Mallaber – drums ("The Ghost Of Tom Joad,"
"Straight Time," "Youngstown," "Dry Lightning,"
and "Across The Border")
Chuck Plotkin – keyboard ("Youngstown")
Marty Rifkin – pedal steel guitar ("The Ghost Of
Tom Joad," "Straight Time," "Youngstown," and
"Across The Border")
Patti Scialfa – background vocals
("Across The Border")
Garry Tallent – bass ("The Ghost Of Tom Joad" and
"Dry Lightning")
Soozie Tyrell – violin ("Straight Time," "Youngstown,"
"Dry Lightning," and "Across The Border"), background
vocals ("Across The Border")

Cover art
Sandra Choron – art direction
Eric Dinyer – artwork

Side one
"The Ghost Of Tom Joad"
"Straight Time"
"Highway 29"
"Youngstown"
"Sinaloa Cowboys"
"The Line"

Side two
"Balboa Park"
"Dry Lightning"
"The New Timer"
"Across The Border"
"Galveston Bay"
"My Best Was Never Good Enough"

Release date
November 21, 1995

Label and catalogue numbers
Vinyl: US & UK Columbia C 67484
CD: US Columbia CK 67484, UK CBS COL 481650 2

Highest chart position on release
US 11, UK 16

Notes
All songs written by Bruce Springsteen.

THE RISING 2002
Recorded at Southern Tracks, Atlanta
Additional recording at: Thrill Hill East
(Springsteen's home studio in New Jersey);
Sound Kitchen Studios, Franklin, Tennessee;
Henson Studios, Los Angeles
Produced by Brendan O'Brien

Personnel
The E Street Band
Bruce Springsteen – lead vocals, lead guitar, acoustic
guitar, baritone guitar, harmonica
Roy Bittan – keyboards, piano, mellotron, Kurzweil,
pump organ, Korg M1, Crumar
Clarence Clemons – saxophone, background vocals
Danny Federici – B3 organ, Vox Continental, Farfisa
Nils Lofgren – electric guitar, dobro, slide guitar, banjo,
background vocals
Patti Scialfa – background vocals
Garry Tallent – bass
Steve Van Zandt – electric guitar, mandolin,
background vocals
Max Weinberg – drums

Additional musicians
Alliance Singers – choir ("Let's Be Friends (Skin To Skin)"
and "Mary's Place")
Asif Ali Khan and Group – special vocal guests
("Worlds Apart")
Jere Flint – cello ("Lonesome Day" and "You're Missing")

Larry Lemaster – cello ("Lonesome Day" and
   "You're Missing")
Ed Manion – baritone saxophone ("Mary's Place")
Nashville String Machine – strings ("Countin' On A
   Miracle" and "You're Missing")
Brendan O'Brien – hurdy-gurdy, glockenspiel,
   orchestra bells
Mark Pender – trumpet ("Mary's Place")
Rich Rosenberg – trombone ("Mary's Place")
Jane Scarpantoni – cello ("Into The Fire," "Mary's Place,"
   "The Rising," and "My City Of Ruins")
Mike Spengler – trumpet ("Mary's Place")
Soozie Tyrell – violin, background vocals
Jerry Vivino – tenor saxophone ("Mary's Place")

Cover art
Chris Austopchuk – art direction
Dave Bett – art direction and design
Danny Clinch – photography
Michelle Holme – design

Track listing
"Lonesome Day"
"Into The Fire"
"Waitin' On A Sunny Day"
"Nothing Man"
"Countin' On A Miracle"
"Empty Sky"
"Worlds Apart"
"Let's Be Friends (Skin To Skin)"
"Further On (Up The Road)"
"The Fuse"
"Mary's Place"
"You're Missing"
"The Rising"
"Paradise"
"My City Of Ruins"

Release date
July 30, 2002

Label and catalogue numbers
US Columbia CK 86600, UK COL 508000 2

Highest chart position on release
US 1, UK 1

Notes
All songs written by Bruce Springsteen.
Also released in the US and Europe on vinyl as a double
   album (US Columbia C2 86600/Europe COL 508000 1).
"Tour Edition" issued in Europe and Australia in 2003
   (COL 508000 3). It features a bonus DVD containing
   the MTV Video Awards performance of "The Rising,"
   the promo video for "Lonesome Day," and footage
   of "Waitin' On A Sunny Day," "Mary's Place," and
   "Dancing In The Dark" performed in Barcelona on
   October 16, 2002.

DEVILS & DUST 2005
Recorded at Thrill Hill East and Thrill Hill West
   (Springsteen's home studios in New Jersey and
   Beverly Hills)
Additional recording at: Southern Tracks, Atlanta;
   Masterfonics, Nashville
Produced by Brendan O'Brien ("All The Way Home"
   and "Long Time Comin'" by Brendan O'Brien, Bruce
   Springsteen, and Chuck Plotkin)

Personnel
Bruce Springsteen – lead vocals, guitar, keyboards,
   bass, drums, harmonica, tambourine, percussion
Steve Jordan – drums
Brendan O'Brien – hurdy-gurdy, electric sarangi, sitar,
   bass, tambora
Patti Scialfa – background vocals
Soozie Tyrell – violin, background vocals

Additional musicians
Brice Andrus – horn section
Danny Federici – keyboards ("Long Time Comin'")
Lisa Lowell – background vocals ("Jesus Was An Only
   Son" and "All I'm Thinkin' About")
Nashville String Machine – strings
Mark Pender – trumpet ("Leah")
Chuck Plotkin – piano ("All The Way Home")
Marty Rifkin – steel guitar ("All The Way Home" and
   "Long Time Comin'")
Donald Strand – horn section
Susan Welty – horn section
Thomas Witte – horn section

Cover art
Chris Austopchuk – art direction
Dave Bett – art direction and design
Anton Corbijn – photography
Michelle Holme – art direction and design

Track listing
"Devils & Dust"
"All The Way Home"
"Reno"
"Long Time Comin'"
"Black Cowboys"
"Maria's Bed"
"Silver Palomino"
"Jesus Was An Only Son"
"Leah"
"The Hitter"
"All I'm Thinkin' About"
"Matamoros Banks"

Release date
April 25, 2005

Label and catalogue numbers
US Columbia CN 93900, UK COL 520000 2

Highest chart position on release
US 1, UK 1

Notes
All songs written by Bruce Springsteen.
Also released in the US on vinyl as a double album
   (C2 93900).
Standard CD release features a bonus DVD containing
   filmed acoustic performances of "Devils & Dust,"
   "Long Time Comin'," "Reno," "All I'm Thinkin' About,"
   and "Matamoros Banks."

WE SHALL OVERCOME:
THE SEEGER SESSIONS 2006
Recorded at Thrill Hill East (Springsteen's home studio
   in New Jersey)
Produced by Bruce Springsteen

Personnel
The Seeger Sessions Band
Bruce Springsteen – lead vocals, guitar, mandolin,
   B3 organ, piano, percussion, harmonica, tambourine
Sam Bardfield – violin, background vocals
Art Baron – tuba
Frank Bruno – guitar, background vocals
Jeremy Chatzky – upright bass, background vocals
Mark Clifford – banjo, background vocals
Larry Eagle – drums, percussion, background vocals
Charles Giordano – B3 organ, accordion, piano,
   pump organ
Lisa Lowell – background vocals ("Jacob's Ladder,"
   "Eyes On The Prize," and "Froggie Went A Courtin'")
Ed Manion – saxophone, background vocals
Mark Pender – trumpet, background vocals
Richie "La Bamba" Rosenberg – trombone,
   background vocals
Patti Scialfa – background vocals
Soozie Tyrell – violin, background vocals

Cover art
Chris Austopchuk – art direction
Danny Clinch – photography
Meghan Foley – design
Michelle Holme – art direction and design

Track listing
"Old Dan Tucker"
"Jesse James"
"Mrs. McGrath"
"O Mary Don't You Weep"
"John Henry"
"Erie Canal"
"Jacob's Ladder"
"My Oklahoma Home"
"Eyes On The Prize"
"Shenandoah"
"Pay Me My Money Down"
"We Shall Overcome"
"Froggie Went A Courtin'"

Release date
April 24, 2006

Label and catalogue numbers
US Columbia 82876 82867 2, UK 82876 83074 2

Highest chart position on release
US 3, UK 3

Notes
All songs trad./public domain except: "Jesse James" (by Billy Gashade); "Erie Canal" (by Thomas S. Allen); "Jacob's Ladder" (additional words by Pete Seeger); "My Oklahoma Home" (by Bill and Agnes "Sis" Cunningham); "Eyes On The Prize" (additional words by Alice Wine); and "We Shall Overcome" (adaptation by Guy Carawan, Frank Hamilton, Zilphia Horton, and Pete Seeger). All songs arranged by Bruce Springsteen.
Also released in the US on vinyl as a double album (82876 83439 1).
Standard CD release features a bonus DVD containing the entire album in PCM stereo, two extra tracks— "Buffalo Gals" and "How Can I Keep From Singing" (additional words by Doris Plenn)—and a thirty-minute film about the making of the album, including filmed performances of "John Henry," "Pay Me My Money Down," "Buffalo Gals," "Erie Canal," "O Mary Don't You Weep," and "Shenandoah."
"American Land Edition" issued in the US and Europe in October 2006 (US 82876 82867 2/Europe 88697009162). As well as everything on the standard edition, it features an additional three bonus tracks— "How Can A Poor Man Stand Such Times And Live" (by "Blind" Alfred Reed with additional words by Bruce Springsteen), "Bring 'Em Home" (by Pete Seeger with additional words by Jim Musselman), and "American Land" (by Bruce Springsteen). The film contains an additional ten minutes and there are also promo videos for "American Land" and "Pay Me My Money Down" and live footage of "How Can A Poor Man Stand Such Times And Live" and "Bring 'Em Home."

MAGIC 2007
Recorded at Southern Tracks, Atlanta
Produced by Brendan O'Brien

Personnel
The E Street Band
Bruce Springsteen – lead vocals, guitars, pump organ, harmonica, synthesizer, glockenspiel, percussion
Roy Bittan – piano, organ
Clarence Clemons – saxophone, background vocals
Danny Federici – organ, keyboards
Nils Lofgren – guitars, background vocals
Patti Scialfa – background vocals
Garry Tallent – bass
Steve Van Zandt – guitars, mandolin, background vocals
Max Weinberg – drums

Additional musicians
Jeremy Chatzky – upright bass ("Magic")
Daniel Laufer – cello ("Devil's Arcade")
Soozie Tyrell – violin
Patrick Warren – Chamberlin, tack piano

String section ("Your Own Worst Enemy" and "Girls In Their Summer Clothes"):
Justin Bruns, Jay Christy, Sheela Lyengar, John Meisner, William Pu, Christopher Pulgram, Olga Shpitko, Kenn Wagner – violins
Amy Chang, Tania Maxwell Clements, Lachlan McBane – violas
Karen Freer, Charae Kruege, Daniel Laufer – cellos

Cover art
Chris Austopchuk – art direction
Danny Clinch – photography
Michelle Holme – art direction
Mark Seliger – photography

Track listing
"Radio Nowhere"
"You'll Be Comin' Down"
"Livin' In The Future"
"Your Own Worst Enemy"
"Gypsy Biker"
"Girls In Their Summer Clothes"
"I'll Work For Your Love"
"Magic"
"Last To Die"
"Long Walk Home"
"Devil's Arcade"
"Terry's Song"

Release date
October 2, 2007

Label and catalogue number
Columbia 88697 17060 2

Highest chart position on release
US 1, UK 1

Notes
All songs written by Bruce Springsteen.
"Terry's Song" is a hidden track.
Also released in the US and Europe on vinyl (88697 17060 1).

WORKING ON A DREAM 2009
Recorded at Southern Track, Atlanta
Additional recording at: Avatar Studios, New York City; Clinton Studios, New York City; Henson Studios, Los Angeles; Thrill Hill East (Springsteen's home studio in New Jersey)
Produced by Brendan O'Brien

Personnel
The E Street Band
Bruce Springsteen – lead vocals, guitars, harmonica, keyboards, glockenspiel, percussion
Roy Bittan – piano, organ, accordion
Clarence Clemons – saxophone, background vocals
Danny Federici – organ
Nils Lofgren – guitars, background vocals
Patti Scialfa – background vocals
Garry Tallent – bass
Steve Van Zandt – guitars, background vocals
Max Weinberg – drums

Additional musicians
Jason Federici – accordion ("The Last Carnival")
Eddie Horst – string and horn arrangements ("Outlaw Pete," "Tomorrow Never Knows," "Kingdom Of Days," and "Surprise, Surprise")
Soozie Tyrell – violin, background vocals
Patrick Warren – organ ("Outlaw Pete"), piano ("This Life"), keyboards ("Tomorrow Never Knows")

Cover art
Chris Austopchuk – art direction
Dave Bett – art direction
Danny Clinch – photography
Michelle Holme – art direction
Jennifer Tzar – photography

Track listing
"Outlaw Pete"
"My Lucky Day"
"Working On A Dream"
"Queen Of The Supermarket"
"What Love Can Do"
"This Life"
"Good Eye"
"Tomorrow Never Knows"
"Life Itself"
"Kingdom Of Days"
"Surprise, Surprise"
"The Last Track"
"The Wrestler" (bonus track)

Release date
January 27, 2009

Label and catalogue number
Columbia 88697 41355 2

Highest chart position on release
US 1, UK 1

Notes
All songs written by Bruce Springsteen.
Also released in the US and Europe on vinyl as a double album (US 88697 41355 1/Europe 88697 45316 1).
"Deluxe Edition" (88697 43931 2) features a bonus "Sessions DVD" containing a video of extra song "A Night With The Jersey Devil" (by Bruce Springsteen

with elements of "Baby Blue" by Robert Jones and Gene Vincent), and a forty-minute "making of" film, including studio performances of "My Lucky Day," "Queen Of The Supermarket," "Kingdom of Days," "Tomorrow Never Knows/What Love Can Do/ This Life," "Life Itself," "Working On A Dream," and "The Last Carnival."

WRECKING BALL 2012

Recorded at Stone Hill Studio (Springsteen's home studio in New Jersey)
Additional recording at MSR Studios, New York City
Produced by Ron Aniello and Bruce Springsteen

Personnel
Bruce Springsteen – lead vocals, guitars, banjo, piano, organ, drums, percussion, loops
Ron Aniello – guitar, bass, keyboards, piano, drums, loops, background vocals
Art Baron – euphonium, tuba, sousaphone, penny whistle
Clarence Clemons – saxophone ("Wrecking Ball" and "Land Of Hope And Dreams")
Clark Gayton – trombone
Charles Giordano – accordion, piano, B3 organ
Stan Harrison – clarinet, alto saxophone, tenor saxophone
Dan Levine – alto horn, euphonium
Lisa Lowell – background vocals
Ed Manion – tenor saxophone, baritone saxophone
Curt Ramm – trumpet, cornet
Patti Scialfa – background vocals, vocal arrangements
Soozie Tyrrell – violin, background vocals
Max Weinberg – drums ("Wrecking Ball" and "We Are Alive")

Additional musicians
Tiffeny Andrews – background vocals ("Easy Money")
Lilly Brown – background vocals ("Easy Money")
Kevin Buell – drums and background vocals ("Death To My Hometown")
Corinda Carford – background vocals ("Easy Money")
Matt Chamberlain – drums and percussion ("Shackled And Drawn," "Death To My Hometown," and "You've Got It")
Soloman Cobbs – background vocals ("Easy Money")
Steve Jordan – percussion ("Easy Money")
Rob Lebret – electric guitar ("Wrecking Ball"), background vocals ("Death To My Hometown," "Wrecking Ball," and "You've Got It")
Greg Leisz – banjo, mandola, lap steel ("We Are Alive" and "You've Got It")
Darrell Leonard – trumpet and bass trumpet ("We Are Alive")
Cindy Mizelle – background vocals ("Shackled And Drawn")
Michelle Moore – background vocals ("Easy Money," "Rocky Ground," and "Land Of Hope And Dreams")

Tom Morello – electric guitar ("Jack Of All Trades" and "This Depression")
Marc Muller – pedal steel guitar ("Wrecking Ball")
New York Chamber Consort – strings ("We Take Care Of Our Own," "Jack Of All Trades," and "Wrecking Ball")
Clif Norrell – background vocals
Ross Peterson – background vocals
Antoinette Savage – background vocals ("Easy Money")
Victorious Gospel Choir – choir ("Rocky Ground" and "Land Of Hope And Dreams")

Cover art
Dave Bett – art direction and design
Danny Clinch – photography
Michelle Holme – art direction and design

Track listing
"We Take Care Of Our Own"
"Easy Money"
"Shackled And Drawn"
"Jack Of All Trades"
"Death To My Hometown"
"This Depression"
"Wrecking Ball"
"You've Got It"
"Rocky Ground"
"Land Of Hope And Dreams"
"We Are Alive"

Release date
March 6, 2012

Label and catalogue number
Columbia 88691 94254 2

Highest chart position on release
US 1, UK 1

Notes
All songs written by Bruce Springsteen. "Shackled And Drawn" contains elements of "Me And My Baby Got Our Own Thing Going" (by James Brown, Lyn Collins, Fred Wesley, and Charles Bobbitt); "Death To My Hometown" contains excerpts from "The Last Words Of Copernicus" (Alabama Sacred Harp Convention); "Rocky Ground" contains an excerpt from "I'm A Soldier In The Army Of The Lord" (traditional); "Land Of Hope And Dreams" contains elements of "People Get Ready" (by Curtis Mayfield).
Also released in the US and Europe on vinyl as a double album (88691 94254 1). The package contained a copy of the standard album on CD.
"Special Edition" (88691 94836 2) features two bonus tracks—"Swallowed Up (In The Belly Of The Whale)" and "American Land" (inspired by "He Lies In The American Land" by Andrew Kovaly and Pete Seeger).

HIGH HOPES 2014

Recorded at: Thrill Hill Recording/Stone Hill Studio (Springsteen's home studio in New Jersey); Very Loud House, Los Angeles; Renegade Studio, New York City; Veritas Studio (Tom Morello's home studio in Los Angeles); Southern Tracks, Atlanta; East West Studios, Los Angeles; NRG Studios, Los Angeles; Village Studios, Los Angeles; Studios 301, Byron Bay and Sydney, Australia; Record Plant, Los Angeles; Electric Lady Studios, New York City; Avatar Studios, New York City; Sear Sound, New York City; Berkeley Street Studio, Santa Monica, California
Produced by Ron Aniello with Bruce Springsteen ("Harry's Place," "Down In The Hole," and "Hunter Of Invisible Game" by Brendan O'Brien; "Heaven's Wall" by Brendan O'Brien, Ron Aniello, and Bruce Springsteen)

Personnel
The E Street Band
Bruce Springsteen – lead vocals, guitars, bass, banjo, mandolin, organ, piano, synthesizer, vibraphone, harmonium, drums, percussion loop
Roy Bittan – piano, organ
Clarence Clemons – saxophone ("Harry's Place" and "Down In The Hole")
Danny Federici – organ ("Down In The Hole" and "The Wall")
Nils Lofgren – guitars, background vocals
Patti Scialfa – background vocals
Garry Tallent – bass
Steve Van Zandt – guitars, background vocals
Max Weinberg – drums

Special guest
Tom Morello – guitar, background vocals (and lead vocals on "The Ghost Of Tom Joad")

Additional musicians
Tawatha Agee – background vocals ("Heaven's Wall")
Ron Aniello – drum and percussion loops, bass, synthesizers, guitar, twelve-string guitar, percussion, organ, Farfisa, accordion, vibraphone
Atlanta Strings – strings ("Harry's Place" and "Hunter Of Invisible Game")
Sam Bardfeld – violin ("Heaven's Wall," "Frankie Fell In Love," and "This Is Your Sword")
Everett Bradley – background vocals, percussion
Jake Clemons – saxophone, background vocals
Barry Danielian – trumpet
Keith Fluitt – background vocals ("Heaven's Wall")
Josh Freese – drums ("This Is Your Sword")
Clark Gayton – trombone, tuba
Charles Giordano – organ, accordion, keyboards
Stan Harrison – saxophone
John James – background vocals ("Heaven's Wall")
Jeff Kievit – piccolo trumpet ("Just Like Fire Would")
Curtis King – background vocals
Ed Manion – saxophone

Cindy Mizelle – background vocals
Michelle Moore – background vocals
New York Chamber Consort Strings – strings
  ("Just Like Fire Would," "Heaven's Wall," and
  "Dream Baby Dream")
Curt Ramm – trumpet, cornet
Evan, Jessie, and Sam Springsteen – background vocals
  ("Down In The Hole")
Al Thornton – background vocals ("Heaven's Wall")
Scott Tibbs – horn orchestration
Soozie Tyrell – violin, background vocals
Cillian Vallely – uilleann pipes, hi & lo whistle
  ("This Is Your Sword")
Brenda White – background vocals ("Heaven's Wall")

Cover art
Danny Clinch – photography
Michelle Holme – art direction and design

Track listing
"High Hopes"
"Harry's Place"
"American Skin (41 Shots)"
"Just Like Fire Would"
"Down In The Hole"
"Heaven's Wall"
"Frankie Fell In Love"
"This Is Your Sword"
"Hunter Of Invisible Game"
"The Ghost Of Tom Joad"
"The Wall"
"Dream Baby Dream"

Release date
January 13, 2014

Label and catalogue number
Columbia 88843 01546 2

Highest chart position on release
US 1, UK 1

Notes
All songs written by Bruce Springsteen except:
  "High Hopes" (by Tim Scott McConnell); "Just Like Fire
  Would" (by Chris J. Bailey); and "Dream Baby Dream"
  (by Martin Rev and Alan Vega).
Also released in the US and Europe on vinyl as a double
  album (88843 01546 1). The package contained a
  copy of the standard album on CD.
"Limited Edition" (88843 03210 2) features a bonus
  DVD—*Born in the U.S.A. Live* (88843 02903 2)—which
  is a recording of a full-album performance at Hard
  Rock Calling, Queen Elizabeth Olympic Park, London
  on June 30, 2013.

LIVE ALBUMS

LIVE/1975–85 1986
Recorded at various venues from October 1975 to
  September 1985
Produced by Jon Landau, Chuck Plotkin, and Bruce
  Springsteen

Personnel
The E Street Band
Bruce Springsteen – lead vocals, electric guitar,
  harmonica, acoustic guitar
Roy Bittan – piano, synthesizer, background vocals
Clarence Clemons – saxophone, percussion,
  background vocals
Danny Federici – organ, accordion, glockenspiel, piano,
  synthesizer, background vocals
Nils Lofgren (from 1984) – electric guitar, acoustic
  guitar, background vocals
Patti Scialfa (from 1984) – background vocals,
  synthesizer
Garry Tallent – bass, background vocals
Steve Van Zandt (up to 1981) – electric guitar,
  acoustic guitar, background vocals
Max Weinberg – drums

Additional musicians
Flo and Eddie (Howard Kaylan and Mark Volman) –
  background vocals ("Hungry Heart")
The Miami Horns – horns ("Tenth Avenue Freeze-Out")

Cover art
Sandra Choron – art direction
Neal Preston – cover photography

Side one
"Thunder Road"
"Adam Raised A Cain"
"Spirit In The Night"
"4th Of July, Asbury Park (Sandy)"

Side two
"Paradise By The 'C'"
"Fire"
"Growin' Up"
"It's Hard To Be A Saint In The City"

Side three
"Backstreets"
"Rosalita (Come Out Tonight)"
"Raise Your Hand"

Side four
"Hungry Heart"
"Two Hearts"
"Cadillac Ranch"
"You Can Look (But You Better Not Touch)"
"Independence Day"

Side five
"Badlands"
"Because The Night"
"Candy's Room"
"Darkness On The Edge Of Town"
"Racing In The Street"

Side six
"This Land Is Your Land"
"Nebraska"
"Johnny 99"
"Reason To Believe"

Side seven
"Born In The U.S.A."
"Seeds"
"The River"

Side eight
"War"
"Darlington County"
"Working On The Highway"
"The Promised Land"

Side nine
"Cover Me"
"I'm On Fire"
"Bobby Jean"
"My Hometown"

Side ten
"Born To Run"
"No Surrender"
"Tenth Avenue Freeze-Out"
"Jersey Girl"

Release date
November 10, 1986

Label and catalogue numbers
Vinyl: US Columbia C5X 40558, UK CBS 450227 1
CD: US Columbia C3K 40558, UK CBS 450227 2

Highest chart position on release
US 1, UK 4

Notes
All songs written by Bruce Springsteen except:
  "Raise Your Hand" (by Steve Cropper, Eddie Floyd,
  and Alvertis Isbell); "Because The Night" (by Bruce
  Springsteen and Patti Smith); "This Land Is Your Land"
  (by Woody Guthrie); "War" (by Barrett Strong and
  Norman Whitfield); and "Jersey Girl" (by Tom Waits).
Reissued and repackaged in the US in 1997
  (C3K 65328); and in the US and Europe in 2002
  (US C3K 86570, Europe 508125 2).

IN CONCERT/MTV PLUGGED 1993
Recorded at Warner Hollywood Studios, Los Angeles, September 22, 1992
Produced by Jon Landau and Bruce Springsteen

Personnel
Bruce Springsteen – lead vocals, lead and rhythm guitar, harmonica
Zachary Alford – drums
Roy Bittan – keyboards
Gia Ciambotti – background vocals
Carol Dennis – background vocals
Shane Fontayne – lead and rhythm guitar
Cleopatra Kennedy – background vocals
Bobby King – background vocals
Angel Rogers – background vocals
Patti Scialfa – acoustic guitar, harmony vocals ("Human Touch")
Tommy Sims – bass
Crystal Taliefero – acoustic guitar, percussion, background vocals

Cover art
Sandra Choron – art direction
Neal Preston – cover photography

Side one
"Red Headed Woman"
"Better Days"
"Atlantic City"
"Darkness On The Edge Of Town"

Side two
"Man's Job"
"Human Touch"
"Lucky Town"

Side three
"I Wish I Were Blind"
"Thunder Road"
"Light Of Day"

Side four
"If I Should Fall Behind"
"Living Proof"
"My Beautiful Reward"

Release date
April 12, 1993

Label and catalogue numbers
Vinyl: Europe only COL 473860 1
CD: US COL CK 68730, Europe COL 473860 2

Highest chart position on release
US 189, UK 4

Notes
All songs written by Bruce Springsteen.
First released in the US in August 1997.

Footage from this event was first released on a two-hour VHS video in 1992 with the following track listing: "Red headed Woman"/"Better Days"/ "Local Hero"/"Atlantic City"/"Darkness On The Edge Of Town"/"Man's Job"/"Growin' Up"/"Human Touch"/"Lucky Town"/"I Wish I Were Blind"/"Thunder Road"/"Light Of Day"/"The Big Muddy"/"57 Channels (And Nothin' On)"/"My Beautiful Reward"/"Glory Days" plus bonus songs not included in the MTV show— "Living Proof," "If I Should Fall Behind," and "Roll Of The Dice." The video was reissued on DVD in 2004.

LIVE IN NEW YORK CITY 2001
Recorded at Madison Square Garden, New York City, June 29 and July 1, 2000
Produced by Bruce Springsteen and Chuck Plotkin

Personnel
The E Street Band
Bruce Springsteen – lead vocals, guitars, harmonica
Roy Bittan – keyboards
Clarence Clemons – percussion, saxophone
Danny Federici – keyboards
Nils Lofgren – electric guitar, background vocals
Patti Scialfa – background vocals, acoustic guitar
Garry Tallent – bass
Steve Van Zandt – electric guitar, background vocals
Max Weinberg – drums

Cover art
Sandra Choron – art direction
Neal Preston – cover photography

Disc one
"My Love Will Not Let You Down"
"Prove It All Night"
"Two Hearts"
"Atlantic City"
"Mansion On The Hill"
"The River"
"Youngstown"
"Murder Incorporated"
"Badlands"
"Out In The Street"
"Born To Run"

Disc two
"Tenth Avenue Freeze-Out"
"Land Of Hope And Dreams"
"American Skin (41 Shots)"
"Lost In The Flood"
"Born In The U.S.A."
"Don't Look Back"
"Jungleland"
"Ramrod"
"If I Should Fall Behind"

Release date
March 27, 2001

Label and catalogue numbers
US COL C2K 85490, Europe COL 500000 2

Highest chart position on release
US 5, UK 12

Notes
All songs written by Bruce Springsteen. "Two Hearts" includes a brief rendition of "It Takes Two" (by Sylvia Moy and William "Mickey" Stevenson); "Tenth Avenue Freeze-Out" incorporates sections of "Take Me To The River" (by Al Green and Mabon "Teenie" Hodges), "It's All Right" (by Curtis Mayfield), and "Rumble Doll" (by Patti Scialfa).
Also released in 2001 on vinyl as a triple album (US COL C3 85490, Europe COL 500000 1).
A double-DVD package (SONY 54071 9) of the same name contained, on disc one, a special band interview with Bob Costas, plus footage of the following songs: "My Love Will Not Let You Down"/"Prove It All Night"/"Two Hearts"/"Atlantic City"/"Mansion On The Hill"/"The River"/"Youngstown"/"Murder Incorporated"/"Badlands"/"Out In The Street"/ "Tenth Avenue Freeze-Out"/"Born To Run"/"Land Of Hope And Dreams"/"American Skin (41 Shots)." Disc two contained previously unseen performances of: "Backstreets"/"Don't Look Back"/"Darkness On The Edge Of Town"/"Lost In The Flood"/"Born In The U.S.A."/"Jungleland"/"Light Of Day"/"The Promise"/"Thunder Road"/"Ramrod"/"If I Should Fall Behind." The DVD package also included a limited-edition bonus CD containing "My Hometown" and "This Hard Land."

HAMMERSMITH ODEON LONDON '75 2006
Recorded at the Hammersmith Odeon, London, November 18, 1975
Produced by Bruce Springsteen and Jon Landau

Personnel
The E Street Band
Bruce Springsteen – lead vocals, guitars, harmonica
Roy Bittan – piano, background vocals
Clarence Clemons – percussion, saxophone
Danny Federici – keyboards
Garry Tallent – bass
Steve Van Zandt – guitar, slide guitar, background vocals
Max Weinberg – drums

Cover art
Christopher Austopchuk – art direction
David Bett – art direction
Michelle Holme – art direction

Disc one
"Thunder Road"
"Tenth Avenue Freeze-Out"

"Spirit In The Night"
"Lost In The Flood"
"She's The One"
"Born To Run"
"The E Street Shuffle"
"It's Hard To Be A Saint In The City"
"Kitty's Back"
"Backstreets"

Disc two
"Jungleland"
"Rosalita (Come Out Tonight)"
"4th Of July, Asbury Park (Sandy)"
"Detroit Medley"
"For You"
"Quarter To Three"

Release date
February 28, 2006

Label and catalogue number
Columbia 82876 77995 2

Highest chart position on release
US 93, UK 33

Notes
All songs written by Bruce Springsteen except: "Detroit Medley," which consists of "Devil With A Blue Dress On" (by William Stevenson and Frederick "Shorty" Long), "C. C. Rider" (by Gertrude "Ma" Rainey and Lena Arant), "Good Golly Miss Molly" (by Robert Blackwell and John Marascalco), and "Jenny Takes A Ride" (by Bob Crewe, Enotris Johnson, and Richard Penniman); and "Quarter To Three" (by Gene Barge, Frank J. Guida, Joseph F. Royster, and Gary Anderson). "Spirit In The Night" contains a section of "Stagger Lee" (traditional); "The E Street Shuffle" contains a portion of "Having A Party" (by Sam Cooke); "Kitty's Back" contains a portion of "Moondance" (by Van Morrison); "Rosalita (Come Out Tonight)" contains portions of "Come A Little Closer" (by Tommy Boyce, Bobby Hart, and Wes Ferrell) and "Theme From *Shaft*" (by Isaac Hayes).
First released as a DVD in 2005 as part of the *Born to Run* Thirtieth Anniversary Edition box set (C3K 94175).

LIVE IN DUBLIN 2007
Recorded at the Point Theatre, Dublin, November 17–19, 2006
Produced by Bruce Springsteen and Jon Landau

Personnel
The Sessions Band
Bruce Springsteen – lead vocals, guitar, harmonica
Sam Bardfield – violin, background vocals
Art Baron – sousaphone, trombone, mandolin, penny whistle, euphonium
Frank Bruno – acoustic guitar, field drum, background vocals

Jeremy Chatzky – upright bass, bass guitar
Larry Eagle – drums, percussion
Clark Gayton – trombone, percussion, background vocals
Charles Giordano – accordion, piano, Hammond organ, background vocals
Curtis King Jr. – percussion, background vocals
Greg Leisz – banjo, background vocals
Lisa Lowell – background vocals, percussion
Ed Manion – tenor saxophone, baritone saxophone, percussion, background vocals
Cindy Mizelle – background vocals, percussion
Curt Ramm – trumpet, percussion, background vocals
Marty Rifkin – steel guitar, dobro, mandolin
Patti Scialfa – acoustic guitar, background vocals
Soozie Tyrell – violin, background vocals

Cover art
Christopher Austopchuk – art direction
Michelle Holme – art direction, design

Disc one
"Atlantic City"
"Old Dan Tucker"
"Eyes On The Prize"
"Jesse James"
"Further On (Up The Road)"
"O Mary Don't You Weep"
"Erie Canal"
"If I Should Fall Behind"
"My Oklahoma Home"
"Highway Patrolman"
"Mrs. McGrath"
"How Can A Poor Man Stand Such Times And Live"
"Jacob's Ladder"

Disc two
"Long Time Comin'"
"Open All Night"
"Pay Me My Money Down"
"Growin' Up"
"When The Saints Go Marching In"
"This Little Light Of Mine"
"American Land"
"Blinded By The Light" (bonus track)
"Love Of The Common People" (bonus track)
"We Shall Overcome" (bonus track)

Release date
June 5, 2007

Label and catalogue numbers
US COL 886970958226, Europe COL 88697095822

Highest chart position on release
US 23, UK 21

Notes
See listing for *We Shall Overcome: The Seeger Sessions* for songwriting credits from that album.

All other songs written by Bruce Springsteen except: "When The Saints Go Marching In" and "This Little Light Of Mine" (traditional); and "Love Of The Common People" (by John Hurley and Ronnie Wilkins).
Also released in a DVD package (US COL 886971013924, Europe COL 88697108762).
A special edition of the DVD was given as a thank you for donating to PBS and contains five extra songs: "Bobby Jean"/"The Ghost Of Tom Joad"/"Johnny 99"/"For You"/"My City Of Ruins."

COMPILATIONS

GREATEST HITS
Released February 27, 1995
US COL C2 67060, Europe COL 478555 2
US 1, UK 1

Track listing
"Born To Run"
"Thunder Road"
"Badlands"
"The River"
"Hungry Heart"
"Atlantic City"
"Dancing In The Dark"
"Born In The U.S.A."
"My Hometown"
"Glory Days"
"Brilliant Disguise"
"Human Touch"
"Better Days"
"Streets Of Philadelphia"
"Secret Garden"
"Murder Incorporated"
"Blood Brothers"
"This Hard Land"

Notes
All songs written by Bruce Springsteen.

TRACKS
Released November 10, 1998
US COL CXK 69475, Europe COL 492605 2
US 27, UK 50

Disc one
"Mary Queen Of Arkansas"
"It's Hard To Be A Saint In The City"
"Growin' Up"
"Does This Bus Stop At 82nd Street?"
"Bishop Danced"
"Santa Ana"
"Seaside Bar Song"
"Zero And Blind Terry"
"Linda Let Me Be The One"

"Thundercrack"
"Rendezvous"
"Give The Girl A Kiss"
"Iceman"
"Bring On The Night"
"So Young And In Love"
"Hearts Of Stone"
"Don't Look Back"

Disc two
"Restless Nights"
"A Good Man Is Hard To Find (Pittsburgh)"
"Roulette"
"Dollhouse"
"Where The Bands Are"
"Loose Ends"
"Living On The Edge Of The World"
"Wages Of Sin"
"Take 'Em As They Come"
"Be True"
"Ricky Wants A Man Of Her Own"
"I Wanna Be With You"
"Mary Lou"
"Stolen Car"
"Born In The U.S.A."
"Johnny Bye-Bye"
"Shut Out The Light"

Disc three
"Cynthia"
"My Love Will Not Let You Down"
"This Hard Land"
"Frankie"
"TV Movie"
"Stand On It"
"Lion's Den"
"Car Wash"
"Rockaway The Days"
"Brothers Under The Bridges ('83)"
"Man At The Top"
"Pink Cadillac"
"Two For The Road"
"Janey, Don't You Lose Heart"
"When You Need Me"
"The Wish"
"The Honeymooners"
"Lucky Man"

Disc four
"Leavin' Train"
"Seven Angels"
"Gave It A Name"
"Sad Eyes"
"My Lover Man"
"Over The Rise"
"When The Lights Go Out"
"Loose Change"
"Trouble In Paradise"
"Happy"
"Part Man, Part Monkey"

"Goin' Cali"
"Back In Your Arms"
"Brothers Under The Bridge"

Notes
All songs written by Bruce Springsteen.

18 TRACKS
Released April 13, 1999
COL 494200 2
US 64, UK 23

Track listing
"Growin' Up"
"Seaside Bar Song"
"Rendezvous"
"Hearts Of Stone"
"Where The Bands Are"
"Loose Ends"
"I Wanna Be With You"
"Born In The U.S.A."
"My Love Will Not Let You Down"
"Lion's Den"
"Pink Cadillac"
"Janey, Don't You Lose Heart"
"Sad Eyes"
"Part Man, Part Monkey"
"Trouble River"
"Brothers Under The Bridge"
"The Fever"
"The Promise"

Notes
All songs written by Bruce Springsteen.
Contains a selection of the songs from *Tracks*, as well as
    two additional songs: "The Fever" and "The Promise."

THE ESSENTIAL BRUCE SPRINGSTEEN
Released November 11, 2003
US COL C2K 90773, Europe COL 513700 9
US 14, UK 28

Disc one
"Blinded By The Light"
"For You"
"Spirit In The Night"
"4th Of July, Asbury Park (Sandy)"
"Rosalita (Come Out Tonight)"
"Thunder Road"
"Born To Run"
"Jungleland"
"Badlands"
"Darkness On The Edge Of Town"
"The Promised Land"
"The River"
"Hungry Heart"
"Nebraska"
"Atlantic City"

Disc two
"Born In The U.S.A."
"Glory Days"
"Dancing In The Dark"
"Tunnel Of Love"
"Brilliant Disguise"
"Human Touch"
"Living Proof"
"Lucky Town"
"Streets Of Philadelphia"
"The Ghost Of Tom Joad"
"The Rising"
"Mary's Place"
"Lonesome Day"
"American Skin (41 Shots) (Live)"
"Land Of Hope And Dreams (Live)"

Bonus disc
"From Small Things (Big Things One Day Come)"
"The Big Payback"
"Held Up Without A Gun (Live)"
"Trapped (Live)"
"None But The Brave"
"Missing"
"Lift Me Up"
"Viva Las Vegas"
"County Fair"
"Code Of Silence (Live)"
"Dead Man Walkin'"
"Countin' On A Miracle (Acoustic)"

Notes
All songs written by Bruce Springsteen except:
    "Trapped (Live)" (by Jimmy Cliff); "Viva Las Vegas"
    (by Doc Pomus and Mort Shuman); and "Code
    Of Silence (Live)" (by Bruce Springsteen and
    Joe Grushecky).
Reissued in Europe without the bonus disc
    in 2003 (COL 513700 2) and 2011
    (COL 88697973592).

GREATEST HITS (BRUCE SPRINGSTEEN & THE E STREET BAND)
Released January 13, 2009
US COL 88697439302, Europe COL 88697532812
US 43, UK 3

Track listing
"Blinded By The Light"
"Rosalita (Come Out Tonight)"
"Born To Run"
"Thunder Road"
"Badlands"
"Darkness On The Edge Of Town"
"Hungry Heart"
"The River"
"Born In The U.S.A."
"Glory Days"
"Dancing In The Dark"

"The Rising"
"Lonesome Day"
"Radio Nowhere"

Notes
All songs written by Bruce Springsteen.
The US edition was initially available exclusively at Wal-Mart. The European limited tour edition also includes "Long Walk Home" as the final track, as well as two bonus tracks: "Because The Night (Live)" (by Bruce Springsteen and Patti Smith) and "Fire (Live)."

THE PROMISE
Released November 16, 2010
COL 88697 76177 2
US 16, UK 7

Disc one
"Racing In The Street ('78)"
"Gotta Get That Feeling"
"Outside Looking In"
"Someday (We'll Be Together)"
"One Way Street"
"Because The Night"
"Wrong Side Of The Street"
"The Brokenhearted"
"Rendezvous"
"Candy's Boy"

Disc two
"Save My Love"
"Ain't Good Enough For You"
"Fire"
"Spanish Eyes"
"It's A Shame"
"Come On (Let's Go Tonight)"
"Talk To Me"
"The Little Things (My Baby Does)"
"Breakaway"
"The Promise"
"City Of Night"

Notes
All songs written by Bruce Springsteen except "Because The Night" (by Bruce Springsteen and Patti Smith). There is a hidden track at the end of the second disc: "The Way."
The Promise: The Darkness on the Edge of Town Story six-disc box set (US 88697 76525 2, Europe 88697 78230 2) was released on the same day. As well as the two-CD compilation described above, it contained: a remastered CD of the original album; a documentary DVD, *The Promise: The Making of Darkness on the Edge of Town*; a DVD containing a 2009 live performance of the full album at the Paramount Theater, Asbury Park, as well as archive footage from rehearsals, sessions, and concerts dating from 1976–1978; and a DVD of a full concert, *Houston '78 Bootleg: House Cut*.

COLLECTION: 1973–2012
Released March 8, 2013
Australia/Europe COL 88765 453852
US not released, UK did not chart

Track listing
"Rosalita (Come Out Tonight)"
"Thunder Road"
"Born To Run"
"Badlands"
"The Promised Land"
"Hungry Heart"
"Atlantic City"
"Born In The U.S.A."
"Dancing In The Dark"
"Brilliant Disguise"
"Human Touch"
"Streets Of Philadelphia"
"The Ghost Of Tom Joad"
"The Rising"
"Radio Nowhere"
"Working On A Dream"
"We Take Care Of Our Own"
"Wrecking Ball"

Notes
All songs written by Bruce Springsteen.
Initially released only in Australia as a limited tour edition. Released in Europe in April 2013. Not officially released in the US, but given away as a free promo (88765 456062) to attendees of the 2013 MusiCares Person of the Year awards.

SINGLES AND EPS

This selection is not exhaustive and does not include, for example, promos, reissues, or every alternative B-side.

1973
"Blinded By The Light"/"The Angel" (US did not chart)
"Spirit In The Night"/"For You" (US DNC)

1974
"4th of July, Asbury Park (Sandy)"/"The E Street Shuffle" (Germany)

1975
"Born To Run"/"Meeting Across The River" (US 23, UK 93)
"Tenth Avenue Freeze-Out"/"She's The One" (US 83, UK DNC)
"Rosalita (Come Out Tonight)"/"Night" (Netherlands)

1978
"Prove It All Night"/"Factory" (US 33, UK DNC)
"Badlands"/"Streets Of Fire" (US 42, UK DNC)
"The Promised Land"/"Streets Of Fire" (Europe)

1980
"Hungry Heart"/"Held Up Without A Gun" (US 5, UK 44)

1981
"Fade Away"/"Be True" (US 20)
"Sherry Darling"/"Be True" (UK DNC)
"Cadillac Ranch"/"Wreck On The Highway" (UK DNC)
"I Wanna Marry You"/"Be True" (Japan)
"The River"/"Independence Day" (UK 35)
"Point Blank"/"Ramrod" (Europe)
"The Ties That Bind"/"I'm A Rocker" (South Africa)

1982
"Atlantic City"/"Mansion On The Hill" (Europe & Canada)
"Open All Night"/"The Big Payback" (Europe)

1984
"Dancing In The Dark"/"Pink Cadillac" (US 2, UK 4)
"Cover Me"/"Jersey Girl (Live)" (US 7, UK 16)
"Born In The U.S.A."/"Shut Out The Light" (US 9)

1985
"I'm On Fire"/"Johnny Bye Bye" (US 6)
"I'm On Fire"/"Born In The U.S.A." (double A-side) (UK 5)
"Glory Days"/"Stand On It" (US 5, UK 17)
"I'm Going Down"/"Janey, Don't You Lose Heart" (US 9)
"My Hometown"/"Santa Claus Is Coming To Town (Live)" (US 6, UK 9)

1986
"War (Live)"/"Merry Christmas Baby (Live)" (US 8, UK 18)

1987
"Fire (Live)"/"Incident On 57th Street (Live)" (US 46)
"Fire (Live)"/"For You (Live)" (UK 54)
"Born To Run (Live)"/"Johnny 99 (Live)" (UK 16)
"Brilliant Disguise"/"Lucky Man" (US 5, UK 20)
"Tunnel Of Love"/"Two For The Road" (US 9, UK 45)

1988
"One Step Up"/"Roulette" (US 13)
"Tougher Than The Rest"/"Tougher Than The Rest (Live)" (UK 13)
Chimes of Freedom EP: "Tougher Than The Rest (Live)"/"Be True (Live)"/"Chimes Of Freedom (Live)"/"Born To Run (Live)"
"Spare Parts"/"Spare Parts (Live)" (UK 32)

1992
"Human Touch"/"Better Days" (double A-side) (US 16)
"Human Touch"/"Souls Of The Departed" (UK 11)
"Better Days"/"Tougher Than The Rest (Live)" (UK 34)
"57 Channels (And Nothin' On)"/"Part Man, Part Monkey" (US 68)
"57 Channels (And Nothin' On)"/"Stand On It" (UK 32)
"Leap Of Faith"/"Leap Of Faith (Live)" (UK 46)
"If I Should Fall Behind"/"If I Should Fall Behind (Live)" (UK DNC)

1993

"Lucky Town"/"Leap Of Faith (Live)" (Europe)
"Lucky Town (Live)"/"Lucky Town" (UK 48)

1994

"Streets Of Philadelphia"/"If I Should Fall Behind (Live)"
   (US 9, UK 2)

1995

"Murder Incorporated"/"Because The Night (Live)"
   (Europe)
"Secret Garden"/"Thunder Road (Live)" (US 63, UK 44)
"Hungry Heart"/"Streets Of Philadelphia (Live)" (UK 28)

1996

"The Ghost Of Tom Joad"/"Straight Time (Live)"
   (UK 26)
"Dead Man Walkin'"/"This Hard Land (Live)" (Europe)
"Missing"/"Darkness On The Edge Of Town (Live)"
   (Europe)
Blood Brothers EP: "Blood Brothers"/"High Hopes"/
   "Murder Incorporated (Live)"/"Secret Garden (String
   Version)"/"Without You"

1999

"Sad Eyes"/"Missing" (Europe)
"I Wanna Be With You"/"Where The Bands Are"/
   "Born In The U.S.A."/"Back In Your Arms Again"
   (Europe & Japan)

2002

"The Rising"/"Land Of Hope And Dreams (Live)"
   (US 52, UK 94)
"Lonesome Day"/"Spirit In The Night (Live)"/"The Rising
   (Live)"/"Lonesome Day (Video)" (US DNC, UK 39)

2003

"Waitin' On A Sunny Day"/"Born To Run
   (Live)"/"Darkness On The Edge Of Town
   (Live)"/"Thunder Road (Live)" (UK DNC)

2005

"Devils & Dust" (download) (US 72)

2007

"Radio Nowhere" (download) (US 102, UK 96)

2008

"Girls In Their Summer Clothes (Winter Mix)"/"Girls In
   Their Summer Clothes (Album Version)"/"Girls In Their
   Summer Clothes (Video)" (download) (US 52, UK 94)
Magic Tour Highlights EP: "Always A Friend" (with
   Alejandro Escovedo)/"The Ghost Of Tom Joad"
   (with Tom Morello)/"Turn! Turn! Turn!" (with Roger
   McGuinn)/"4th Of July, Asbury Park (Sandy)"
   (Danny Federici's final performance with the
   E Street Band) (US 48)
"Working On A Dream" (download) (US 95, UK 133)
"My Lucky Day" (download) (US DNC, UK DNC)
"The Wrestler" (download) (US 120, UK 93)

2009

"What Love Can Do"/"A Night With The Jersey Devil"
   (limited-edition seven-inch single for 2009 Record
   Store Day)

2010

"Wrecking Ball (Live)"/"The Ghost Of Tom Joad
   (Live with Tom Morello)" (limited-edition ten-inch
   single for 2010 Record Store Day)
"Save My Love"/"Because The Night"
   (limited-edition seven-inch single for 2010
   Black Friday Record Store Day)

2011

Live from the Carousel: "Gotta Get That Feeling"/
   "Racing In The Street ('78)" (limited-edition ten-inch
   single for 2011 Record Store Day)

2012

"We Take Care Of Our Own" (download)
   (US 106, UK 111)
"Death To My Hometown" (download)
   (US DNC, UK DNC)
"Rocky Ground"/"The Promise (Live)" (limited-edition
   seven-inch single for 2012 Record Store Day)

2013

"High Hopes" (download) (US DNC, UK 167)

2014

"Just Like Fire Would" (download) (US DNC, UK DNC)
American Beauty EP: "American Beauty"/"Mary Mary"/
   "Hurry Up Sundown"/"Hey Blue Eyes"
   (limited-edition twelve-inch EP for 2014
   Record Store Day)

OTHER RECORDINGS

1979

No Nukes (Musicians United for Safe Energy)
   "Stay" (with Jackson Browne and Rosemary Butler)
   and "Devil With The Blue Dress Medley"

1987

A Very Special Christmas
   "Merry Christmas Baby"

1988

Folkways: A Vision Shared
   "I Ain't Got No Home" and "Vigilante Man"

1990

Harry Chapin Tribute
   "Remember When The Music"

1991

For Our Children
   "Chicken Lips And Lizard Hips"

1994

A Tribute to Curtis Mayfield
   "Gypsy Woman"

1996

The Concert for the Rock and Roll Hall of Fame
   "Shake, Rattle And Roll," "Great Balls Of Fire," and
   "Whole Lotta Shakin' Goin' On" (with Jerry Lee Lewis)

1998

*Where Have All the Flowers Gone:
   The Songs of Pete Seeger*
   "We Shall Overcome"

2000

Til We Outnumber 'Em
   "Riding My Car" and "Deportee (Plane Wreck
   At Los Gatos)"

2001

America: A Tribute to Heroes
   "My City Of Ruins (Live)"

2002

Kindred Spirits: A Tribute to the Songs of Johnny Cash
   "Give My Love To Rose"

2004

Enjoy Every Sandwich: The Songs of Warren Zevon
   "My Ride's Here"

2007

We All Love Ennio Morricone
   "Once Upon A Time In The West"
Sowing the Seeds: The 10th Anniversary
   "The Ghost Of Tom Joad" (with Pete Seeger)
Give Us Your Poor
   "Hobo's Lullaby" (with the Sessions Band and
   Pete Seeger)

2010

The 25th Anniversary Rock & Roll Hall Of Fame Concerts
   (box set)
   "The Ghost Of Tom Joad" (with Tom Morello),
   "Fortunate Son" (with John Fogerty), "Oh, Pretty
   Woman" (with John Fogerty), "Jungleland," "A Fine
   Fine Boy" (with Darlene Love), "London Calling"
   (with Tom Morello), "New York State Of Mind" (with
   Billy Joel), "Born To Run" (with Billy Joel), "(Your Love
   Keeps Lifting Me) Higher And Higher" (with Darlene
   Love, John Fogerty, Sam Moore, Billy Joel, and Tom
   Morello), "Because The Night" (with U2, Patti Smith,
   and Roy Bittan), "I Still Haven't Found What I'm
   Looking For" (with U2)
Hope for Haiti Now
   "We Shall Overcome (Live)"

2011

The Bridge School Concerts 25th Anniversary Edition
   "Born In The U.S.A. (Live)"

2013

12-12-12: The Concert for Sandy Relief
"Land Of Hope And Dreams (Live)" and
"Wrecking Ball (Live)"

2014

Looking into You: A Tribute to Jackson Browne
"Linda Paloma" (with Patti Scialfa)

GUEST APPEARANCES

1977

Ronnie Spector and the E Street Band: "Say Goodbye
To Hollywood"/"Baby, Please Don't Go"
acoustic guitar

1978

Robert Gordon with Link Wray:
Fresh Fish Special
piano on "Fire"
The Dictators: *Bloodbrothers*
vocal on "Faster And Louder"
Lou Reed: *Street Hassle*
spoken word on "Street Hassle"

1980

Graham Parker: *The Up Escalator*
background vocal on "Endless Night and "Paralyzed"

1981

Gary U.S. Bonds: *Dedication*
co-producer, co-lead vocal on "Jolé Blon"; guitar,
vocal on "This Little Girl"

1982

Gary U.S. Bonds: *On the Line*
co-producer
Donna Summer: *Donna Summer*
guitar, background vocal on "Protection"
Little Steven and the Disciples of Soul:
Men Without Women
harmony vocal on "Men Without Women,"
"Angel Eyes," and "Until The Good Is Gone"

1983

Clarence Clemons and the Red Bank Rockers: *Rescue*
producer, guitar on "Savin' Up"; guitar on "Summer On
Signal Hill"

1985

USA for Africa: *We Are the World*
shared lead vocal on "We Are The World"
Artists United Against Apartheid: *Sun City*
shared lead vocal on "Sun City"

1986

Jersey Artists for Mankind: "We've Got The Love"
guitar solo

1987

Little Steven: *Freedom—No Compromise*
co-lead vocal on "Native American"

1989

Roy Orbison and Friends: *A Black and White Night Live*
guitar, background vocal
L. Shankar with the Epidemics: *Eye Catcher*
harmonica on "Up To You"

1991

Nils Lofgren: *Silver Lining*
background vocal on "Valentine"
Southside Johnny and the Asbury Jukes: *Better Days*
co-lead vocal on "It's Been A Long Time"; keyboard,
guitar, background vocal on "All The Way Home"
John Prine: *The Missing Years*
background vocal on "Take A Look At My Heart"

1993

Patti Scialfa: *Rumble Doll*
guitar, keyboard

1995

Elliott Murphy: *Selling the Gold*
vocal on "Everything I Do (Leads Me Back To You)"
Joe Ely: *Letter to Laredo*
background vocal on "All Just To Get To You" and
"I'm A Thousand Miles From Home"
Joe Grushecky and the Houserockers: *American Babylon*
producer, background vocal

1999

Mike Ness: *Cheating at Solitaire*
vocal, guitar on "Misery Loves Company"
Joe Grushecky and the Houserockers:
Down the Road Apiece—Live
guitar, vocal on "Talking To The King," "Pumping Iron,"
and "Down The Road Apiece"

2000

Emmylou Harris: *Red Dirt Girl*
harmony vocal on "Tragedy"
John Wesley Harding: *Awake*
co-lead vocal on "Wreck On The Highway"

2002

Marah: *Float Away with the Friday Night Gods*
background vocal, guitar solo on "Float Away"

2003

Soozie Tyrell: *White Lines*
guitar on "White Lines"; vocal on "Ste. Genevieve"
Warren Zevon: *The Wind*
guitar, background vocal on "Disorder In The House";
background vocal on "Prison Grove"

2004

Clarence Clemons: *Live in Asbury Park Vol. II*
guitar, vocal on "Raise Your Hand"

Patti Scialfa: *23rd Street Lullaby*
guitar, keyboard on "You Can't Go Back," "Rose,"
and "Love (Stand Up)"
Gary U.S. Bonds: *Back in 20*
vocal on "Can't Teach An Old Dog New Tricks"
Jesse Malin: *Messed Up Here Tonight*
guitar, vocal on "Wendy"

2006

Joe Grushecky: *A Good Life*
vocal, guitar on "Code Of Silence," "Is She The One,"
"A Good Life," and "Searching For My Soul"
Sam Moore: *Overnight Sensational*
vocal on "Better To Have And Not Need"
Jerry Lee Lewis: *Last Man Standing*
background vocal on "Pink Cadillac"

2007

Jesse Malin: *Glitter in the Gutter*
vocal on "Broken Radio"
Patti Scialfa: *Play It as It Lays*
guitar

2009

Bernie Williams: *Moving Forward*
guitar, vocal on "Glory Days"
John Fogerty: *The Blue Ridge Rangers Rides Again*
vocal on "When Will I Be Loved"
Roseanne Cash: *The List*
vocal on "Sea Of Heartbreak"

2010

Alejandro Escovedo: *Street Songs of Love*
vocal on "Faith"
Ray Davies: *See My Friends*
co-lead vocal on "Better Things"

2011

Dropkick Murphys: *Going out in Style*
co-lead vocal on "Peg O' My Heart"
Stewart Francke: *Heartless World*
vocal on "Summer Soldiers (Holler If Ya Hear Me)"

2012

Pete Seeger and Lorre Wyatt: *A More Perfect Union*
co-lead vocal on "God's Counting On Me …
God's Counting On You"
Jimmy Fallon: *Blow Your Pants off*
co-lead vocal on "Neil Young Sings 'Whip My Hair'"

2013

Dropkick Murphys: *Rose Tattoo—For Boston Charity EP*
vocal on "Rose Tattoo"

Overleaf: Atlanta, 2007.

Page 288: Amnesty International
Human Rights Now! tour, 1988.

SOURCES

BOOKS

Alterman, Eric. *Ain't No Sin to Be Glad You're Alive: The Promise of Bruce Springsteen.*
New York: Little, Brown, 1999.

Burger, Jeff, ed. *Springsteen on Springsteen: Interviews, Speeches, and Encounters.*
Chicago: Chicago Review Press, 2013.

Carlin, Peter Ames. *Bruce.* New York: Touchstone, 2012.

Clemons, Clarence, and Don Reo. *Big Man: Real Life & Tall Tales.* New York: Grand Central, 2009.

Cross, Charles R. *Backstreets: Springsteen, the Man and His Music.* New York: Harmony, 1989.

Dylan, Bob. *Chronicles: Volume One.* New York: Simon & Schuster, 2004.

Gilmore, Mikal. *Night Beat: A Shadow History of Rock & Roll.* New York: Doubleday, 1998.

Maharidge, Dale, and Michael S. Williamson. *Journey to Nowhere: The Saga of the New
Underclass.* Rev. ed. New York: Hyperion, 1996.

———. *Someplace Like America: Tales from the Great Depression.* Rev. ed. Berkeley and
Los Angeles: University of California Press, 2011.

Marcus, Greil. *Mystery Train: Images of America in Rock 'n' Roll Music.* Rev. ed.
New York: Plume, 2008.

Marks, Craig, and Rob Tannenbaum. *My MTV: The Uncensored Story of the Music Video
Revolution.* New York: Plume, 2012.

Marsh, Dave. *Born to Run: The Bruce Springsteen Story.* New York: Thunder's Mouth Press, 1979.

Masur, Louis P., and Christopher Phillips, eds. *Talk about a Dream: The Essential Interviews of
Bruce Springsteen.* New York: Bloomsbury, 2013.

O'Connor, Flannery. *A Good Man Is Hard to Find and Other Stories.* New York: Harcourt,
Brace & Company, 1955.

Rolling Stone magazine, ed. *Bruce Springsteen: The Ultimate Compendium of Interviews,
Articles, Facts, and Opinions from the Files of* Rolling Stone. Boston: Hyperion, 1996.

Santelli, Robert. *Greetings from E Street: The Story of Bruce Springsteen and the E Street Band.*
San Francisco: Chronicle, 2006.

Spera, Keith. *Groove Interrupted: Loss, Renewal, and the Music of New Orleans.* New York:
St. Martin's Press, 2011.

Springsteen, Bruce. *Songs.* New York: HarperCollins, 1998.

St John, Lauren. *Hardcore Troubadour: The Life and Near Death of Steve Earle.* New York:
Fourth Estate, 2003.

FEATURES AND INTERVIEWS

Arax, Mark, and Tom Gorman. "California's Illicit Farm Belt Export." *Los Angeles Times*,
March 13, 1995.

Bangs, Lester. Review of *Greetings from Asbury Park, N.J. Rolling Stone*, July 5, 1973.

———. Review of *Born to Run, Creem*, November 1975.

Binelli, Mark. "Bruce Springsteen's American Gospel." *Rolling Stone*, August 22, 2002.

Block, Melissa. "Springsteen Speaks: The Music of Pete Seeger." *All Things Considered*,
NPR, April 26, 2006.

Caramanica, Jon. "Everything Old Is Praised Again." *New York Times*, February 14, 2012.

Colbert, Stephen. Comments about Bruce Springsteen. *Colbert Report*, Comedy Central,
October 10, 2007.

Corn, David. "Bruce Springsteen Tells the Story of the Secret America." *Mother Jones*,
March/April 1996.

Crouch, Ian. "The Original Wrecking Ball: Bruce Springsteen's *Nebraska*." *New Yorker*, March 6, 2012.

DiMartino, Dave. "Bruce Springsteen Takes It to the River." *Creem*, January 1981.

Einstein, Damian. Interview with Bruce Springsteen. WHFS-FM, June 2, 1973.

Flanagan, Bill. "Bruce Springsteen: Interview." *Musician*, November 1984.

———. "Ambition, Lies, and the Beautiful Reward: Bruce Springsteen's Family Values." *Musician*,
November 1992.

Flippo, Chet. Interview with Bruce Springsteen. *Musician*, November 1984.

Fricke, David. "Bruce Springsteen: Bringing It All Back Home." *Rolling Stone*, February 5, 2009.

———. "Q&A: Bruce Springsteen on Touring Europe, the E Street Band and a Half-Century
of Rock." *Rolling Stone*, June 20, 2013.

Fussman, Cal. "Bruce Springsteen: It Happened in Jersey." *Esquire*, August 1, 2005.

Gibbons, Fiachra. "Bruce Springsteen: 'What Was Done to My Country was Un-American.'"
Guardian, February 17, 2012.

Gilmore, Mikal. "The *Rolling Stone* 20th Anniversary Interview: Bruce Springsteen."
Rolling Stone, November 5, 1987.

Greene, Andy. "Bruce Springsteen on 'Anomaly' of New Album *High Hopes*: Exclusive."
Rolling Stone, December 17, 2013.

———. "Tom Morello: 'Springsteen Concerts Are Orthopedically Exhausting.'"
Rolling Stone, January 3, 2014.

Hagen, Mark. "Meet the New Boss." *Observer*, January 18, 2009.

Henke, James. "The *Rolling Stone* Interview: Bruce Springsteen Leaves E Street."
Rolling Stone, August 6, 1992.

Hepworth, David. Interview with Bruce Springsteen. *Q*, August 1992.

Herman, Dave. Interview with Bruce Springsteen. *King Biscuit Flower Hour*, DIR Radio Network,
July 9, 1978.

Hilburn, Robert. Interview with Bruce Springsteen. *Melody Maker*, August 24, 1974.

Humphries, Patrick, and Roger Scott. Interview with Bruce Springsteen. *Hot Press*,
November 2, 1984.

Kandell, Steve. "The Feeling's Mutual: Bruce Springsteen and Win Butler Talk about the Early
Days, the Glory Days and Even the End of Days." *Spin*, December 2007.

Knobler, Peter, and Greg Mitchell. "Who Is Bruce Springsteen and Why Are We Saying All These
Wonderful Things About Him?" *Crawdaddy!*, March 1973.

Koppel, Ted. Interview with Bruce Springsteen. *Nightline*, ABC, August 4, 2004.

Landau, Jon. "Loose Ends." *Real Paper*, May 22, 1974.

Lauer, Matt. "'The Boss' Is Back with a New CD." *Today*, NBC, April 25, 2005.

Letterman, David. Interview with Bruce Springsteen. *Late Show with David Letterman*,
CBS, August 1, 2002.

Lillianthal, Steven B. "More than One Balloon." *New York Times*, December 8, 2002.

Loder, Kurt. "The *Rolling Stone* Interview: Bruce Springsteen on *Born in the U.S.A.*"
Rolling Stone, December 6, 1984.

Lombardi, John. "The Sanctification of Bruce Springsteen and the Rise of Mass Hip."
Esquire, December 1988.

Lustig, Jay. "The Boss Says It Feels Good to Be Home." *Star-Ledger*, March 19, 1999.

Marcus, Greil. Review of *Born to Run. Rolling Stone*, October 9, 1975.

———. "The Great Pretender: Bruce Springsteen Appears at Once as the Anointed
Successor to Elvis and as an Impostor Who Expects to Be Asked for His Stage Pass."
New West, December 22, 1980.

Marsh, Dave. "A Rock Star Is Born: Bruce Springsteen and the E Street Band at the Bottom Line."
Rolling Stone, September 25, 1975.

———. Interview with Bruce Springsteen. *Musician*, February 1981.

———. Interview with Bruce Springsteen. *Live from E Street Nation*, E Street Radio,
January 10, 2014

Martin, Gavin. "Hey Joad, Don't Make It Sad … (Oh, Go on Then)." *New Musical Express*,
March 9, 1996

Nelson, Paul. Review of *The River. Rolling Stone*, December 11, 1980.

O'Reilly, Bill. Comments about Bruce Springsteen. *The O'Reilly Factor*, Fox News, October 3, 2007.

Pareles, Jon. "Music: His Kind of Heroes, His Kind of Songs." *New York Times*, July 14, 2002.

———. "Bruce Almighty." *New York Times*, April 24, 2005.

———. "The Rock Laureate." *New York Times*, January 28, 2009.

Pelley, Scott. Interview with Bruce Springsteen. *60 Minutes*, CBS News, October 7, 2007.

Percy, Will. "Rock and Read: Will Percy Interviews Bruce Springsteen." *DoubleTake*, Spring 1998.

Pond, Steve. Review of *Nebraska. Rolling Stone*, October 28, 1982.

———. Review of *Tunnel of Love. Rolling Stone*, October 3, 1987.

Rockwell, John. "Rock: Bruce Springsteen at the Garden." *New York Times*, November 29, 1980.

Rose, Charlie. Interview with Bruce Springsteen. *Charlie Rose*, PBS, November 20, 1998.

Rotella, Sebastian. "Children of the Border." *Los Angeles Times*, April 3, 1993.

Schruers, Fred. "Bruce Springsteen and the Secret of the World." *Rolling Stone*, February 5, 1981.

Sciaky, Ed. Interview with Bruce Springsteen. 93.3 WMMR (Philadelphia), November 3, 1974.

Scott, A. O. "The Poet Laureate of 9/11." *Slate*, August 6, 2002.

———. "In Love with Pop, Uneasy with the World." *New York Times*, September 30, 2007.

Smith, R. J. "Springsteen Looks Back and Drives On." *Michigan Daily*, October 5, 1980.

Springsteen, Bruce. "A Statement from Bruce Springsteen." *brucespringsteen.net*, April 22, 2003.

———. "Chords for Change." *New York Times*, August 5, 2004.

Stewart, Jon. "Bruce Springsteen's State of the Union." *Rolling Stone*, March 29, 2012.

Sutcliffe, Phil. Interview with Bruce Springsteen. *MOJO*, January 2006.

Sweeting, Adam. "Bruce Springsteen: 'I Think I Just Want to Be Great.'" *Uncut*, September 2002.

Tucker, Ken. Review of *Nebraska*. *Philadelphia Inquirer*, October 3, 1982.

———. "Springsteen Talks." *Entertainment Weekly*, February 28, 2003.

Tyler, Andrew. "Bruce Springsteen and the Wall of Faith." *New Musical Express*, November 15, 1975.

Tyrangiel, Josh. "Reborn in the USA." *Time*, August 5, 2002.

Werbin, Stuart. "Bruce Springsteen: It's Sign Up a Genius Month." *Rolling Stone*, April 26, 1973.

Wilkinson, Alec. "The Protest Singer: Pete Seeger and American Folk Music." *New Yorker*, April 17, 2006.

Will, George. "Bruce Springsteen: 'The Blue-Collar Troubadour.'" *Observer-Reporter* (Washington), September 15, 1984.

Wolcott, James. "The Hagiography of Bruce Springsteen." *Vanity Fair*, December 1985.

"Bruce Springsteen: The Seeger Sessions." PRX, June 30, 2006.

"Q&A: Pete Seeger." *Billboard*, June 26, 2006.

"Random Notes." *Rolling Stone*, November 25, 1982.

———. *Rolling Stone*, May 12, 1983.

———. *Rolling Stone*, September 1, 1983.

———. *Rolling Stone*, February 2, 1984.

———. *Rolling Stone*, March 17, 1984.

"Rock Concert Rocks Community." *Courier*, September 17, 1970.

VH1 Storytellers, "Bruce Springsteen." VH1, April 23, 2005.

"Working on a Dream: A Super Bowl Journal." NFL Network, September 7, 2009.

PRESS CONFERENCES AND SPEECHES

Earle, Justin Townes, and Joe Pug. Speaking during performance in Carrboro, North Carolina, March 9, 2010.

Kerry, John. "How Do You Ask a Man to Be the Last Man to Die in Vietnam?" Statement made before the Senate Foreign Relations Committee, April 23, 1971.

Obama, Barack. Speech made at the 32nd annual Kennedy Center Honors, Washington, DC, December 6, 2009.

Seeger, Pete. Interviewed by the House Un-American Activities Committee, August 18, 1955.

Springsteen, Bruce. Speech inducting Bob Dylan into the Rock and Roll Hall of Fame, January 20, 1988.

———. Super Bowl XLIII press conference, Tampa, Florida, January 29, 2009.

———. Eulogy for Clarence Clemons (delivered June 21, 2011), published in *Rolling Stone*, June 29, 2011.

———. Press conference, Théâtre Marigny, Paris, February 16, 2012.

———. Keynote speech, SXSW music festival, NPR, March 15, 2012.

———. Speech given at the Obama for America presidential campaign, Des Moines, Iowa, C-SPAN, November 5, 2012.

CDS AND DVDS

Springsteen, Bruce. Liner notes. *Tracks*. CD box set. Columbia. Released November 10, 1998.

———. Commentaries. *Devils & Dust*. Bonus DVD, directed by Danny Clinch. Columbia. Released April 25, 2005.

———. Liner notes. *Bruce Springsteen and the E Street Band: Hammersmith Odeon, London '75*. DVD, directed by Derek Burbidge. Columbia. Released November 15, 2005.

———. Liner notes. *We Shall Overcome: The Seeger Sessions*. CD/DVD. Columbia. Released April 24, 2006.

———. "Behind the Scenes." *We Shall Overcome: The Seeger Sessions*. Bonus DVD, directed by Thom Zimny. Columbia. Released April 24, 2006.

———. "The Sessions." *Working on a Dream*, deluxe edition. Bonus DVD, directed by Thom Zimny. Columbia. Released January 27, 2009.

———. Liner notes. *High Hopes*. CD. Columbia. Released January 14, 2014.

In Concert: MTV Plugged. Recorded September 22, 1992. DVD. Columbia. Released November 9, 2004.

The Promise: The Making of Darkness on the Edge of Town. DVD, directed by Thom Zimny. Columbia. Released November 16, 2010.

Wings for Wheels: The Making of Born to Run. DVD, directed by Thom Zimny. Columbia. Released November 15, 2005.

PICTURE CREDITS

Every effort has been made to trace and acknowledge the copyright holders. We apologize in advance for any unintentional omissions and would be pleased, if any such case should arise, to add appropriate acknowledgment in any future edition of the book.

T: top; B: bottom; L: left; R: right; C: center

Corbis: Endpapers, 128–129 (Brooks Kraft); 13, 24 L, 83, 90 B, 91, 96 (Lynn Goldsmith); 28–29, 37 L & R (Found Image Press); 45, 48 T (Jeff Albertson); 75 (Bettmann); 113 (Aaron Rapoport); 182 (Albert Ferreira/Reuters); 206 L, 241 T (Saed Hindash/*Star-Ledger*); 209 L; 237 (Andy Mills/*Star-Ledger*); 240 (Ron Sachs/Pool/CNP); 242–243 (Joe Skipper/Reuters); 247 T (Julia Robinson/Reuters); **Getty Images:** 1, 53 B, 268–269 (Tom Hill/WireImage); 2, 3, 9, 191, 192 L, 196, 199, 200–201, 205, 206–207, 211, 222–223, 228–229, 231, 233, 240 B, 284–285 (Danny Clinch); 15, 39, 40–41, 42, 46, 49, 52–53, 88–89, 94, 118, 120 (The Estate of David Gahr); 19 C, 27, 31, 43 L, 109 L (Michael Ochs Archives); 30 (Bob Parent/Hulton Archive); 51 (Terry O'Neill); 53 C, 74 (Fin Costello/Redferns); 66–67 (Chalkie Davis); 77, 105 R (*New York Daily News*); 82 (Donna Santisi/Redferns); 90 T (Chris Walter/WireImage); 109 R (Eric Schaal/*LIFE* Picture Collection); 110, 245 (AFP); 121 (Janette Beckman/Redferns); 136 (Jim Steinfeldt); 141 (Ron Galella/WireImage); 151 (Brian McLaughlin); 155, 168 T (Ebet Roberts); 158 L, 181 T, 184, 185, 194, 198, 202, 203, 208, 212, 226, 234, 235 L & R, 247 B (Kevin Mazur Archive/WireImage); 168 B (*Washington Post*); 177 (Mitch Jenkins); 178–179 (Bob King); 181 B (Doug Kanter/AFP); 186 (Peter Pakvis/Redferns); 188–189 (Justin Sullivan); 192–193 (Harry Scott/Redferns); 195 (Timothy A. Clary); 213 (David Redfern/Redferns); 215 (Paul Bergen/Redferns); 218–219 (Edd Westmacott/Photoshot); 227 (Joe Raedle); 232 T (Roger Kisby); 232 C (Peter Still/Redferns); 246 (Barry Chin/*Boston Globe*); 247 C (Heidi Gutman/NBCUniversal); 248 (John Shearer/WireImage); 249 (James Nielsen/AFP); 250 (John Cohen); 251, 260–261, 262 (Lloyd Bishop/NBC/NBCU Photo Bank); 252–253, 254 (Kevin Mazur/WireImage/SiriusXM); 255 (Buda Mendes); 256 (Kevin Nixon/*Classic Rock Magazine*/TeamRock); 257 (Jewel Samad/AFP); 259 (Will Russell); 260 L (Debra L. Rothenberg); 265 (Leaane Stander/Foto24/Gallo Images); © **Neal Preston:** 10, 24–25, 98–99, 114, 115, 116, 119, 122, 123, 124–125, 126, 131, 132–133, 134 B, 137, 138–139, 142–143, 150, 152–153, 157, 158–159, 161, 163, 166–167, 169, 170, 288; **Photoshot:** 19 B (MPTV); 55 (Michael Putland/Retna); 105 L (UPPA); 135 (HBO-Cinemax/Photofest/Retna); 164 (Neal Preston/Retna); 174–175 (Caserta/DALLE/Idols); 209 R (Starstock); 232 B (InfoPhoto/Retna); © **Chuck Pulin/DavidMcGough.com:** 32, 35, 48 B; © **Peter Cunningham:** 33; © **Art Mailett:** 36; © **Carl Dunn:** 40 L; © **Barbara Pyle:** 53 T, 58–59, 64; © **Eric Meola, 2005, 2011:** 56, 57, 60–61, 62–63, 72, 81, 84–85; © **Frank Stefanko:** 69, 70–71, 76–77, 87, 92, 96 T & C, 97, 102 L, 104, 111, 172–173; **Rex Features:** 79–80 (Andre Csillag); 165 (Everett Collection); © **David Michael Kennedy:** 101, 102–103, 107, 108; **PA Images:** 106, 140, 146–147, 149, 187, 220 B, 222 L; **Eyevine:** 145 (Keith Meyers/*New York Times*); 217, 224 (Todd Heisler/*New York Times*); **Alpha:** 156; **Heidi Gutman/NBC NewsWire:** 221; © **Michael Gallagher:** 266.

Album covers: Columbia (see Discography for details of art direction and photography).

We would like to thank Ian Whent, for his invaluable help with our picture research, and Guy White at Snap Galleries, London, and Aaron Zych at the Morrison Hotel Gallery, New York.

ACKNOWLEDGMENTS

Foremost, thanks to Bruce Springsteen for a career that's so fun to write about. This book exists without Peter Ames Carlin, but I wouldn't have had the pleasure of writing it. Thank you for a friendship that's been above and beyond (and access to your archives). Zachary Schisgal was calm and cool when I needed someone to be both those things. Thanks, also, to Colin Webb at Palazzo Editions for entrusting me with the gig. James Hodgson battled time zones to carefully edit these words. The websites www.backstreets.com and brucebase.wikispaces.com are priceless resources for any Springsteen fan and I returned to them time and again. A lot of fantastic words have been written about Springsteen, and I've read most over the years. Legal team (and pals) Tom Johnson and Yoona Park worked pro bono. Helen Jung and Patrick Green offered moral support (and beer). Mom and Dad are just great at being Mom and Dad. Always have been. And April and Stella: This is for you. Thanks for everything. Always, and forever.
Ryan White

Palazzo Editions thanks David Costa for his initial presentations and constant design inspiration.

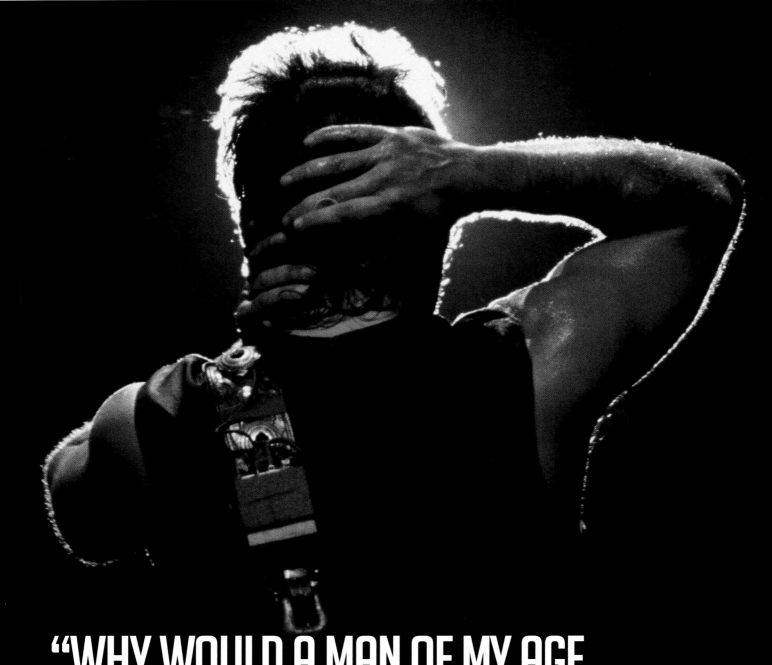

"WHY WOULD A MAN OF MY AGE WANT TO GO OUT AND DRENCH HIMSELF, AND EXHAUST HIMSELF AT THIS LATE DATE? THERE'S ONLY ONE REASON: BECAUSE HE HAS TO."

Bruce Springsteen, 2014